PERSPECTIVES ON FEMALE SEX OFFENDING

WELFARE AND SOCIETY
STUDIES IN WELFARE POLICY, PRACTICE AND THEORY

Series Editors:
Matthew Colton, Kevin Haines, Peter Raynor, Tim Stainton and Anthea Symonds
School of Social Sciences and International Development,
University of Wales Swansea

Welfare and Society is an exciting series from the University of Wales Swansea, School of Social Sciences and International Development in conjunction with Ashgate, concerned with all aspects of social welfare. The series publishes works of research, theory, history and practice from a wide range of contemporary applied social studies subjects such as Criminal Justice, Child Welfare, Community Care, Race and Ethnicity, Therapeutic and Intervention Techniques, Community Development and Social Policy. The series includes extended research reports of scholarly interest as well as works aimed at both the academic and professional communities.

Perspectives on Female Sex Offending

A Culture of Denial

MYRIAM S. DENOV
Department of Criminology
University of Ottawa, Canada

ASHGATE

Published by
Ashgate Publishing Limited
Gower House
Croft Road
Aldershot
Hampshire GU11 3HR
England

Ashgate Publishing Company
Suite 420
101 Cherry Street
Burlington, VT 05401-4405
USA

Ashgate website: http://www.ashgate.com

British Library Cataloguing in Publication Data
Denov, Myriam S.
    Perspectives on female sex offending : a culture of denial.
    - (Welfare and society)
    1.Female sex offenders 2.Female sex offenders - Psychology
    3.Sexual abuse victims 4.Sexual deviation
    I.Title
    364.1'53'082

Library of Congress Control Number: 2003112474

ISBN 0 7546 3565 1

Printed and bound by Athenaeum Press, Ltd.,
Gateshead, Tyne & Wear.

Contents

List of Figures and Table

Preface

The journey for this research began from a personal experience that profoundly altered my outlook and thinking with regard to gender, sexuality, and professional intervention. I had been working as a social work student in a clinic where I was providing psychological assessments and counseling to victims of child sexual abuse, as well as male sex offenders. I had reached a point in my work where I naively thought I had seen and heard everything, and that nothing that a client disclosed could possibly surprise me. All of this changed when one of my clients disclosed that he had been sexually abused by his mother. I had never before heard of sexual abuse by women and the training that I received in both social work and criminology had never mentioned or even insinuated that women could be perpetrators of sexual abuse. Sexual abuse had always been presented as a problem committed by males, mostly against females. When my client made his disclosure, I felt very ill-equipped to deal with the issue and I wondered how my reaction would affect him. I listened to my client's disclosure, trying to mask my discomfort.

Following the disclosure, I sought out more experienced professionals for information and advice on the topic and suggestions for a plan of action for my client. Many of the professionals I consulted not only questioned whether it was possible for a woman to commit a sexual offence, but also questioned whether sexual abuse by a woman would be harmful to the victim. Later on, when I consulted professionals who had worked with female sex offenders, many described feelings of shock, and revulsion with regard to the issue. One female social worker described a therapy session with a female sex offender who was disclosing details of her sexual offences. Feeling disgusted and repulsed by what she was hearing, the social worker politely excused herself from her client, shut her office door and hung onto a wall, hoping that she would not be physically sick. She reminded me that such a response had never before occurred under similar circumstances while working with male sex offenders.

My own reaction and the reaction of others persuaded me to investigate the reality of female sex offending and, in particular, its impact on victims. When I turned to the empirical literature, I found a few studies that examined the characteristics and motivations of female perpetrators of sexual abuse, but very little dedicated to their victims. It was then that I realized the importance of research in the area and embarked on a small study of victims sexually abused by females for a master's degree. During the course of in-depth interviews, victims frequently spoke of their difficulties with disclosure, and negative experiences that they had had upon disclosing female perpetrated sexual abuse to helping professionals. These findings, and my earlier encounters with professionals, encouraged me to expand on my initial study and to examine both victim and professional perspectives on female sex offending for my doctoral studies.

The topic of female sex offending is one that often evokes passionate reactions: surprise, disbelief, shock, intrigue, or utter revulsion. Throughout the research process, some of the reactions to my study served as reminders of the difficulty and resistance to addressing the topic. For example, several social service organizations refused my request to display a poster to recruit potential participants claiming that the topic of female sex offending was 'anti-feminist' and that supporting my study went against the mandate of their agency. When attempting to recruit professionals to participate in the study, I was hung up on by several psychiatrists who did not want to discuss the issue. During an interview for a doctoral scholarship, my panel of academic assessors began to laugh and make derogatory comments when I began to discuss males who were sexually abused by females. Such reactions convinced me even more that this was a topic that needed to be explored.

It is my hope that this book, which seeks to illuminate the experiences and voices of victims of female sex offenders and the professionals who are called upon to work with them, will help to fill the empirical void that surrounds the topic of female sexual offending, and ultimately increase our awareness and understanding of the complex issue of child sexual abuse. More specifically however, I hope that the book will contribute to the training of different professional groups involved in child sexual abuse, as well as to policy and practice issues relating to victims and to child protection. This book forms part of the *beginning* of our attempts to understand the perspectives of victims and professionals in relation to female sex offending. We have much more to learn about the issue, particularly from victims, who have been a largely silenced group and whose disclosures, experiences, strength and courage continue to challenge and inspire us as professionals.

Acknowledgements

It is impossible to give adequate thanks to the many people who provided me with information, advice, encouragement, and much needed laughter during the writing of this manuscript, first as a Ph.D. dissertation at the Institute of Criminology, University of Cambridge, and later, during its conceptualization as a book.

My sincere thanks and appreciation go to the men and women who consented to be interviewed, giving their time and opening their lives to a complete stranger. I thank them for their candour, their insights, and for sharing with me their personal experiences. I owe them all a debt of gratitude and can only hope that this work does justice to their trust and generosity.

For their generous financial support during the course of my Ph.D., I would like to thank the Commonwealth Scholarship Commission, the Wakefield Trust, the Cambridge Commonwealth Trust, the Canadian Centennial Scholarship Fund, and the University of Cambridge.

I owe a special debt of gratitude to Loraine Gelsthorpe who, in her capacity as my Ph.D. supervisor, provided constant intellectual stimulation, and guidance. Loraine's commitment and support over the years, both practical and personal, have been invaluable and it has been my good fortune to have worked with her.

I would like to thank the many Canadian agencies who allowed me to conduct my research within their organizations. I am particularly grateful to Jim Worling, Harvey Armstrong, Bruce Leslie, Grant Fair, Kim Madden and John Dalzell for their interest in my work, and assistance in finding study participants.

Many individuals, from near and from far, have offered invaluable support, as well as intellectual stimulation during the research for and preparation of this book. Many thanks are due to Jennifer Brown, Kathryn Campbell, Eric Chui, Myna Denov, Bryson Gordon, Cyril Greenland, Derek Janhevich, Leah Richards, Julian Roberts, Guy Schmit, Alix Youtz. I am particularly grateful to Julia Gotz who has been a constant source of insight, and who has been steadfast in her support and generosity. I would also like to thank Peter Raynor for his careful editing of the book, and for providing me with the opportunity to be a part of this series at Ashgate.

A very special thank you goes to Celia Denov and Robert Bell for their unrelenting support, encouragement, humour and most of all, their wisdom. They have each contributed to the completion of this book and I am truly grateful for all they have given me.

Finally, I would like to thank André for his unwavering commitment, insights, and practical support. From the early conception of the research to the final draft of this book, he has been a constant source of support acting as editor, computer doctor, companion, and best friend. His intelligence, wit and warmth have inspired and sustained me throughout this work – *merci!*

For André

Introduction

Societal Values and the Recognition of Child Sexual Abuse

There is little doubt that variations in values, beliefs and practices pertaining to all aspects of sexuality have occurred throughout time. Attitudes concerning sexual practices between adults and children are no exception. Although sexual relations between adults and children have existed throughout history and across cultures, whether such behaviour was conceived of and defined as 'abuse' has been dependent on the societal values of the particular period (Mrazek, 1981; Mitterauer, 1994). For example, it is reported that in ancient Greece and Rome there was an atmosphere of acceptance of sexual practices between adults and children (de Mause, 1974; King, 1994). Child prostitution was widespread and slave children, particularly boys, were used for sexual gratification by adult men with the approval of the community (Banning, 1989). Castration of young boys to 'feminize' them for sexual purposes was apparently not uncommon, as was anal intercourse between male teachers and their male pupils (Mrazek, 1981). In other ancient civilizations, such as the Incan of pre-Spanish Peru, the Ptolemaic Egyptian, and old Hawaiian, certain types of incest were permitted in isolated, privileged classes (Mead, 1968; Davenport, 1977; Schultz, 1982; Banning, 1989; Mitterauer, 1994). Mrazek (1981) argues that changes in thought about particular sexual practices have occurred in a continuous cycle rather than in a linear progression. Clearly, what is defined as 'normal' in one period in history may be later defined as immoral and then criminal and then as psychopathological. There is usually a predominant attitude in a particular society at a specific point in history based largely on the socio-historical context.

The twentieth century has seen a series of shifts in attitudes and beliefs regarding the prevalence of adult-child sexual relations, particularly within the family. Early writers considered incest to be a very rare occurrence (Herman, 1981; Miller, 1985; Russell, 1986). For example, Weinberg (1955) and Freedman, Kaplan and Sadock (1975) suggested that the incidence of father-daughter incest was one in a million. However, between 1976 and 1985, reports of sexual abuse in the United States rose eighteenfold. The American Humane Association recorded fewer than two thousand cases in 1976 but almost 23,000 in 1982. Statistics Canada, the country's national statistical agency, reports that in 1997, 30,735 sex offences were reported to police. Thirty per cent of these victims were children under twelve.

Many authors relate the source of early denial of incest and other forms of sexual abuse to Sigmund Freud (Masson, 1984; Miller, 1985; Howitt, 1992). In an 1896 article about hysterical patients entitled 'Heredity and the Aetiology of the Neuroses', Freud described the crux of his theory which attributed hysterical symptoms to repressed memories of sexual abuse (Mendel, 1995; Russell, 1995). Freud described female patients who were recalling childhood incestuous interactions with their fathers or other adult men. Initially, Freud understood these recollections to be repressed traumatic memories of actual early life events. He theorized that these events, the anxiety they evoked, and the consequent necessity to repress them, resulted in later pathology. A year later, however, Freud retracted his theory and redefined the experiences of these women as sexual fantasy (Rush, 1980; Herman, 1981; Masson, 1984; Miller, 1985; Russell, 1986; Howitt, 1992). There has been a great deal of speculation about Freud's motives for his sudden retraction including hypotheses about the power of social forces in Europe at that time, Freud's own family history and possible childhood abuse by his father, the failure to convince his colleagues of the merits of his theory, and Freud's exhaustion from working with such difficult to treat patients (Freyd, 1996). However, Freud's reformulation of his original theory from the seduction theory to his later positing of the Oedipus complex profoundly influenced attitudes about sexual abuse in the decades that followed (Finkelhor, 1984; Allen, 1990). Masson (1984) argues that in abandoning his seduction theory, Freud not only did a disservice to psychoanalysis as a theory and clinical practice, but also silenced thousands of patients and exonerated child sexual abusers.

It was perhaps with the introduction of second-wave feminism that the issue of sexual assault was brought to the forefront (Mendel, 1995; Donat & D'Emilio, 1997; Brandon et al., 1998). Feminist analyses of sexual assault underscored that all forms of sexual violence should be viewed within the context of male power and masculinities whereby men use their power as a form of social control by denying women freedom and autonomy (Kelly, 1988; Radford & Stanko, 1996). Sexual assault is not sexually motivated, but used by men as a form of domination and control, a weapon used to enforce women's subordinate role to men. Feminism has been a powerful influence in how sexual assault is now understood and in the last two decades, there has been a surge of attention to the issue, particularly as it pertains to children (Finkelhor, 1984; Driver & Droisen, 1989; Nava, 1992; Child Abuse Studies Unit, 1993).

Similar to perceptions of adult sexual relations with children, images of the sex offender have changed dramatically and cyclically over time, evoking varied societal reactions and responses. According to Jenkins (1998), the imagery of the 'malignant sex fiend' was prominent in the decade after World War II, only to be succeeded by a more liberal view of sex offenders over the next quarter century. Recently, the pendulum has swung back to the predator model and sex offenders are now perceived as being highly dangerous, close to the worst multiple killers and torturers.

Although there may be fluctuations in public attitudes toward sexual contact with children, its etiology, and perceptions of sexual offenders, what is common to most constructions is that the offenders are inevitably male and the victims inevitably female. The words 'sexual assault', 'sexual aggression' and 'sexual coercion' tend to conjure up an image of a male perpetrator and a female victim (Byers & O'Sullivan, 1996). Even titles of books such as *The Sexual Offender and His Offenses* (Karpman, 1954), work to remind us that sexual assault is, without exception, a male crime. To quote Brownmiller (1975), '[sexual assault] is nothing more or less than a conscious process of intimidation by which *all men* keep *all women* in a state of fear' (p.5; italics in original). Even scholarly work which aims to deconstruct the image of the sex offender frequently fails to question the concept of gender. In his book *Moral panic: The changing concepts of the child molester in modern America*, Jenkins (1998) traces the shifting constructions and social responses to adult sexual contact with children without calling into question or even noting that constructions of sexual offenders are inevitably male. There is little doubt that males commit the vast majority of sexual offences and their victims are predominantly female (Home Office, 2001; Snyder, 2000; Canadian Centre for Justice Statistics, 2001). However, the notion of male abusers and female victims has become paradigmatic within the field of child sexual abuse. This has, I would argue, obscured the recognition of male victims and female perpetrators to some degree.

Female Sexual Offending: An Unexplored Phenomenon

To perceive of a woman as sexually aggressive, or worse, as a sexual offender, is contrary to traditional 'sexual scripts' which are heterosexual and gendered (Jackson, 1978; Koss & Harvey, 1991; Byers, 1996). Specific sex roles are assigned to men and others are assigned to women. Traditional sexual scripts exclude the image of women as sexual aggressors, as initiating sex with men, as indicating their sexual interest and, at times, coercing their reluctant partners to engage in unwanted sexual activities (Byers & O'Sullivan, 1998). Women are expected to influence men to avoid sex, not to have sex (Clark & Hatfield, 1989). These scripts also exclude the image of men as sexually reluctant or as victims of sexual coercion or assault (Lew, 1990; Hunter, 1990; Mendel, 1995). In fact, men are perceived to be highly sexually aggressive. Once a man's sexual response has been set in motion, he is thought to have difficulty controlling it (Smart, 1976; Jackson, 1978).

Reflecting traditional sexual scripts, until the late 1980s research and clinical studies focused almost entirely on male sex offenders and their female victims. Female sexual offenders and their victims, whether male or female, have been virtually ignored or neglected from serious study. Although the evidence that women sexually abuse children has been available for many years, it is only within the last decade that as a society we have begun to accept that it occurs and to explore it. Some effort has been made to study female perpetrators, particularly in the United Kingdom, the United States and Canada, from both a psychological/psychodynamic perspective (McCarty, 1986; O'Connor, 1987; Fehrenbach & Monastersky, 1988; Cooper et al., 1990; Rowan, Rowan & Langelier, 1990;) and a sociological perspective (Faller, 1987; Knopp & Lackey, 1987; Cavanaugh-Johnson, 1989; Mathews, Matthews & Speltz, 1989; Saradjian, 1996; Davin, Hislop & Dunbar 1999), but our understanding of these women is still in its infancy. Meanwhile, scant research has been conducted on victims of female perpetrators and the impact of the sexual abuse. We have little in-depth understanding of the experiences of these victims and their perceptions, reactions, and the meaning that they attach to the sexual abuse, as well as the consequences of the abuse. Moreover, we have limited knowledge of victims' experiences with child sexual abuse professionals.

In a similar vein, there has been minimal research focusing on professional responses to female sexual offending. Studying professional perspectives on this issue is important. Professionals, particularly those at the early end of the child welfare continuum such as police officers, and those at the later end of the continuum, such as psychiatrists, play a pivotal role in the identification and treatment of child sexual abuse. Their beliefs systems and 'ways of seeing' have an impact on everyday policy and practice. Their perceptions of victims and offenders and their approach to investigation and intervention will have an enormous impact on who is labelled an 'offender', a 'victim' and what behaviours are reported, charged and treated as 'sexual abuse'.

In an attempt to go beyond traditional sexual scripts and to fill the critical gaps in the empirical literature, this book aims to elucidate professional perspectives on female sexual offending – to ascertain how two professional groups, police officers and psychiatrists, portray, explain, and manage cases involving a female sex offender and the implications of their perspectives for both professional and child sexual abuse policy and practice. How, and in what terms, do police officers and psychiatrists understand and explain the phenomenon of female sexual offending as well as the offender? Does the gender of the perpetrator influence professional perceptions of sexual abuse cases and the way(s) in which professionals handle such cases?

The book also aims to explore victims' perspectives on female sex offending. I examine the life histories and experiences of male and female victims of female sexual offenders, and investigate the impact and consequences of the sexual abuse. How do victims experience women as sexually abusive? Does the gender of the perpetrator influence a victim's experience of abuse? What is the impact and consequences of sexual abuse by females? Finally, how do victims who reported sexual abuse to a professional perceive the response to their disclosure? It is arguable that victims are a valuable and often under-utilized source of information (Beck, 1999). By exploring victims' perspectives, we can gain not only an understanding of the nature and characteristics of female sex offending, but also of victims' treatment and intervention needs. Also, by providing information on victims' experiences it is hoped that more effective interventions can be made on their behalf.

In exploring professional and victim perspectives, it will become apparent that female sex offending challenges traditional sexual scripts concerning 'appropriate' female behaviour. As a result, efforts are made to transform the offender and her offence, realigning them with culturally acceptable notions of female behaviour, ultimately denying women's potential for sexual aggression. We will see that female sex offending is viewed, assessed and understood within gendered narratives and from a gendered lens. The gender of the offender is central to the meaning of the offence and can never be conceptualized without its context. Thus, similar events acquired different significances for male and female sex offenders. For police officers, psychiatrists and victims, it means something different to be abused by a woman – and because the meaning of the abuse is gendered, so too are the responses to the abuse. The study ultimately seeks to determine how and why particular responses to female sex offending emerge and are maintained and reproduced within a given society.

Definition of Terms

Sexual Abuse

Definitional issues are of crucial importance when researching sexual abuse (Johnson & Shrier, 1987; Lawson, 1993). Fromuth and Burkhart (1987) suggest that the range in sexual abuse prevalence estimates are a product of different criteria used to define abuse; the more restrictive the criteria, the lower the estimates of abuse. This study does not intend to provide an estimate of the prevalence of sexual abuse by females and thus the criteria used to define abuse do not have as far-reaching methodological implications. However, it remains an important issue. The definition of sexual abuse used for this study was adapted from Schecter and Roberge (1976), considered one of the most widely accepted definitions of sexual abuse (Mrazek, 1981; Watkins & Bentovim, 1992). Sexual abuse is defined as 'the involvement of dependent developmentally immature children or adolescents in sexual activities they do not truly comprehend, and to which they are unable to give informed consent and that violate the sexual taboos of family roles' (Schecter & Roberge, 1976). Sexual abuse was limited to activities that involved direct sexual contact.

Victims of Child Sexual Abuse

For the purposes of this study, 'victims' or 'survivors'[1] of sexual abuse are defined as those who experienced sexual abuse when they were 14 years old or younger at the time of the first sexual contact, and where the female perpetrator was at least five years older. No stipulations were made about the relationship between the victim and the perpetrator.

Perpetrator of Child Sexual Abuse

'Perpetrator' of child sexual abuse refers to any individual who commits sexual abuse as defined above.

Overview of the Book

The book consists of seven chapters. Chapter one explores the prevalence of female sexual offending and addresses the debate as to whether female sexual abuse is a rare phenomenon or an under-recognized one. The chapter provides an overview of both case and self-report data, and highlights the paradoxes and controversies that exist within the available data. It also examines the barriers in place which may act to obscure the extent of female sex offending.

Chapter two explores the issue of denial and how the denial of particular social issues emerges and is sustained within a given society. The chapter outlines two social processes; the dialectical process and the transformation process. These two processes offer a framework for understanding the emergence and perpetuation of denial and may provide a suitable model from which to understand responses to female sex offending.

Chapter three discusses the research methodology; how the information to be described in later chapters was collected and analyzed. It also addresses fieldwork issues, and the implications of researching a sensitive topic.

Chapter four describes police perspectives on female sex offending. It traces the ways in which twelve police officers working in a Canadian Sexual Assault Unit constructed and managed cases of sexual assault involving a female perpetrator. It examines how broader structural considerations as well as the individual action of police officers influence the ways in which police officers construct female sex offending within the context of their everyday work and investigative practice.

Chapter five investigates psychiatrists' perspectives on female sexual offending. The chapter explores the views of ten Canadian psychiatrists and the ways in which they came to understand and construct cases of sexual assault involving a female perpetrator. It explores how individual psychiatrists draw upon both societal and institutional ideologies as well as their individual beliefs in their understandings and representations of female sex offending.

Chapter six explores female sex offending from the perspective of the victim. This chapter examines the life histories and experiences of 15 self-identified survivors of female sexual offenders from Canada. The chapter begins by describing the characteristics of the sample and outlines the ways in which survivors experienced women as sexually abusive. It then addresses the meaning that survivors attached to the sexual abuse and how they negotiated the sexual abuse experience both as children and as adults. Following this, the chapter explores the long-term impact and consequences of the sexual abuse on survivors. It also examines how survivors perceived the professional responses to their sexual abuse disclosures and the implications of these responses.

Chapter seven provides an overview of the study's main findings and discusses their implications for professional and child sexual abuse policy and practice. This concluding chapter considers how the research contributes to current debates about organizational cultures, criminal justice responses to female offenders, and feminist theory. Finally, it offers some directions for future research.

This study involves an original piece of research which adds to the currently available knowledge on perspectives on female sex offending. It is obviously an exploratory study because of the small sample, but it nevertheless forms the beginning of our attempts to understand victim and professional perspectives on the issue.

Note

1   The terms 'victim' and 'survivor' are not unproblematic. Upon the 'discovery' of child sexual abuse in the mid-1970s, children believed to have experienced it were referred to by clinicians as 'victims' of child sexual abuse. Recently, however, feminists, clinicians, as well as 'victims' themselves have taken issue with the term. They have argued that the term 'victim' denotes powerlessness, hopelessness and vulnerability (Lew, 1990). It also makes invisible the other side of victimization – the active and positive ways in which people cope, resist and survive (Kelly, 1988; Walklater, 1995). Some effort has been made to modify the use of the word 'victim' and replace it with 'survivor', considered by some to be a more positive and empowering term (Lew, 1990). Nonetheless, the term 'survivor' is also controversial as those who have experienced child sexual abuse may not have overcome the experience as the term suggests. Moreover, it has become a 'catch phrase' for many types of victimization. One male participant interviewed for this study expressed his discomfort with both terms: 'I can't stand being called a *victim*, I loathe it'. But I also hate the term *survivor*. I just hate it. I don't want to be lumped in a group. This happened to me, yes, but please, don't call me a victim or a survivor'. Within the book, I use the term 'victim' in the sense of being a victim of a criminal offence. Nevertheless, I also use and acknowledge the importance of the term 'survivor' for those who have survived sexual violence. The terms are employed interchangeably, acknowledging that both fail to adequately capture the experience of sexual abuse.

1 The Prevalence of Female Sex Offending: Rare or Under-Recognized ?

The issue of female sexual offending has received very little attention and recognition in both clinical and empirical literature on sexual abuse. The disregard for the topic has frequently been justified by those who argue that the scant number of reported cases reveal an insignificant social problem. However, this stance has not only assumed that the literature accurately reflects the true incidence of female sexual offending, but has also failed to consider the problems that exist within the available data – namely, methodological problems as well as the fact that case-report studies and self-report studies provide two often conflicting portraits of the prevalence of the phenomenon. In an attempt to discern whether female sexual offending is rare or under-recognized, the first half of this chapter will provide an overview of the current case and self-report data on its prevalence. By drawing upon the literature, I show that while the prevalence rates of female sex offending are small when compared to rates of male sex offending, there is evidence to suggest that sexual abuse by females may be under-recognized.

In the second half of the chapter, I discuss some of the possible reasons for the under-recognition of the problem. This section critically analyzes the societal response to the issue. It highlights empirical data on societal perceptions of gender and its relation to sexual assault, the criminal law pertaining to female sexual perpetration, as well as professional and victim perceptions of sexual abuse by females. On the whole, these responses point to a widespread denial of women as potential sexual aggressors that could work to obscure the true dimensions of the problem.

The Controversy

Early work on sexual offenders suggested that female sexual offending was 'virtually unknown among women' (Mohr, 1977). Mathis claimed that sexual offending among females was so rare that it was 'of little significance' (Mathis, 1972: 54). Similarly, Freund et al. declared that 'pedophilia ... does not exist at all in women' (Freund et al., 1984: 193). Other authors have proposed that the scant number of reported cases of female sexual abuse reveals an insignificant social problem (Russell, 1984). Nonetheless, more recent studies have begun to acknowledge the existence of female sexual offenders (McCarty, 1986; Faller, 1987; O'Connor, 1987; Fehrenbach & Monastersky, 1988; Cavanaugh-Johnson, 1989; Mathews et al., 1989; Cooper et al., 1990; Rowan et al., 1990; Mayer, 1992; Saradjian, 1996; Anderson & Struckman-Johnson, 1998; Davin et al., 1999). These studies, which have been conducted in three different countries (the United Kingdom, Canada and the United States), and have included a wide range of data gathering techniques including large-scale self-report surveys, in-depth interviews, and case file analyses have all pointed to the existence of female sexual offending. However, the empirical literature concerning its prevalence is contradictory (Finkelhor & Russell, 1984; Faller, 1987; Dimock, 1988; Fromuth & Burkhart, 1989; Faller, 1989; Allen, 1990; Elliott, 1993; Jennings, 1993; Mendel, 1995) and the dimensions of the problem remain an issue of controversy. For example, in self-report studies based on samples of college men, Fritz, Stoll and Wagner (1981), and Fromuth and Burkhart (1989), found very high rates of female perpetration; 60 per cent and 78 per cent respectively. Conversely, case-report studies of child protection service data reveal very low rates of female perpetration, ranging from one to eight per cent (Pierce & Pierce, 1985; Reinhart, 1987; Faller, 1989; Roane, 1992). In order to understand these discrepancies, the literature needs to be examined in more detail. The following literature review will survey the data on female sexual offending from three countries; the United Kingdom, Canada and the United States.

Case Report Studies

Case report studies, which are based on data collected by the state and its agencies, provide an efficient and relatively simple method of obtaining statistics on a given phenomenon. However, to have confidence in official statistics, we must be sure that they fulfil the criteria of both validity and reliability (May, 1993). Research is said to be valid when the conclusions are accurate and reliable when the findings are repeatable (Kidder, 1981).

There are several important reasons why data originating from case report studies should be regarded with caution. First, May (1993) suggests that official criminal statistics reflect crimes that are visible, such as street crime, rather than crimes that take place within the conventional working environment such as white-collar crime, or the domestic sphere such as domestic violence. Indeed, sexual abuse would conform to the category of less visible offences as it often occurs within the domestic sphere, thereby making it less likely to come to the attention of official agencies.

Second, definitional factors within the criminal law will have an important bearing on whether a behaviour is regarded as 'criminal' and whether or not it will end up in official crime statistics. May (1993) argues that there are two factors that determine whether or not behaviour is to be regarded as 'criminal'. First, the act must be defined as 'criminal' in law and second, it must be detectable. Sexual offences by females have only recently been considered 'criminal' within the annals of both English and Canadian law[1] (Edwards, 1984; Nelson, 1994). It is also said to be largely undetected (Justice & Justice, 1979; Plummer, 1981). As such, it does not correspond with either of the components noted above and may be overlooked in official data.

Third, professional and organizational practices play a crucial role in the construction of official crime statistics. For example, individual police officers often use their discretion in whether or not to record a reported incident (Ericson, 1982; Griffiths & Verdun-Jones, 1989). Also, organizational policies which officers are instructed to follow, as well as the culture of the police organization itself, will have an impact on what acts are recorded as criminal (Ericson, 1982; Brookman, 1999; Holdaway, 1999). As May indicates: 'Criminal facts do not speak for themselves, but may tell us more about organizational practices and power relations in society' (May, 1993: 55).

Fourth, victim under-reporting is likely to contribute to the low official numbers. Surveys conducted by interviewing a random sample of the general public have shown that only 36 per cent, or just under four out of every ten crimes committed on a daily basis are reported to the police (May, 1993). According to these estimates, six in every ten crimes committed never even reach the attention of police who act as gatekeepers of official crime statistics (May, 1993). Victim under-reporting may be further complicated in cases of sexual abuse. The majority of child sexual abuse cases are not officially reported to the police, or to child protection agencies (Russell, 1983; Finkelhor, 1986; Fromuth & Conn, 1997). To add to the complexity of the issue, female sexual offending may be even less likely to be reported than sexual abuse involving a male perpetrator (Sgroi & Sargent, 1993; Rosencrans, 1997). In fact, victim under-reporting is considered a significant barrier to understanding the true dimensions of female sexual offending (Knopp & Lackey, 1987; Mathews, 1996). This is said to stem from the taboo nature of female sexual abuse, and the complexities of male victimization (Lew, 1990; Jennings, 1993).

Finally, case-report studies on female sexual offending may prove to be unreliable and misleading as a result of the way in which authors define 'perpetrators' of sexual abuse and the way in which findings are presented in case report studies. For example, in 1981 the National Incidence Study on Child Abuse and Neglect provided figures in which a reader might conclude that 46 per cent of the sexual experiences encountered by children involved a female perpetrator. However, when the data was reanalyzed by Finkelhor and Russell (1984), they found that according to the study's definitions, a caretaker could be a perpetrator not only if he or she had sexual contact with a child, but also if he or she 'permitted acts of sexual abuse to occur'. In many cases of intrafamilial sexual abuse, mothers (or other female caretakers) are aware that the abuse is occurring and fail to stop it (Cooper & Cormier, 1990). In this particular study, these women were listed as perpetrators. When Finkelhor and Russell reanalyzed the data and subtracted these 'perpetrators', leaving only those who actually committed the abuse, the percentage of female perpetrators was estimated to be 13 per cent in the case of female victims and 24 per cent in the case of male victims. Finkelhor and Russell assert that the most accurate estimate of sexual abuse by older females is about five per cent for female children (ranging from zero to ten per cent) and approximately 20 per cent for male children[2] (ranging from 14 to 27 per cent). This particular case demonstrates the importance of ensuring appropriate definitions when analyzing case report studies on child sexual abuse.

Case Report Data on Female Sex Offending: A Rare Phenomenon

Data from official sources on offender populations lend to the conclusion that female sex offending is indeed a rare phenomenon. According to the U.S. Department of Justice (2002), in the United States in 2001, 1.2 per cent of those charged with forcible rape,[3] and eight per cent charged with sexual offences[4] were female. In a statistical report using data from the U.S. National Incident-Based Reporting System, Snyder (2000) found that between 1991 and 1996 in 12 States, four per cent of offenders in sexual assaults[5] against children were female. In the United Kingdom, Home Office Criminal Statistics indicate that between 1975 and 1984, less than one per cent of all sexual offences[6] were committed by women (O'Connor, 1987). More recent Home Office figures show little variation in these earlier rates. In 2000, two percent of adults convicted of a sexual offence were female (Home Office, 2001). Within the Canadian context, the Canadian Badgley Commission (1984) which carried out a nation wide study on sexual offences[7] against children in Canada from 1876 to 1972, found that 1.2 per cent of sexual offenders were female. Recent statistics from the Canadian Centre for Justice Statistics (2001) reveal that in 2000, 1.5 per cent of adults convicted of sexual assault were female.

Smaller case-report studies stemming from victim populations also serve to confirm the low numbers of female perpetrators. Pierce and Pierce (1985) reviewed 304 cases of sexual abuse reported to a child abuse hotline between 1976 and 1979. Of the 304 cases, child protection workers determined that sexual abuse had occurred in 205 cases – 180 victims were female, 25 victims were male. The authors found that only one per cent of female victims and four per cent of male victims reported having been abused by a female. Faller (1989) analyzed 87 validated cases where boys had been sexually abused and were subsequently referred to the University of Michigan Project on Child Abuse and Neglect. She found that eight per cent of victims had been sexually abused by a lone female. Roane (1992) reviewed 77 cases of sexually abused boys referred to a multi-disciplinary child protection team. Six of the boys (7.8 per cent) reported abuse by a female offender. Finally, Reinhart (1987) analyzed case reports between 1983 and 1985 of 189 sexually abused boys who had been identified, evaluated and referred to a centre for child sexual abuse. Reinhart reported that 4.2 per cent of the perpetrators of sexual abuse against the boys were female.

The case-report literature points to the rarity of female sex offending. However, case-report data reflects only those who come into contact with the criminal justice system or social service systems as a consequence of sexual abuse. This data may be fraught with inconsistencies given that societal taboos may deter many from reporting female sex offending to the police and child welfare agencies (Elliott, 1993). Studies employing other methodologies, particularly self-report studies, provide a different portrait of the prevalence of this phenomenon.

Self-Report Studies

The strength of the self-report study arguably lies in its versatility, efficiency and its generalizability (Hammersley, 1989). In terms of versatility, self-report studies can test hypotheses, help us to learn about social processes, and enhance our understanding of a myriad of social issues. They are efficient in the sense that data can be collected from a large number of people quickly and at relatively low cost. The findings of self-report studies can be generalized, and inferences can be made about the attitudes and characteristics of a population with calculable margins of error, from a sample of only a small fraction of that population. Finally, self-report studies are helpful methodological tools as they are able to access information relating to behaviours that are frequently unreported and unrecognized (Binder & Geis, 1983).

The limitations of self-report studies stem from the fact that researchers must rely completely on the participants' answers, which may be inaccurate or imprecise. Those completing questionnaires may under-report or over-report what is being asked of them and they may be unaware of their feelings or unable to accurately remember a past occurrence (Scott, 1996).

In his critique of self-report studies, May (1993) argues that surveys may be inherently biased. He emphasizes that presuppositions on the part of researchers lead them to ask participants particular questions. Given that these questions restrict the way in which people can answer, it becomes inevitable that the theories are 'proven'. May also argues that events can hardly be understood by compartmentalizing them into fixed categories (closed-questions) at one point in time (the actual completion of the questionnaire). By compartmentalizing in this way, researchers are providing simplifications of the complexities of the social world, and they take no account of changes in opinion over time.

Self-report studies are also dubious in the sense that a researcher cannot guarantee that their questions will be interpreted by participants in the manner in which they intended, particularly when there is no opportunity for dialogue or clarification (Binder & Geis, 1983). Furthermore, if the questions posed in self-report surveys are too narrow in spectrum, experiences that lie outside of the definitional realm will be overlooked. For example, it has been proposed that narrow definitions of sexual abuse, which are frequently found in studies of female sexual abuse, contribute to under-reporting (Bolton, Morris & MacEachron, 1989; Kasl, 1990). Many surveys neglect to include a broad range of behaviours that may be experienced by victims, particularly more subtle or covert forms of behaviour that may or may not be perceived as abusive. For example,

Rothstein (1979) describes the case of an adult psychotherapy patient who experienced subtle maternal sexual abuse that involved no genital contact but resulted in long-term destructive consequences that were apparent in the patient's marital and sexual relationship. These subtle forms of female sexual abuse may not be reflected in survey questions.

   Lawson (1993) argues that methodological errors in previous self-report studies on female sexual offending, particularly in the areas of questionnaire design and implementation, may also provide an inaccurate picture of the phenomenon. In self-report studies, the appropriate use of language is crucial. Most questionnaires designed to explore sexual abuse by females have inquired into participants' experiences of 'sexual abuse' or 'victimization' by females (Mendel, 1995). However, recent authors have noted the importance of asking participants about child sexual 'interactions' or 'experiences' rather had than about 'sexual abuse' or 'victimization' when exploring female perpetration (Johnson & Shrier, 1985, 1987; Crewdson, 1988; Mendel, 1995). As a result of the prevalent perceptions that sexual interaction with older females is not considered to be abusive, using 'child sexual interactions' will yield higher rates of positive responses (Mendel, 1995).

   Johnson and Shrier (1985, 1987) provide an excellent example of this phenomenon. They conducted two separate studies on sexually abused adolescent males. In the first study (Johnson & Shrier, 1985), zero participants indicated sexual abuse by a female. In the second study (Johnson & Shrier, 1987), 11 of the 25 sexually abused males indicated they had been sexually abused by a female. The primary difference between the two studies was that in the earlier study, Johnson and Shrier asked the adolescents whether they 'had ever been raped, sexually abused, or forced to engage in a sexual act' (Johnson & Shrier, 1985: 650). In the 1987 study they inquired into their sexual experiences more generally. What led Johnson and Shrier to conduct the second study was that during the earlier (1985) study, several of the adolescents described during interviews sexual interactions with adult females, yet had not indicated that had been sexually abused in the self-report section of the study. Similarly, Crewdson (1988) reports that when a child and family service agency advertised to hear from men who had been sexually abused as children, it received only a few responses. However, when they changed the expression 'sexual abuse' to 'sexual experiences', more than 100 men responded and three quarters of them revealed that, as children, they had had sex with an adult woman.

   Finkelhor maintains that specific types of sexually abusive experiences may be under-reported. These include:

1) Experiences which are blocked and not accessible to retrieval;
2) Experiences which are partially forgotten but retrievable with the right prompting;
3) Experiences that are in memory but are not defined according to the terms referred to in survey questions;
4) Experiences that are in memory but are not volunteered due to embarrassment or to other conscious withholding (Finkelhor, 1986: 48).

Female sexual abuse may conform to all of these experiences and it may be reasonable to assume that because of the nature of these experiences, it is difficult to obtain accurate accounts of the prevalence of female sexual abuse using traditional self-report methods (Lawson, 1993).

Self-Report Studies on Female Sex Offending: An Under-Recognized Phenomenon

On the whole, self-report studies paint a different picture of the relative rates of sexual abuse by females as opposed to sexual abuse by males when compared with case-report data. For example, Fromuth and Conn (1997) explored child molestation committed by females during childhood and adolescents. In a sample of 546 female college students, the authors found that four per cent of the women reported at least one experience that met the criterion for sexually molesting a younger child. While the finding of four per cent does not appear to differ significantly from the numbers of female perpetrators found in case-report studies, it is important to recognize that the four per cent of female perpetrators found in this study is a *higher* number than was found in a similar study conducted on males as perpetrators. Fromuth, Burkhart and Webb Jones (1991) surveyed 582 male college students on their sexual experiences occurring from age 16 or later. They found that three per cent of the college men reported experiences that met the criteria for sexually abusing a child.[8] The main difference in these studies is that in the 1991 study, a 'perpetrator' had to be at least 16 years old. In recognition that sexual abuse by females is often committed at an earlier age (Fromuth & Conn, 1997), the 1997 study did not set a minimum age for the offender.

Other self-report studies of non-clinical populations have found surprisingly high rates of female perpetrators among those sexually abused. Fritz, Stoll and Wagner (1981) administered a questionnaire to 412 male and 540 female college students and found that seven per cent of the women and 4.8 per cent of the men reported having been molested as a child. Ten per cent of the abused women and 60 per cent of the abused men reported having been molested by a female. Similarly, in their research involving college men, Fromuth and Burkhart (1989) found that 15 per cent of 253 men in the first sample and 13 per cent of 329 men in the second sample reported childhood sexual abuse. The majority of perpetrators were female; 78 per cent of respondents in first sample, and 72 per cent in the second sample reported having experienced sexual abuse by a female.

Self-report studies on victim populations yield higher rates of female perpetration as compared to case-report data. Mendel (1995) examined 124 sexually abused males undergoing therapy in both private and community mental health clinics. He found that 60 per cent of his sample reported childhood sexual activity with females; 14 per cent indicated sexual contact with females only, while 46 per cent reported sexual abuse by both males and females. Mendel argues that the high incidence of female perpetration in his sample demonstrates that cases reported to police and child protective services are not representative of the true nature of the phenomenon.

Studies which have explored the backgrounds of convicted sex offenders have uncovered histories of sexual abuse by females. Allen (1991) surveyed 75 males and 65 females convicted of sexual offences against children. Approximately one-third of the male offenders (36 per cent) and about three-quarters of the female offenders (72 per cent) reported they had been sexually abused as children. Of the males who reported being sexually abused, 45 per cent reported that their sexual abuser had been female. Of the female offenders who reported being sexually abused, seven per cent reported that they had been sexually abused by a female. Groth (1979) conducted a study of 348 convicted male rapists and child molesters. Groth found that 106 of these offenders reported histories of childhood sexual trauma. Of those reporting sexual trauma, 51 per cent reported being abused by a male perpetrator, 42 per cent reported being abused by a female perpetrator. Data was unavailable for seven per cent of the sample of offenders.

Petrovich and Templar (1984) found that 59 per cent of 83 prisoners convicted of rape had been molested by a female in their childhood. The boys were a mean age of 11.5 years at the time of the molestation and 82 per cent of cases involved intercourse. Condy et al. (1987) reported that 46 per cent of 212 male prisoners and 16 per cent of 359 male college students reported sexual interaction with older females during childhood. At least half of these sexual interactions involved intercourse.

Carlson described four different categories of abuse by females:

1) Chargeable offences such as oral sex, intercourse, masturbation, fondling or sexual punishment;
2) Less flagrant offences such as voyeurism, exposure, sexualized hugs, kissing on the mouth in a sexual way;
3) Invasions of privacy in a sexual area of the body. This may include enemas, washing the child beyond a reasonable age, obsessive cleaning of the foreskin, and intrusive questions about sexual matters;
4) Inappropriate relationships created by the adult, such as substituting the son for an absent father, sleeping with him, or using him as a confidant about personal or sexual matters (Carlson, 1990).

According to Carlson's data, 31 per cent of men who completed a long-term sex offender treatment program had experienced the first form of abuse. When the second form was added, the proportion of males sexually abused by women rose to 50 per cent. Carlson reports that nearly all of the men had experienced some form of sexual intrusion included in the third and fourth levels.

The review of the current literature on female sex offending highlights that self-report studies yield higher proportions of female sex offending than case-report studies. This not only reveals that female sexual offending may be under-reported to official agencies, but also throws into question the accuracy of case-report data. Although the limitations of self-report surveys impact on their validity and reliability, the findings of the self-report data appear more convincing than case-report data. This stems from the fact that self-report studies are able to tap the hidden source of unreported crime, the so-called 'dark figure'.

While there is little doubt that males commit the vast majority of sexual offences, the literature review bids us to question the notion that female sex offending is a rare phenomenon as portrayed by official statistics. If female sex offending is indeed under-recognized, it may be helpful to begin to address the source(s) of the under-recognition. The next section of the chapter discusses factors that appear to contribute to the lack of recognition of the phenomenon.

Barriers to Recognizing Female Sex Offending

When authors speak of prevalence rates in relation to female sexual offending, they often speak of under-recognition, uncertainty and controversy (Elliott, 1993; Lawson, 1993; Rudin, Zalewski & Bodmer-Turner, 1995). Many have contended that societal attitudes to the phenomenon act to obscure the true extent of the problem (Groth, 1979;

Plummer, 1981; Allen, 1990; Hunter, 1990; Mendel, 1995). This section of the chapter critically examines societal responses to the issue by drawing on empirical data of perceptions of gender and its relation to sexual assault, the criminal law pertaining to female sexual perpetration, victim reporting practices, as well as professional responses to sexual abuse by females. There appears to be a pervasive denial of women as potential sexual aggressors in each of these areas. It is this denial that may play a role in the under-recognition of sexual abuse by females.

Societal Perceptions of Female Sexuality

Despite the increasing recognition of female sexual abuse as evidenced in self-report studies, pervasive societal beliefs regarding the passive nature of female sexuality have continued to propagate the notion that women are incapable of sexual aggression. For example, Mathis dismissed the possibility that females could sexually abuse because it was 'unthinkable' that a woman 'might seduce a helpless child into sex play', and even if she did, 'what harm could be done without a penis?' (Mathis, 1972: 54). Lawson (1991) suggests that the cultural bias towards viewing mothers as asexual is one of the primary reasons that cases of maternal sexual abuse are rarely identified. Abuse, particularly sexual abuse, does not fit with the cultural construction of femininity (Banning, 1989; Scavo, 1989; Howitt, 1992; Saradjian, 1996). To be considered 'feminine' means to be nurturing, protecting, caring, there to meet the needs of others, to be non-aggressive and non-sexual. To believe that a woman could sexually abuse a child requires one to challenge powerful stereotypes about motherhood and female-child relationships that are deeply held, even cherished by our society. As Larson and Maison state:

> Socially, we, as a culture, find it particularly difficult to think that women would sexually abuse children. Our Judeo-Christian heritage places enormous emphasis on women as warm, nurturing mothers. Furthermore, we are, at best, culturally ambivalent about female sexuality. We struggle with the notion of women – particularly mothers – being sexual at all (Larson & Maison, 1987: 30).

The difficulty accepting the notion of a sexually aggressive female has been substantiated in several empirical studies of the general population. For example, Broussard, Wagner and Kazelskis (1991) asked 180 female and 180 male undergraduate students their perceptions of child sexual abuse on the victim. Participants tended to view the interaction of a male victim with a female perpetrator as less representative of child sexual abuse. They also believed that male victims of female perpetrators would experience less harm than if the victim was a female and the perpetrator a male.

Finkelhor (1984) found that his survey participants tended to view the sexual offences of women as relatively insignificant. When he asked 521 parents about the seriousness of different types of sexual abuse, they rated adult female perpetrators' actions with both male and female victims as less abusive than those of adult male perpetrators with male or female victims. As Finkelhor aptly points out, these perceptions are important as they affect which cases get identified and treated as child sexual abuse.

In their study on social cognitions concerning adult male victims of female sexual assault, Smith, Pine and Hawley (1988) compared social judgements about male and female victims of heterosexual and homosexual rape. Based on a sample of 77 male and 89 female college students, the researchers found that male victims of sexual assault by a woman were judged more likely to have initiated or encouraged the sex acts and were viewed as experiencing less stress as a result of the experience than were female victims of male assault or same-gender assault victims. Male victims of women were also seen as experiencing the most pleasure from the assault.

Perhaps as a result of the common perception that women are incapable of being sexual aggressors, victims of female sexual abuse have difficulty accepting that a woman perpetrated the abuse. Sgroi and Sargent (1993) found that all seven adult female survivors that they interviewed reported that it was harder for them to sustain the belief that they had been sexually abused by a female relative than to acknowledge that they had been physically and/or emotionally abused by their mothers and sexually and/or physically abused by their fathers. All participants reported that the sexual abuse by a first degree relative (mother or sister) was the most shameful and damaging form of childhood victimization they had suffered. As one survivor noted:

> It's odd that the (sexual) abuse by my father was not as awful as the (sexual) abuse by my mother. There's something about a mother. When you're small, she should be the first person you go to if you're hurt, the first person to cuddle you. She should clothe you, feed you and give you physical love and care, as well as emotional support. So when she's the one who abuses, it leads to an even greater sense of despair than when your father abuses you (Elliott, 1993: 138).

This section has revealed the denial of women as potentially harmful sexual aggressors within the perceptions of the general population. In the following section, I will explore how this denial is reproduced within the annals of the criminal law.

The Criminal Law and Female Sex Offending

The criminal law is said to have a distinctly social basis; it both shapes and is shaped by the society in which it operates (Comack & Brickley, 1991). An examination of the laws governing sexual assault in both Canada and the United Kingdom reveal that the denial of women as potential sexual aggressors has not only been accepted and affirmed in the beliefs of the general population, but has also been cemented in everyday practices of law.

Within the Canadian Criminal Code (CCC), until 1983 a woman could not be charged with committing rape or indecent assault, and a male could not be a victim of such an assault. The legal definition of rape (Section 143) stated that 'a *male* person commits rape when he has sexual intercourse with a *female* person ...' (emphasis added). In a similar vein, prior to 1986, Section 150 of the CCC, which outlined the crime of incest, assumed that a female, and not a male, would be the victim of such an offence. Furthermore, female sexual passivity was reaffirmed in law by implying that females could not be the 'instigator' or 'aggressor' in cases of incest. Subsection (3) of the statute on incest noted:

> Where a female person is convicted of an offence under this section and the court is satisfied that she committed the offence by reason only that she was under restraint, duress or fear of the person with whom she had the sexual intercourse, the court is not required to impose any punishment upon her.

In a concerted effort to eradicate the gender specificity within the law and replace it with gender neutrality, the recent changes made to the CCC have ensured that it is now possible for a woman to be charged with a sexual offence and males can now be victims of incest.

The situation in the United Kingdom is particularly important as the majority of laws governing sexual offences continue to be gender specific, whereby a victim must be female and a perpetrator must be male (Keenan & Maitland, 1999). At the time of writing, a woman cannot be charged with committing rape and a male cannot be a victim of rape.[9] Section 1 (1) of the Sexual Offences (Amendment) Act 1976 provides that:

A *man* commits rape if:

1) *he* has unlawful sexual intercourse with a *woman* who at the time of the intercourse does not consent to it; and
2) at the time he knows that *she* does not consent to the intercourse or *he* is reckless as to whether *she* consents to it (emphasis added).

Under the current law, a woman can only be convicted of aiding or abetting a man to have sexual intercourse with another woman knowing that the other woman does not consent. As such, the construction of rape within UK law precludes the possibility of a woman acting as the principal sexual aggressor and that a male be a potential victim. Moreover, past judicial decisions propagated the belief that young children, particularly boys, did not need to be protected from the sexual advances of older women, as women were perceived to be sexually harmless. In the case of Upward (1976) the judge declared:

> It has never been an offence for a woman to have sexual intercourse with a boy, perhaps for the simple reason that Parliament has never thought it fit to legislate for it, or alternatively it may be that Parliament, which passes these Acts, takes the view that no great moral harm is done (cited in Edwards, 1984: 11).

The fact that historically, under both English and Canadian criminal law, women could not commit sexual offences, not only underscores the denial of women as potential sexual aggressors, but also provides some explanation of the low number of reported cases. The criminal law has not had the language to represent these cases or the political will to prosecute these cases.

Victim Under-Reporting

As noted earlier, victim under-reporting is considered a significant barrier to understanding the true dimensions of female sexual offending (Knopp & Lackey, 1987; Mathews, 1996; Rosencrans, 1997; Davin et al., 1999). There are several possible explanations for victim under-reporting, which include the taboo nature of female sexual abuse, the complexities of male victimization, and the nature of victim disclosures. These factors are intrinsically linked to the denial of women as potential sexual aggressors. Given the fear of challenging traditional sexual scripts of female sexual passivity, victims may refrain from reporting sexually abusive experiences by women in both self-report and case-report studies.

The taboo nature of female sex offending prevents many victims from coming forward with their experiences (Renvoize, 1982; Kasl, 1990; Elliott, 1993; Koonin, 1995). Victims often anticipate hostile reactions to their disclosures. As Elliott notes:

> Uncovering cases of female sexual abuse has been traumatic. There is a strongly held view that the issue of female sexual abuse should not be raised publicly, but should only be dealt with in private ... Secrecy, distress, anger, controversy, and fear surround the issue ... secrecy is deemed necessary because of the hostile reaction many have had to the subject of female sexual abuse ... it isn't safe yet (Elliott 1993: 1, 11).

Longdon (1993) claims that either from a fear of ridicule or from having previously received negative responses upon disclosure many survivors of female sexual abuse have, in desperation, and from a desire to receive help of any sort, said that their abuser was a man.

Rosencrans' (1997) study reveals that victims of female sexual abusers, both male and female, are unlikely to report the abuse. Rosencrans conducted a self-report study of women and men who were sexually abused by their mothers. The study relied upon participants to come forward with their histories of abuse and all participants were recruited by announcing the study at conferences, or through personal or professional referrals. A far greater number of females than males came forward to participate in the study (93 women versus nine men). Rosencrans' work revealed that victims of female perpetrated sexual abuse, both male and female, are unlikely to report the abuse. She noted that 80 per cent of the women and men in her sample viewed their sexually abusive treatment by their mother as the 'most hidden' aspect of their lives. Rosencrans found that only three per cent of the women, and none of the men told anyone about the sexual abuse during their childhood even though 100 per cent reported that it was damaging.

It has also been argued that boys, who are more often than girls the victims of female perpetrators, are especially reluctant to come forward and report the abuse, thus the low numbers of reported cases (Nasjleti, 1980; Fritz et al., 1981; Dimock, 1988; Vander Mey, 1988; Faller, 1989; Krug, 1989). Johnson and Shrier's (1987) research revealed that boy victims of female perpetrators experienced sexual abuse as highly traumatic. However, none of the boys reported the abuse to a mental health, social service, or criminal justice agency. Similarly, of 216 college men identified by Risin and Koss (1987) as having been sexually abused in childhood (47 per cent of whom were abused by a woman), 81 per cent had told no one about the sexual abuse.

Several authors have suggested several possible explanations as to why males may not report sexual offences by women. The explanations have centered on the denial of females as potential sexual aggressors and males as sexual abuse victims. As Krug notes:

1) Males do not get pregnant, and the evidence of sexual abuse has not been present;
2) A double standard in belief systems has existed in which fathers have the potential for evil and mothers are 'all good';
3) Adult males have been too embarrassed to reveal their sexual activity with and arousal by their mothers;
4) Male children have been presumed to be unaffected by sexual abuse, and reports by sons have been ignored; and/or
5) Patients and therapists alike have been unaware of the connection between the sexual abuse of males by mothers and later interpersonal relationship problems (Krug, 1989: 117-8).

Nasjleti (1980), Dimock (1988), and Bolton et al. (1989) have suggested that the failure of boys to report sexual contact with an older female is related to their gender socialization and perceptions of males as 'incapable' of sexual victimization. Boys are socialized to be physically aggressive, self-reliant, independent, and are not permitted to express feelings of helplessness, fear, weakness, or vulnerability. To report such victimization would highlight their vulnerability and emphasize their 'unmanliness'. As a result, male survivors have 'suffered silently' (Nasjleti, 1980).

Other studies have speculated that males are less likely to report abuse by females because they do not consider such sexual interaction to be abusive (Fromuth & Burkhart, 1987; Vander Mey, 1988; Johnson & Shrier, 1987; Mathews, 1996). Male sexual socialization encourages men to define sexual experiences as favourable as long as there is no homosexual involvement (Fromuth & Burkhart, 1987). Furthermore, sexual interaction between boys and older females is often treated by Western cultures as something desirable and enviable (Dimock, 1988; Lew, 1990; Mendel, 1995; Hunter, 1990; Trivelpiece, 1990). Mathews (1996) argues that such ideologies force males to minimize or reconstruct the meaning and impact of their victimization by females, and to see it as beneficial, harmless, a learning experience, or a rite of passage. As such, it is less likely that a sexual experience with an older female would be recognized as 'abuse', and therefore less likely to be reported (Dimock, 1988).

It has also been suggested that the socialization messages given to children, both male and female, are that males are the sexual perpetrators

(Etherington, 1995). This may contribute to the child's inability to interpret his or her experience as 'abuse' when approached sexually by a female.

The character and nature of victim disclosures are important factors when considering victim reporting, prevalence rates, and the denial of women as potential sexual aggressors. Research has shown that victims may be more inclined to disclose female sexual abuse within the context of a long-term therapeutic relationship (Marvasti, 1986; Margolin, 1987; Krug, 1989; Lawson, 1991, 1993). Therefore, these cases, which are usually managed by solely by clinicians, are unlikely to make it into official statistics or self-report studies.

Several authors have documented that both children and adults seem to experience more distress when disclosing sexual abuse by female perpetrators (Kendall-Tackett & Simon, 1987; Lew, 1990; Rudin et al., 1995). Sgroi and Sargent (1993) document that all of the adult survivors in their study found it more difficult to disclose the sexual abuse by their mothers than any other experiences of victimization by males. Lawson argues that 'in cases of mother-son sexual abuse, the taboo against disclosure is far stronger than the taboo against the behaviour itself' (Lawson, 1993: 264). However, within a therapeutic relationship based on mutual trust and respect, victims of female perpetrators and even perpetrators themselves may feel more comfortable disclosing inappropriate sexual interactions (Lawson, 1993; Sgroi & Sargent, 1993). For example, Chasnoff et al. (1986) document that three of their female patients voluntarily disclosed that they had sexually abused their infant sons. These cases were disclosed during individual or group therapy sessions conducted at a treatment program for chemically dependent women. Similarly, Marvasti (1986) found that it was only after several months of individual and group therapy, that five of his female patients disclosed that they had sexually abused their sons. None of the women in either study had been implicated in the criminal justice system.

Krug (1989) began a systematic inquiry of possible maternal sexual abuse among his patients after two individuals disclosed such histories. Krug states: 'After therapeutic rapport has been established, a surprising number have revealed their involvement with their mothers' (Krug, 1989: 112). During the course of psychiatric treatment, Margolin (1987) documented 16 cases of mother-son incest. Sarrel and Masters (1982) explored the cases of 11 males sexually assaulted by women who had requested treatment for sexual dysfunctions or disorders. Of the 11 men, only one sought sex therapy because of his molestation experience. All the others came for help with sexual dysfunctions and had not consciously connected the sexual abuse to subsequent sexual problems. After establishing a therapeutic rapport, the men revealed their sexually abusive pasts. Few of the men had ever disclosed their experiences prior to entering therapy.

Given that it seems to be more common to disclose sexual abuse by women in the context of therapy, therapists are often surprised and bewildered by official statistics. One therapist noted:

> When I started to work as a therapist in this four years ago the first child I worked with had been abused by his mother ... about 25 per cent of the hundreds of children I have worked with since that time have said a woman sexually assaulted them ... It is no longer a surprise to me when children mention a woman as an assailant, but what is a surprise is the figure of two per cent [from official statistics]. If that's true, the whole two per cent workload for the country is somehow ending up in my casebook (cited in Howitt, 1992: 105).

It must be acknowledged however, that even in the context of therapy, victims have difficulty revealing abuse by a female perpetrator. Kendall-Tackett and Simon (1987) and Sgroi and Sargent (1993) have noted that victims are more likely to disclose childhood sexual abuse by a male perpetrator and may wait until later in the treatment relationship before disclosing sexual abuse by a female perpetrator. Goodwin and DiVasto (1979) cite two cases in which clients initially presented with a complaint of after-effects of sexual abuse by males and only after the clients had developed sufficient trust in the therapeutic relationship did they reveal that they were abused by their mothers. Very few of the clinical cases mentioned above were ever reported to child abuse authorities and as such, they represent the 'dark figure' of female sexual abuse.

The context of victim disclosures is an important factor in establishing accurate prevalence rates. Both self and case-report studies may under-report the prevalence of female perpetrated abuse because victims are more likely to disclose such abuse within the confines of a trusted therapeutic relationship with clinicians, who are infrequently consulted in data collection surveys.

In the next section, I explore the available literature on professional responses to sexual abuse and their potential impact on the recognition of the female sex offending.

Professional Attitudes to Female Sex Offending

> Recognition of sexual molestation in a child is dependent upon the individual's inherent willingness to entertain the possibility that the condition may exist (Sgroi, 1975: 18).

Professionals working in the area of child sexual abuse such as social workers, psychiatrists, police officers, or judges, play a pivotal role in the identification and treatment of cases of child sexual abuse. As mentioned in the introduction, professionals' approach to inquiry and investigation, their reactions to disclosures, and procedures with regard to intervention, may have an enormous impact on who is labelled a 'victim', an 'offender', and what behaviours are identified, reported, and charged as 'sexual abuse'. In fact, professionals' initial perceptions of a disclosure can affect its entire course and outcome (Attias & Goodwin, 1985). In this sense, professional attitudes about female sexual abuse are likely to have a critical influence on prevalence rates.

Some professionals working in the area of child sexual abuse have shown a strong resistance to acknowledging and identifying cases involving female perpetrators (Lawson, 1993; Sgroi & Sargent, 1993; Holmes & Offen, 1996; Crawford, 1997). The emerging literature on female sexual offending has begun to underscore the ambivalent and sometimes dismissive professional responses to allegations of female child sexual abuse at all points in the child abuse system, whether it be police officers (Nelson, 1994; Hetherton & Beardsall, 1998), child protection workers (Howitt, 1992; Freel, 1995) or other professionals (Finkelhor, 1983; Finkelhor, Williams & Burns, 1988; Ramsay-Klawsnik, 1990; Williams & Farrell, 1990).

Many authors have proposed that the belief that women do not commit sexual offences has contributed to the professional bias (Banning, 1989; Allen, 1990; Howitt, 1992; Longdon, 1993; Mendel, 1995). Friedman (1988) argues that professionals, who have a tendency to see things within a gender specific schema, observe sexual misbehaviour in fathers and ignore that of mothers. Allen (1990) proposes that sexually abusive females may be permitted to drop out of the system that exists to protect children from abuse and that professionals may be less likely to 'report occurrences of female sexual abuse of children, investigators less diligent in conducting inquiries, attorneys less likely to prosecute, and judges more likely to dismiss or reduce charges' (Allen, 1990: 117).

Research has highlighted the professional denial of female sex offending. Cavanaugh-Johnson (1989) studied 13 girls between the ages of four and 12 who had sexually abused other children. All of the girls were patients in a sex offender treatment program specifically designed for children. Cavanaugh-Johnson argues that in all 13 cases, child protection workers and the criminal justice system failed to appropriately intervene. Despite the severity of the sexual abuse perpetrated by the girls, and the fact that the girls had a number of victims (ranging from one to 15), professionals tended to dismiss the sexual acts of these girls. Cavanaugh-Johnson writes:

> Mental health professionals appear to want to deny the existence of these children who are acting out sexually and often aggressively with other children ... In incest situations where the older sibling is molesting a younger one, children's service workers do not move to protect the younger child. None of the girls in the present study were filed on by the police, and therefore none were prosecuted. None of these girls ever spoke to a probation officer, and none of them were placed on probation. Child abuse reports were not filed. Not one of these children was mandated for treatment (Cavanaugh-Johnson, 1989: 572, 583).

What is puzzling about this study is that although Cavanaugh-Johnson criticizes the lack of professional intervention in relation to these girls, all of the girls were involved in a treatment program. Unfortunately, Cavanaugh-Johnson provides no explanation to account for this contradiction.

Nelson (1994) found that police officers who dealt with cases of involving female sex offenders reconstructed the offender and the offence in accordance with a 'fantasy model' that was more fitting with conventional images of gender and sexuality. In doing so, the severity of the sexual offence, and the impact on the victim were greatly diminished. Nelson outlines one case in which a mother, whose five-year old son had been sexually abused by a female babysitter, was frustrated at the police inaction in charging the female perpetrator. When Nelson questioned a police officer about the case, he responded:

> I wish that someone that looked like her (the babysitter) had sexually abused me when I was a kid ... the kid's mother is overreacting because someone popped her kid's cherry. Hell, it's every guy's dream (Nelson, 1994: 74).

Incidentally, no criminal charges were laid against the alleged perpetrator.

Hetherton and Beardsall (1998) identified gender biases in the decisions of social workers and police working in child protection. They found that sexually abusive females may be permitted to drop out of the child welfare system simply by virtue of their gender. The authors presented police officers and social workers with identical case vignettes of sexual abuse involving either a male or a female perpetrator. Both professional groups considered that social service involvement and investigation were less warranted when the perpetrator was female. Case registration and imprisonment of the male perpetrator was considered more important by both professional groups. The authors argue that victims of female sexual abuse may be less likely to receive the protection afforded victims of male sexual abuse. They argue that professionals may actually contribute to the low reported rates of female sex offending which perpetuates the view that the phenomenon is a rarity and less harmful than abuse committed by males.

In their study of sexual abuse in day care, Finkelhor et al. (1988) found that the social response to females who committed sex acts with children was more ambivalent that males committing similar acts. Cases involving female perpetrators were systematically decriminalized; they were less likely to be founded or to result in arrest or prosecution. The authors suggest that the criminal justice system may be more comfortable prosecuting, convicting and punishing whose who fit the traditional stereotype of a sex offender (that is, male) – the sample of cases in their study that made it to court included a disproportion of cases in which perpetrators and victims fit the stereotypes about sexual abuse.

Williams and Farrell (1990) analyzed 43 cases of alleged sexual abuse in day care. They found that cases fitting the popular stereotype of child molestation (a mature white middle to lower class male perpetrating against a young white female) is more likely to elicit a formal response, whereas cases at variance with this imagery (for example, a female perpetrator) require that aggravating conditions (such as force or oral sex) be present before formal actions are taken.

Research has also shown that even when victims disclose their victimization to a professional, they are often not believed (Ramsay-Klawsnik, 1990; Etherington, 1995; Holmes & Offen, 1996). Elliott (1993) reports that 78 per cent of her sample of 127 male and female survivors of female sexual abusers said they could find no one willing to help or believe them. In fact, one survivor in her sample was told that the abuser 'must have been male' and was offered help to deal with the 'real' abuser.

Krug (1989) initially questioned the validity of his private practice patients who reported being sexually abused by their mothers. However, the emotional distress that accompanied the disclosures convinced Krug that they were not fabrications. Many professionals working in the area of child sexual abuse concur that victims of sexual abuse by women have not received appropriate concern or attention. Many of these professionals have resorted to creative ways of ensuring that their clients receive attention. As one therapist noted:

> When I first began working in a mental health clinic, I would contact child protection workers as required by law when I suspected child abuse in a family.

After several cases I began to notice a disturbing pattern. When I reported a case involving a girl or boy being abused by an adult male, there was rapid action. However, when I reported a boy being abused by an adult female, very little was done; in many cases nothing was done. My clients saw the agency's lack of concern as a sign that what had been done to them was acceptable and that they had no business calling it abuse; this only added to the trauma they had experienced. In anger, I began calling the agency, saying, 'I have a case here where it appears that a 23 year old male is having intercourse with a 13 year old female. Do you think a child abuse investigation is in order?' Only after I was told 'Absolutely, this clearly is a case of abuse' would I say that I must have 'misspoken,' that I meant to say that it was a 23 year old *female* having sex with a 13 year old *male*. I found then that my clients began to get better attention (Hunter, 1990: 37, italics in original).

Allen (1990) proposes that the beliefs and attitudes that many professionals hold against the occurrence of female child abuse may have actually prepared them not to see it. For example, in a book for professionals working with survivors of child sexual abuse, O'Hagan (1989: 113) cites a case example in which a boy was sexually abused by his mother. However, the author later includes this disclaimer:

The examples of mothers sexually abusing their own children, which have been mentioned in previous chapters, *can be safely interpreted as aberrations, having little or no significance for the training of professionals in working with child sexual abuse* (O'Hagan, 1989: 113, emphasis added).

The refusal to acknowledge female sexual abuse may also be related to the strong feelings of fear, and revulsion that such abuse may rouse. Gentry (1978) and Cooper and Cormier (1990) note that the aforementioned feelings are frequent responses to child sexual abuse and that these responses will usually lead to widespread denial.

Banning (1989) suggests that the current cultural and professional bias against recognizing females as sexual offenders is reminiscent of Freud's struggle to persuade a disbelieving audience in 1896 of the possibility of father-daughter incest among his female patients. Howitt concurs:

Child abuse theoreticians have contributed a lot to the construction of notions about child sexual abuse by women. Indeed, some of them go through the denial and redefining processes which are analogous to those which have been seen as evidence of Freud's denial of sexual abuse (Howitt, 1992: 106).

This section has revealed the denial that appears to exist within the professional realm. This denial inevitably affects how cases of female perpetrated sexual offences are managed, and recorded, and whether or not they end up in official statistics.

Upon examining the social responses to female sex offending, there appears to be a denial of women as potential sexual aggressors. This denial, which was apparent in societal perceptions of female sexuality, the criminal law as it pertained to sexual assault, victim reporting practices, and professional attitudes to sexual offending, could work to obscure the true dimensions of the problem. The next chapter further examines the notion of denial and the processes by which denial may emerge, be maintained and reproduced within a given society.

Notes

1   This issue will be explored further on in this chapter.
2   Allen (1991) has noted that even when considering these low numbers, the actual number of children affected by female sex offending is substantial. Prevalence studies show that in the United States, an estimated 23 per cent of females are sexually abused in childhood. If five per cent of female children are abused by women, approximately 1.5 million females in the United States may have been sexually abused by females. Similarly, estimating that roughly 6.75 per cent of males experience sexual abuse in childhood, and that 20 per cent of those will have been abused by a female, approximately 1.6 million males will have been sexually abused by a female.
3   Forcible rape is defined as the carnal knowledge of a female forcibly and against her will. Included are rapes by force and attempts or assaults to rape. Statutory offences are excluded.
4   Sex offences (excluding forcible rape, prostitution and commercialized vice) are defined as statutory rape and offences against chastity, common decency, morals, and the like.
5   Sexual assaults are defined as any sexual act directed against another person, forcible and/or against that person's will; or not forcibly or against that person's will where the victim is incapable of giving consent because of his/her temporary or permanent mental or physical incapacity.
6   Sexual offences include buggery, rape, incest, indecent assault, gross indecency with a child, and unlawful sexual intercourse with a girl under 13, unlawful intercourse with a girl between 13 and 16.
7   Under the Canadian Criminal Code, sexual offences include sexual interference, invitation to sexual touching, sexual exploitation, incest, and bestiality.
8   It is important to acknowledge the difference in the two studies' definition of age criteria for perpetration. Amongst other criteria, the 1991 study required the male perpetrator to be at least 16 years old, which was not the case for the

1997 study of female perpetration. This was done in recognition of the authors' argument that sexual abuse by females is committed at a younger age. Given this difference in age criteria, comparing these studies' data could be problematic. However, assuming that there was no minimum offending age set for the 1991 study, and that the number of male perpetrators thus increased from three per cent to four per cent (an increase of 33 per cent), this would yield a rate of female offending of 50 per cent. This remains a notably higher rate than was found in case report literature.

9   The issue of gender bias in the laws governing sexual offences in the UK is currently being debated in Parliament as part of the major overhaul of the laws on sexual offences (Travis, 2002).

2 Understanding Denial: The Transformation and Dialectical Processes

To begin to understand the denial of women as potential sexual aggressors, it is necessary to place it within a broader social context. In this chapter I provide a framework for understanding the emergence and maintenance of denial using two social processes – a transformation process and a dialectical process. The transformation process helps to understand how denial emerges. I argue that in order to allay the discomfort of a 'deviant' reality – a reality that challenges the set of fundamental beliefs held by society, institutions and individuals – the deviant reality is realigned with more 'acceptable' cultural beliefs and is ultimately transformed. This transformation process leads to the denial of the deviant reality.

The dialectical process is used to illustrate how cultural values (and thus denial) are maintained and perpetuated within a given society. Three core elements are fundamental to the dialectical process – society, institutions and individuals. Although each of the three elements is important in their own right, it is their interconnecting relationship that is crucial to the discussion. The three elements work to simultaneously maintain and reproduce cultural values (and thus denial) in a dialectical and interdependent fashion.

The dialectical and transformation processes may ultimately provide a framework from which the denial of female sex offending can be understood. It should be noted, however, that both processes can be used to understand denial with regard to a vast array of social issues and are not limited to the study of female sex offending.

The Dialectical Process

The main goal of this portion of the chapter is to outline the central features of my proposed dialectical process. Drawing upon Anthony Giddens' notion of the 'duality of structure', which is outlined below, I introduce the concept of a dialectic. The notion of a dialectic illustrates both the idea that humans produce and reproduce social reality, as well as the dynamic relationship that exists between individual agency and larger structural constraints. I argue that social reality, and thus denial, are constructed and transmitted through a complex dialectical process involving three carriers of culture – society, institutions and individuals. These components can be considered 'carriers' of culture as they each play a fundamental role in the transmission and dissemination of cultural values. They do not exist in isolation to each other and one does not exert a greater influence on the others. Rather, they are equally powerful in their potential ability to shape and transmit cultural ideas from the point of view of both action and structure. The three carriers of culture form an interdependent dialectic whereby one relies upon, and simultaneously influences and reproduces the other. I argue that cultural values, and thus denial, are maintained and perpetuated through this dialectical process.

In his theory of structuration, Anthony Giddens (1984) seeks to resolve and reconcile the two valid but seemingly antithetical strands of 'action' and 'structure' in social theory. Giddens suggests that rather than seeing 'action' (individual agency, interaction, and the micro features of society) and 'structure' (structural constraints, collective forces, and the macro features of society) as oppositional elements of a dualism and mutually exclusive domains, we should regard them as the complementary terms of a duality – a 'duality of structure'. 'By the duality of structure' writes Giddens, 'I mean that social structures are both constituted by human agency, and yet at the same time are the very medium of this constitution' (Giddens, 1976: 121). In keeping with the duality of structure, every act of production is at the same time an act of reproduction as people reflexively produce and reproduce their social life (Giddens, 1979). Structure is believed to be internal to the flow of everyday action and it is both enabling and constraining. It is both medium and outcome, that is, as actors draw upon structures in order to provide guidance for their own actions, they reproduce them. The duality of structure is extremely well suited to illustrate the kind of relationship that I am trying to describe with regard to the dialectical process – that being an interactive and dynamic relationship reflecting both action and structure whereby people both draw upon, create and reproduce social structures in the course of their everyday social activity.

Three Components of the Dialectic: Society, Institutions and Individuals

Before outlining the dynamics and relationships within my proposed dialectical process and how it relates to the denial of female sex offending, I explore each component of the dialectic and its role in the dissemination of cultural values. For explanatory purposes, a description of each of the three carriers of culture is necessary. However, the three components (society, institutions and individuals) should not be seen as mutually exclusive, but as an interactive whole. A detailed description of the ways in which society, institutions and individuals interconnect, as well their relationship to denial will be addressed later on in the chapter.

Society

Society, which represents both the entity existing outside of individuals and institutions, and that which would not exist without them, is one carrier of culture within the dialectical process. The notion of 'society' does not exist in a concrete or tangible form in the way that individuals do. Rather, it has a 'virtual' existence (Layder, 1994), which can be understood as traces in the memories of the individuals who draw on the 'rules' that constitute it. It is necessary to explore how these rules or values emerge and their power within the dialectic. To understand this, we can turn to the work of Berger and Luckmann (1966) and Giddens (1984).

In their exploration of how societal values emerge and are transmitted, Berger and Luckmann argue that through the accumulation of consciousness, common sense, language, symbols, and through intense social interaction with others, humanity creates a social stock of knowledge. This social stock of knowledge provides a code of conduct for every day practice, and the standards and values by which one should live and behave in a given society within a particular historical context. Through continual social interaction, the social stock of knowledge is said to be passed down from one generation to the next. With the passage of time and the constant sharing of the stock of knowledge with a new generation, Berger and Luckmann suggest that this knowledge becomes 'institutionalized' – a rigid and structured way in which things are done. These rules, values and practices slowly become 'common sense' or 'conventional wisdom' to societal members (Bash, 1995).

Giddens (1984) provides a similar, yet more dynamic explanation of the development of societal values which reflects both action and structure. He suggests that when actors create society they do not do so from scratch, but draw on pregiven resources. According to Giddens, there are three kinds of such resources; meanings (things known – the social stock of knowledge), morals (value system), and power (patterns of domination and divisions of interest). He argues that all large-scale social phenomena are patterns of interaction yet they can also be thought of as structure in that they are systematic, regular and permanent insofar as actors reproduce them in the future. These patterns of interaction are what he regards as 'social practices' – the behavioural and institutional dimensions of the practical consciousness of reflexive people who draw on shared cultural beliefs and stocks of knowledge.

In essence, Giddens' notion of 'social practices' and Berger and Luckmann's notion of 'institutionalized knowledge' actually embody society. Such knowledge and practices are represented as traces in the memories of individuals who in turn draw upon them. As such, the notion of society can be seen as structurally constraining as it has an impact on the way in which individuals orient their behaviour. However, society is also enabling as individuals (and institutions) can play a crucial role in the shaping of society's rules and knowledge. Moreover, individuals and institutions can choose which values or rules they will incorporate or endorse. Individuals actively shape society while broader structural considerations simultaneously constrain and enable individual behaviour.

It is the capacity to influence both individuals and institutions through such rules (and in turn for individuals and institutions to influence society) that allows society, despite having an intangible and 'virtual' existence, to be seen as a carrier of culture and to argue that it plays a fundamental role in the dissemination of cultural values to both institutions and individuals.

Over time, various forms of societal knowledge and social practices may evolve into what are known as 'traditional scripts'. The following section outlines the meaning of traditional scripts and their role in the dissemination and perpetuation of societal values.

Traditional scripts   Traditional scripts can be considered forms of knowledge and practices that have been informally converted into smaller, more manageable parts. Scripts are an important aspect of society as they embody societal knowledge and practices. These 'scripts' provide behavioural guidelines to a myriad of situations and a means through which we can assess that behaviour. Just as a theatrical script provides an actor with his or her lines and a framework from which to play their character, traditional scripts provide individuals with a framework for viewing the world and acting out situations within it. Scripts emerge from institutionalized knowledge and social practices; they are likely to reflect the values of a given society. As a result, they can be a means through which individuals recall societal 'rules' in a quick and efficient way. However, their scripted format can make them inflexible and thus, if taken in their purest form, they may be regarded as a one-dimensional presentation of a more diverse and multi-faceted phenomenon. Although scripts may be set out in advance, they are not entirely constraining or all-powerful. Just as one actor has the ability to interpret a theatrical script and play the character slightly differently than another, individuals may choose to enact traditional scripts, modify them, or reject them entirely, illustrating how both action and structure are embedded within traditional scripts. Moreover, reflecting the duality of structure, individuals draw on traditional scripts in their interactions with others and in doing so, reproduce them.

It is important to note that what is perceived and established as a script in one culture, may be different in another. There are likely to be variations in traditional scripts from society to society and over time, corresponding to the socio-historical context. Particularly in industrial societies which are characterized by cultural heterogeneity and complexity, there are likely to be subtle variations in scripts according to one's social class, race, ethnicity, gender, and age.

There are several possible reasons why scripts may be relied upon by both individuals and institutions. Scripts can help people to make sense of the world around them. They allow us to compartmentalize behaviour and create order and stability. In fact, traditional scripts may be invoked when there is uncertainty or confusion with regard to a particular situation as they may provide clarity. Scripts are also useful because of their speed and efficiency. They allow us to frame behaviour or sum up situations in a relatively predictable way. They enable us to summarize ambiguous situations and to recall the 'rules' of society in a quick and easy manner. Finally, to some extent, the complexity of the social world requires us to simplify information and to disregard in some measure evidence that is contrary to our own beliefs (Hosking & Morley, 1991). Often, there is a need to justify the relationship between our ideas and actions with a gloss of constancy rather than inconsistency (Holdaway, 1996: 157). Scripts may provide such a gloss of constancy.

There are many different types of scripts that guide a range of behaviours and situations. The type of script that will be discussed in this book are sexual scripts. Gagnon and Simon explain the role of sexual scripts:

[Sexual] scripts are involved in learning the meaning of internal states, organizing the sequences of specifically sexual acts, decoding novel situations, setting the limits on sexual responses, and linking meanings from non-sexual aspects of life to specifically sexual experience (Gagnon & Simon, 1974: 19).

Sexual scripts are said to provide motivations for sexual conduct and are bound up with cultural notions of femininity and masculinity. Women and men are said to learn to be sexual in different ways – 'to enact different roles in the sexual drama' (Jackson, 1978: 30). Though it may appear that sexual behaviour is a private matter, something uniquely personal, each sexual relationship is structured by the cultural values of the society in which it takes place. Conventional sexual scenes appear to be scripted for an active male and a passive female. As Jackson notes:

> From the beginning boys learn to be independent, to seek success actively through their own efforts and abilities while girls are encouraged to be dependent, to seek success passively through pleasing others. It is hardly surprising that when they learn of the erotic implications of relationships between them they should express their sexuality this way. The man becomes the seducer, the woman the seduced, he the hunter, she the prey (Jackson, 1978: 31).

Indeed, traditional sexual scripts are heterosexual and gendered (Jackson, 1978; Koss & Harvey, 1991). Traditional sexual scripts for females centre primarily on sexual passivity and virtuousness (Welldon, 1988; Birch, 1993). They tend to exclude the image of women as sexual aggressors, as initiating sex with men, as indicating their sexual interest and, at times, coercing their reluctant partners to engage in unwanted sexual activities (Byers & O'Sullivan, 1998). Although women may be regarded as 'temptresses' or 'seductresses', this is more often a submissive and coy role than an aggressive one. Women are to be desired by the male onlooker, however they are rarely the active initiators of sexuality. Traditional sexual scripts for males focus mainly on sexual aggression and exclude the image of men as sexually reluctant or as victims of sexual coercion or assault (Hunter, 1990; Lew, 1990; Mendel, 1995). Men are perceived to be highly sexually aggressive and once they become sexually aroused, they are believed to be at the mercy of their desires (Smart, 1976; Jackson, 1978; Tiefer, 1989).

Although individuals can and do defy traditional sexual scripts, there may be consequences to doing so. Women who fail to conform to traditional sexual scripts by evidencing too much sexual desire, excessive sexual activity, or challenging notions of innate female sexual passivity may be labelled as sexually out of control or duplicitous (the whore) (Lunbeck, 1987; Groneman, 1994; Lloyd, 1995; Naylor, 1995). For example, in the late nineteenth century, 'nymphomania', the term used to describe out of control sexuality in women, was believed to be a specific organic disease, classifiable with an assumed set of symptoms, and treatments (Storer, 1856; Walton, 1857; Diethelm, 1971). As it has in the past, the term continues to resonate with a sense of the insatiable sexuality of women, devouring, depraved, and diseased (Groneman, 1994). It conjures up an aggressively sexual female who both terrifies and titillates men (Naylor, 1995). This imagery conveys the idea that sexually aggressive women are somehow not 'real' or 'normal' women. Their sexual interest and desire defy notions of acceptable (passive) femininity and as a result, such women may be pathologized or regarded with disdain. Similar implications may arise for men who act in ways which counter traditional sexual scripts of sexual aggression and prowess. Such men may be regarded as effeminate or even homosexual (Messner & Kimmel, 1989; Lew, 1990). In essence, there may be social costs involved with challenging traditional sexual scripts.

One of the problems with employing the concept of scripts is that the term seems to imply that people are merely passive recipients of an established social order. Clearly, this is not the case. Individuals actively negotiate and contribute to scripts. As Layder (1994) and Giddens (1984) suggest with regard to human action, people are not simply compelled by forces outside of themselves and they do not act mechanically and blindly as if compelled by laws of nature. They are always capable, to some degree, of resisting the constraints imposed on them by society and of influencing and transforming their social situation. Therefore, I use the concept of scripts with the knowledge that they are not static or one-dimensional but are more dynamic, reflecting both individual agency and broader social structural constraints. Regardless of whether scripts accurately reflect social reality, they are an important part of the knowledge that makes up society.

Institutions

Institutions are another component in the dialectic. According to Giddens, institutions and organizations[1] represent the concrete activities of human subjects which are organized, regular and enduring. Institutions are the visible patterns of social relations that have become a routine feature of society by being continually reproduced in people's behaviour. Institutions provide a way of seeing and being to individuals working within them (Jenkins, 1996). Moreover, they are said to order social life, provide predictability, and templates for how things should be done (Berger & Luckmann, 1966; Jenkins, 1996; Holdaway, 1997). As Jenkins writes:

Institutions are an integral part of the social construction of reality, with reference to which, and in terms of which, individuals make decisions and orient their behaviour (Jenkins, 1996: 127).

Research suggests that the surrounding organizational culture is highly influential to individual practice, regardless of the nature of the occupation (Light, 1980; Waddington, 1984; Fielding, 1988; Fook, Ryan & Hawkins, 1994). What is observed, particularly in the context of formal training, is said to mould individual outlooks and contribute to one's overall socialization (Bucher & Stelling, 1977; Light, 1980; Maxmen, 1985). In fact, research has shown that professionals maintain what they have read or been taught even where it is contradicted by their own work experience and knowledge (Dietz & Craft, 1980; La Barbara, Martin & Dozier, 1980). Through training, education, and through organizational shorthands, a concept to be outlined shortly, an organization furnishes a *cultural code* (Atkinson, 1983) promoting unique sets of values, beliefs and practices which individuals within the institution may or may not embrace. It should be noted however, that the development of a cultural code is not only a result of the internal workings of the institution. The cultural code is also likely to be a reflection of broader societal knowledge and contexts, highlighting the important influence of broader societal values have on institutions. Thus Giddens' concept of the duality of structure, whereby the institutional culture draws upon and reproduces broader societal ideologies, is embedded within the conceptualization of institutions.

Despite the constraining aspects of institutions, it is critical to keep in mind that institutions are also enabling as they allow people to act and to make a difference within the work context. As demonstrated above, institutions reflect the 'structure' component of the action-structure duality. However, they can also be seen to reflect the 'action' component of the duality in that they do not exist independently of the reasons, motivations and reflexive behaviour of actual people. Indeed, one must not forget that institutions do not have a life of their own. As Giddens (1984) suggests, social life is made to happen by social actors in the flow of their intentional conduct. Thus, it is apparent that action and structure are embedded within the organizational context both enabling and constraining behaviour. It is the potential power of institutions to influence, and in turn, be influenced by organizational members, which enables them to be considered carriers of culture. With the passage of time, an organization's unique sets of rules and beliefs may evolve into 'organizational shorthands'. This concept and its role in organizational policy and practice will be discussed in the following section.

Organizational shorthands If institutions are carriers of culture, then organizational shorthands are one means through which that that culture is carried, as they exemplify organizational values and beliefs, as well as the everyday practices of those individuals working within organizations. The essence of a 'shorthand' is similar to that of a script – a rigid, one-dimensional presentation of a more diverse and multi-faceted phenomenon. However, they are specific to a particular organizational context and reflect the values of that context.

To simplify information about complex situations, members of an institution may evoke mental and conceptual images which help guide them in assessing persons and situations (Edwards, 1984). Organizational shorthands may develop about individuals, groups, morality, immorality, good and bad people, institutions, practices and community settings and these shorthands may be employed in a routine way (Cicourel, 1968). Shorthands provide quick references as to 'what is going on' and have been found to influence professional responses and decision-making in regard to homicide defendants (Swiggert & Farrel, 1977), the treatment of skid-row residents (Bittner, 1967), juvenile delinquents (Piliavin, 1964), and shoplifters (Steffensmeier & Terry, 1973).

As an example, stereotypical thinking and the use of organizational shorthands have been identified as a characteristic of police thinking and action (Manning, 1977; Holdaway, 1997). In the early 1960s Maureen Cain found that officers divided the population into categories of 'roughs' and 'respectables'. In addition, people were further differentiated by gender and race. 'Coloured immigrants', the term used by officers to characterize all minority ethnic groups, were typified as disorderly, potentially violent and permanently under suspicion. Asians were regarded as devious, liars and potential illegal immigrants (Cain, 1973: 117-9). Holdaway (1983) found that there was a widely shared view among British police officers at Hilton that you could not trust black people. Black people were typified as not liking the police, as disorderly, as having a predisposition to crime, as violent and as a complaining, untrustworthy group. Holdaway (1996, 1999) argues that stereotypical thinking within the police is a stable feature of the occupational culture and is said to amplify racial prejudice and possibly discrimination.

There are several possible explanations as to why members of institutions employ shorthands in the context of their daily work. Like scripts, organizational shorthands provide speed and efficiency. In work contexts that continually demand the immediate summarizing of ambiguous situations, shorthands provide a fast and efficient method for understanding situations and making decisions.

Since organizational shorthands may be a significant part of the organizational culture, there may be pressure to conform to them. Within the context of professional work, rejecting organizational shorthands may be difficult as a result of occupational norms, and expectations. Sanctions may be associated with deviating from the institutionalized routine. Within an organization, 'the ways things are done' may quickly become 'the way things should be done' (Jenkins, 1996: 128). Individuals may be vilified should they depart from the established organizational shorthands.

Like traditional scripts, organizational shorthands can enable and constrain organizational behaviour. They provide the rules and direction in which individuals may feel compelled to orient their behaviour, while simultaneously allowing individuals to choose the direction that their behaviour takes. Regardless of whether organizational shorthands accurately represent social reality, they are crucial to understanding the internal dynamics of institutions.

Individuals

Individuals are another component in the dialectic. It is important to note that what goes on in society and its institutions do not go on 'behind the backs' of individuals. In essence, individual actors' reasons and intentions are centrally involved in the creation and recreation of social life (Giddens, 1984: 71).

There are two types of 'individuals' which are relevant to this discussion; individuals working within institutions and individuals apart from institutions. While the boundaries between these two categories of individuals are in some ways blurred (as individuals can be both within and apart from institutions at the same time), both sets of individuals can be considered carriers of culture as they have the capacity to influence the development of societal values, other individuals within the parameters of their work culture (individuals within institutions), as well as those within their personal context such as family or friends, either through action or even inaction. As Layder writes:

> Each individual is party to collective decisions and plays some part in the outcome of events even if it does not reflect their own wishes and intentions. This holds true even if a person does not appear to be taking any active role in the 'business' of the encounter, since silence or inactivity may be a very effective means of influencing others (Layder, 1974: 66).

However, the individual is not entirely free but is constrained by social determinations. As we have seen from the preceding discussions, individuals are likely to be influenced by both society and institutions. Once again, the dynamic relationship between broader structural constraints and individual human action becomes evident.

It is important to note that individuals may, during the course of their everyday lives, rely upon either traditional scripts or organizational shorthands or both, depending upon the context in which they find themselves and their willingness to endorse them. However, as individuals have the power to embrace or reject their surrounding structures, they may use all, some, or none of scripts or shorthands. The use or rejection of scripts may also depend on the strength of the institutional norms or peer pressure.

Linking Society, Institutions and Individuals

Although society, institutions and individuals each play an important role in the transmission of culture, it is when they are viewed as a complex whole that the true extent of their cultural influence is revealed. Instead of conceptualizing social reality as being made up of the three separate entities of society, institutions and individuals, it may be more helpful to think of them as involved in a dialectical process where one entity relies upon, and informs the others.

Let us first explore the dialectical relationship between society and institutions. The relationship between broader societal values and institutional values is thought to be a close one. Martin and Jurik (1996: 37) suggest that work cultures are not only shaped by cultural factors outside work organizations, but that institutions draw upon these larger societal values and norms in the development of their distinct organizational culture. Organizations are thought to be sites for the construction and display of cultural images, symbols, ideologies that legitimate broader cultural ideologies (Hall, 1982; Martin & Jurik, 1996). In this way, institutions may draw upon and reproduce broader societal values in their organizational context. Concurrently, societal values are likely to be strengthened in the process of being reproduced by institutions.

Institutions and individuals are closely connected. As we have seen, institutions have the power to influence individuals within the organizational context. The institutional training and way of 'seeing' may frame and guide the lens through which individual workers come to view their work. These individuals may also draw on institutional values that may inform their personal beliefs. However, individuals inevitably contribute to, influence, and reproduce the values and culture of their surrounding institution.

Individuals who are apart from institutions remain intimately related to them. Inevitably, individuals will come into contact with a variety of institutions. The policies and practices of these institutions are likely to have an impact on their lives. Conversely, these individuals can have an important influence on organizational policy and practice.

Individuals are also closely linked to society. Individuals may draw upon broader societal values in the development of their personal ideologies and their everyday lives. Simultaneously, they contribute to the formation of societal values and by doing so, strengthen, reinforce and reproduce them. This entire process is exemplified below in figure 2.1.

The dialectical and interdependent relationship between society, institutions and individuals is reflective of Giddens' notion of the duality of structure whereby every act of production is at the same time an act of reproduction, as people reflexively produce and reproduce their social life. As actors draw upon structures in order to provide guidance for their own actions, they reproduce them.

A helpful example illustrating this interconnecting relationship between society, institutions, and individuals can be illustrated using the example of race and racism. Contemporary racism by whites against blacks, for instance, is said to be rooted in centuries of oppression and struggle that formed the foundations of relations between the white majority and black minorities (Essed, 1991). Racism is a complex set of ideologies, attitudes and beliefs claiming racial superiority, and sometimes involving racial discrimination and disadvantage for ethnic minorities (Cashmore, 1996). Racism is thought to be created and reproduced out of a complex set of conditions, drawing on cultural and ideological remnants of previous historical processes and further determined by the economic, political, social, and organizational conditions of society (Essed, 1991: 12). Racist discourse of blacks, for example, has focused on stereotypical imagery of blacks as lazy, untrustworthy, disorderly, or criminal (Holdaway, 1997).

By analyzing police responses to and treatment of racial and ethnic minorities, it is possible to illustrate how institutions appear to construct, sustain and reproduce notions of race within their organizations. Several studies have shown that racist values play an important role in the everyday culture of the police at both the rank and file and command levels (Smith & Gray, 1986; Reiner, 1991; Young, 1991; Keith, 1993; Holdaway, 1983).

Research has found that instead of challenging racist banter and practices, supervisory officers are often drawn into them (Holdaway, 1996: 1650).   This highlights how broader societal beliefs about race may influence institutional ideology and practice and ultimately illustrates the enactment of both the dialectic and the duality of structure.

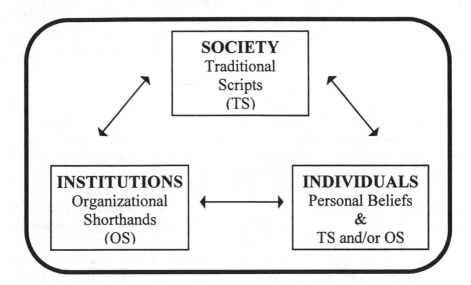

Figure 2.1   The Dialectical Process

The presence of institutional police racism in Britain has been highlighted in the Macpherson (1999) report. The report followed an investigation into the case of Stephen Lawrence, a young black man who was a victim of a racially motivated attack by a gang of white youths. The report defined 'institutional racism' as:

> The collective failure of an organization to provide an appropriate and professional service to people because of their colour, culture or ethnic origin. It can be seen or detected in processes, attitudes and behaviours which amount to discrimination through unwitting prejudice, ignorance, thoughtlessness, and racist stereotyping which disadvantage minority ethnic people (Macpherson, 1999: 28).

Perhaps reflecting racist ideologies in society as a whole, the police have been criticized for making minimal attempts to address racism within police forces (Solomos, 1993). For example, the Macpherson report found that not a single officer had received any training of significance in racism awareness and race relations throughout the course of his or her career (Kushnick, 1999: 2). Furthermore, the Institute of Race Relations, in its evidence of Part two of the Macpherson Inquiry, argued that: 'There is an overwhelming body of evidence to support the proposition that black communities in Britain are the subject to a differential and discriminatory pattern of policing' (Institute of Race Relations, 1999: 1).

Thus far, it is possible to see the enactment of the duality of structure in the dialectical relationship between society and institutions. Broader societal beliefs about race appear to be drawn upon, articulated and reproduced by institutions such as the police service.

The duality of structure where individuals draw upon existing structures and simultaneously reproduce them is also evident in the dialectical relationship between individuals and their surrounding society and institutions. This is demonstrated by the fact that individual police officers appear to draw upon both societal and institutional ideologies concerning race in their everyday practices. Referring again to the case of Stephen Lawrence, this can be identified in police officers' treatment of Duwayne Brooks, Stephen Lawrence's friend who was with him when Lawrence was killed. Following the attack on Lawrence, Brooks reported to the police that the assailants called Lawrence 'nigger'. Officers were reluctant to accept Brooks' statement. Whether unaware or unwilling, the police failed to define the attack as racially motivated. In fact, Brooks was later regarded as a possible suspect in the murder (Holdaway, 1999). The treatment of Duwayne Brooks reveals the ways in which individual officers drew upon broad culturally available meanings of black people as troublesome, as potentially criminal, and as presenting a problem of public order which are widely based ideas about black youth and black people more generally (Solomos, 1993; Holdaway, 1999). It is possible to see how these negative, racializing categorizations which are said to have become institutionalized within policing (Holdaway, 1999) are relied upon and reproduced by individual officers within the context of their daily work.

The example of institutionalized racism and the case of Stephen Lawrence highlight the dynamics of the aforementioned dialectical process as well as the way in which this process is illustrative of Giddens' notion of the duality of structure. Institutions appear to draw upon and perpetuate larger cultural meanings of race in their institutional policies and practices that put ethnic minorities at a significant disadvantage. Concurrently, individual officers may also draw upon these same cultural meanings of race and actively construct, sustain, and reproduce inaccurate and discriminatory views of ethnic minorities.

The dialectical process appears to provide a coherent framework from which to understand how cultural values and beliefs are sustained, transmitted and reproduced through the three carriers of culture. The next portion of the chapter returns to the core issues of the book; the issue of denial and how denial emerges. The transformation process, which will be addressed in the next section, provides a model for understanding the emergence of denial.

Sexual Taboos and the Origins of Denial

Understanding how the denial of a particular issue emerges is complex, as it is not likely to stem from a single source. However, because denial (particularly denial in relation to sexuality) may be linked to societal taboos, it may be helpful to briefly examine the notion of taboos, particularly sexual taboos. Mary Douglas' (1966) work entitled *Purity and Danger* provides some insights into the roots of societal taboos. More specifically, Douglas traces the origins of sexual taboos to the desire of a community to preserve purity within the social order and ensure support for moral values. Any behaviour which is seen to 'pollute' or cross a pre-determined line that should not be crossed is regarded as 'boundary pollution'. According to Douglas, these pollution beliefs provide a kind of impersonal punishment for wrongdoing and a means of supporting the accepted system of morality. Douglas argues that because boundary pollution focuses particularly on sexuality, behaviours such as incest are viewed as sexual pollution and thus vilified in most cultures.

The taboo against sexual relations in the family is said to have existed since our earliest recorded history (Cooper, 1990). Like most sexual taboos, the incest taboo is not likely to have emerged from a single source. Instead, it is likely to stem from a complex array of factors. According to Mitterauer (1994) there are four theories that have been used to explain the root of the incest taboo.[2] The first is the biological approach that asserts that the taboo on incest stems from the danger of inbreeding. Investigation of both humans and animals seems to show that inbreeding has genetically negative consequences for the offspring. In humans, the children of close relatives show a distinctively greater incidence of disease and deformity, often referred to as 'inbreeding degeneration' (Mitterauer, 1994). This is said to motivate a ban on incest.

The second approach to explaining the taboo is the 'theory of indifference' (Mitterauer, 1994). It assumes an innate aversion from sexual intercourse between persons who have lived together from early youth. For example, boys and girls who have grown up together in the same child-group of a kibbutz apparently never enter love relationships or marriage in later life (Shepher, 1971). What is notable about the theory of indifference is that the aversion to incest is related not to biology, but to social proximity.

The third theory concerning the root of the incest taboo stems from cultural anthropology and Lévi-Strauss' 'theory of exchange' (Lévi-Strauss, 1969). Lévi-Strauss holds that the incest taboo is not so much a ban on marrying one's mother, sister, or daughter as a command to give them to a man from another group. From this perspective, societies consist of a series of exchanges and the most valuable items of exchange are women. Thus, the incest taboo is a rule of reciprocity; but it is not a purely social rule. Lévi-Strauss argues that the prohibition of incest is the 'fundamental step because of which, by which, but above all in which, the transition from nature to culture is accomplished' (Lévi-Strauss, 1969: 24).

A fourth theory is a sociological one that is based on a desire for stability in family roles and relationships. It is assumed that the main function of the incest taboo is to avoid tensions that might be created by uncertainty over roles within the family (Mitterauer, 1994). The incest taboo is said to prevent potentially intolerable sexual rivalries within the family.

The origins of sexual taboos such as incest can thus be traced to a multiplicity of factors. However, whatever the source of the taboo, when it is broken it is likely to create varying degrees of conflict and psychological discomfort (Gentry, 1978; Cooper & Cormier, 1990). In the next section, I describe my conceptualization of the transformation process and how it furthers our understanding of sexual taboos as well as denial.

The Transformation Process

The transformation process begins when realities or situations present themselves that challenge accepted traditional scripts or organizational shorthands. In some instances, what are initially perceived as 'deviant' realities may slowly be integrated into the social stock of knowledge, eventually becoming a part of the accepted reality. In other instances, however, 'deviant' realities may evoke conflict or discomfort as they threaten the security of ones model of the world (Saradjian, 1996). In such cases, in order to alleviate the conflict, individuals may attempt to transform the socially aberrant realities. This transformation may be done (either unwittingly or consciously) by employing a particular lens – invoking a particular way of seeing the world. The lens acts as a tool to assist in the transformation process – it focuses one's vision in a particular direction and it works to distort or colour one's perceptions of the 'deviant' reality.

There may be different types of lenses used in this process. For example, racialized or gendered lenses are ones where race or gender become central to the meaning and focus of one's gaze. Although factors well beyond an individual's race or gender are likely to be fundamental to understanding the complexity of a situation or reality, with a gendered lens, for example, it is the individual's gender, and all of the scripts and shorthands that are tied up with that concept, which become paramount in understanding the situation or reality.

Regardless of the type of lens invoked, the lens ultimately serves to distort the 'deviant' reality and bring it into alignment with traditional scripts, organizational shorthands, and accepted cultural views – thus alleviating the initial discomfort. This transformation process necessarily leads to the denial of the deviant reality. By denying, we are refusing to accept a 'deviant' version of reality and attempting to maintain the security in our model of the world. If the denial becomes widespread within a particular group or society, then a *culture of denial* may arise. This process is exemplified below in figure 2.2.

It is important to note that the transformation process can, like the dialectical process, be seen to exemplify the 'real life' enactment of the duality of structure. Individuals, in searching for guidance for their own actions, appear to recall, draw upon, and sometimes reproduce the constraining societal 'rules' that define what behaviours are 'acceptable' as well as those that are considered 'deviant'. It is possible to see how the transformation process reflects the enabling and constraining nature of Giddens' notions of the duality of structure. While broader structural constraints may influence an individual's definition as to what is 'acceptable' and what is 'deviant', an individual may choose to accept or reject the 'deviant' reality and may choose whether or not to enact the transformation process.

To provide a more concrete example of this transformation process, its relationship to the duality of structure, and how this process may lead to denial, I will explore responses to father-daughter incest, and more specifically, the response of the highly influential psychoanalyst, Sigmund Freud. Freud's response to father-daughter incest helps to illustrate the enactment of the transformation process, as well as Giddens' notion of the duality of structure.

Towards the end of the nineteenth century, when Sigmund Freud had a private clinical psychiatric practice, the issue of incest was not perceived to be an issue of great social concern (Russell, 1986). In fact, it was thought to be extremely rare, if not non-existent. However, Freud began to see patients in his practice who appeared to be recalling childhood incestuous

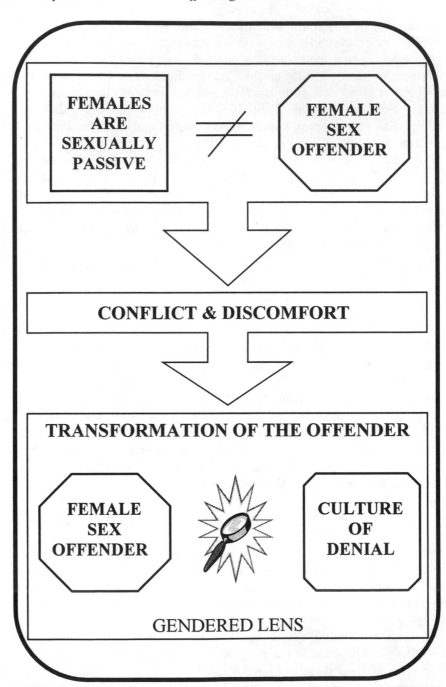

Figure 2.2   The Transformation Process

interactions with their fathers. Freud described the experiences of these female patients in a paper entitled *The aetiology of hysteria* (Freud, 1962).

Initially, Freud understood his patients' recollections to be repressed traumatic memories of actual early life events. In his paper, he theorized that these events, the anxiety they evoked, and the consequent necessity to repress them, resulted in later pathology. The paper ultimately acknowledged that the rather unsavoury reality of father-daughter incest did occur. However, for reasons not entirely clear, Freud retracted his theory and redefined the experiences of these women as sexual fantasy (Herman, 1981; Russell, 1984; Miller, 1985). As was noted in the introduction, there has been a great deal of speculation about Freud's motives for his sudden retraction. Explanations for the sudden change in perspective have included hypotheses about the power of social forces in Europe at that time, Freud's own family history and possible childhood abuse by his father, the failure to convince his colleagues of the merits of his theory, and Freud's exhaustion from working with such difficult to treat patients (Freyd, 1996). Russell (1986) has suggested that his change in perspective was precipitated by the fact that he was disturbed by his own incestuous desires towards his daughter.

Freud's retraction of his initial theory and his subsequent redefinition of these women's experiences can be used to illustrate the enactment of the transformation process. Arguably, the issue of father-daughter incest was controversial and challenged the accepted views of father-daughter relationships at that time. Perhaps in response to the discomfort and conflict that his theory (and its implications) evoked in others, as well as the negative reactions that may have been directed towards him and his work, Freud transformed his initial theory. In keeping with the transformation process, Freud appeared to employ a lens which distorted the reality of father-daughter incest. In altering his 'gaze' Freud was able to realign the experiences of his clients to converge with the accepted views and traditional scripts of the time which upheld the rarity of incest. Although transforming these women's experiences as sexual fantasy may have allayed the discomfort which his theory evoked, Freud ultimately denied the reality of father-daughter incest and contributed to the culture of denial that was already in place at that time.

From the above example, it is possible to see the enactment of Giddens' notion of the duality of structure. In searching for guidance for his actions, Freud appears to have been influenced and constrained by broader structural considerations and societal 'rules' which defined incest as a rare and insignificant phenomenon. As Freud drew upon structures (rules) in order to provide guidance for his actions, he ultimately reproduced those same structures.

Returning to the transformation process, denial thus appears to emerge as a response to 'deviant' social realities – realities which challenge traditional scripts and create discomfort within a given society. However, it is necessary to understand how, once introduced, this denial is sustained and reproduced. This is where the dialectical process comes in. Just as society, institutions, and individuals simultaneously construct, articulate, and reproduce particular cultural values and ideologies in a dialectical fashion, they also maintain and reproduce denial in a similar fashion, reflecting the duality of structure.

The issue of father-daughter incest can once again provide an example of this process. At the societal level, prior to the mid-1970s, there appeared to be both a resistance to identifying individual cases of incest, as well as an overt denial of its occurrence (Herman, 1981; Miller, 1985; Elliott, 1993; Mendel, 1995). Drawing upon and reflecting these broader societal attitudes, during this same period, few if any institutions or organizations provided support for incest survivors and their families (Russell, 1986; Cooper, 1990). Completing the dialectic, individuals also appeared to view incest as either rare or insignificant. Clinicians claimed that incest was a rare phenomenon occurring at rates of one in a million (Weinberg, 1955; Freedman et al. 1975). Once again, it appears that each carrier of culture is informed by the others and simultaneously articulates and reproduces the denial of father-daughter incest in a dialectical and interdependent way. Denial thus can be said to emerge through a transformation process. Once the denial is in place, it appears to be maintained and reproduced through a dialectical process involving the three carriers of culture – society, institutions and individuals.

Returning to the issue of female sex offending, in chapter one it was revealed that at the societal level, there appeared to be a denial of women as potential sexual aggressors. In that chapter, I showed that the notion of female sex offending posed a significant challenge to traditional sexual scripts and elicited varying degrees of discomfort. Perhaps to alleviate the conflict and discomfort, sex offending appeared to be viewed through a particular lens – a gendered lens – whereby an offender's gender became central to the construction of the reality of sexual assault. The gendered lens worked to distort the reality of female sex offending and appeared to transform the female sex offender into a harmless woman incapable of sexual assault, ultimately leading to a denial of the problem. This demonstrates the enactment of the transformation process. It is also illustrative of the duality of structure in relation to female sex offending whereby, through a dialectical process, individuals draw upon broader structures and rules in their activities and practices and in doing so ultimately reinforce and reproduce them.

If the transformation and dialectical processes are suitable ways to understand the denial of female sex offending, because society, institutions and individuals are interconnected and because we found denial at the societal level (as revealed in chapter one), we should find denial at both the institutional and individual levels. However, this needs to be confirmed. The examination of professional and victim perspectives on female sex offending is thus of crucial importance. Through such an analysis, we can not only ascertain how these groups portray and understand female sex offending, but also assess whether the transformation and dialectical processes are at play at the institutional and individual levels. We can thus determine the significance of the two processes in understanding a culture of denial. Before embarking on this analysis, however, in the following chapter I outline the methodology employed.

Notes

1   'Institutions' and 'organizations' are used interchangeably.
2   For further overviews of incest theories see Wolfram (1987) and Hopkins (1980).

3   The Research Methodology

This chapter outlines how the data were collected and analyzed. It also addresses the implications of researching a sensitive topic (for both the researcher and the researched), and fieldwork issues.

The Sensitive Nature of the Research

Lee and Renzetti (1993) define a sensitive research topic as one that potentially poses a substantial threat for those involved in the research and which may have an impact on the collection, holding or dissemination of research data. Sensitive topics are ones that delve into deeply personal and valued experiences – experiences that those being studied do not wish to be misused. In sensitive research there may be psychic costs to the researched – possibly guilt, shame, or embarrassment. The sensitive nature of the research can affect almost every stage of the research process from formulation through design to implementation, and dissemination (Brewer, 1993; Sieber, 1993).

Few would dispute the sensitive nature of this research. Professionals were being asked to reflect on a controversial issue that throws into question traditional ideas of female behaviour and may contradict elements of their own professional training. They were also being encouraged to reflect on personal experiences and responses to their work, which may evoke negative feelings. The potential psychic costs for survivors are even more apparent. Survivors of female sex offenders were being asked to share, with a complete stranger, what may be their most painful childhood memories. Participants could become highly distressed at the recollection of these upsetting incidents. Those who are still suffering from the trauma may experience heightened anxiety by speaking about it in detail. Individuals who have come to terms with their experiences of sexual abuse and have moved forward in their lives are being asked to reopen old wounds.

The sensitive nature of the research, and the potential difficulty with disclosures made gaining the trust of participants of crucial importance.

Trust is not a 'one shot agreement' (Johnson, 1975) but is continually negotiated during fieldwork (Emerson, 1983; Reinharz, 1992; Brewer, 1993). Establishing trust and rapport with police officers is said to be difficult for female researchers (Warren & Rasmussen, 1977). Some hold the view that researchers on the police have to be male in order to be able to participate fully in the occupational culture (Van Maanen, 1981: 480). Moreover, obtaining top-level access, which is how I came to do my fieldwork within the police, does not guarantee sustained co-operation (Buchanan, Boddy & MacCalman, 1988; Reiner, 2000). However, I found that when rapport was established with a reluctant detective, the trust of the other officers came more easily. I shared an office with a detective who had the reputation in the unit of being rather cold and uncommunicative. I received warnings from the other officers about him: 'Don't pay to much attention to him ... he's a grouch, but a real teddy bear underneath'. With time, this detective became interested in my research. In fact, he ended up being one of the most helpful detectives in the unit, and assisted me in selecting officers to interview by informing me as to who was 'a good talker'. The other officers were shocked to see that we got on so well. Once I had gained this detective's trust, the other detectives became more friendly and accepting of my presence.

The Intimate Stranger

'One-off' interviews characterized interviews with psychiatrists and survivors. In these situations, the trust of the participants could not be negotiated. However, Brannen (1988) argues that in researching sensitive topics, the one-off interview can be the ideal situation for disclosure. In her view, the one-off character provides anonymity and facilitates disclosure and trust. Similarly, Simmel asserts that the stranger 'often receives the most surprising openness – confidences which sometimes have the character of a confessional and which would be carefully withheld from a more closely related person' (cited in Wolff, 1950: 404). The anonymity of the relationship did appear to facilitate disclosure and many participants claimed that it was easier to talk about their experiences to a complete stranger. Also, the fact that little research had been done in the area appeared to facilitate disclosure. Many victim-participants had never had the opportunity to discuss their experiences and were extremely eager to talk about them.

The level of intimacy required to discuss experiences of sexual abuse made my relationship with victim-participants an unusual one. On the one hand, the survivors and I were complete strangers. On the other hand, once they shared deeply personal experiences with me, our relationship became more intimate. For example, at the end of one interview, one participant gave me a hug and said: 'I feel as though I'm saying goodbye to an old friend'. However, the complex relationship as 'intimate strangers' at times made me feel as if the interview process was an odd form of prostitution: I would meet a stranger for the first time. They would come into my home or I would be invited to theirs.[1] We would have a pleasant exchange for some time. However, we both knew why we were there and that eventually we would have to 'get down to business'. At this point, I would produce a tape recorder from my bag and they would read and sign a consent form. Following this ritual, I would then ask them to recount what was perhaps the most intimate and painful details of their lives. Although difficult for participants, it was also dehumanizing for me as a researcher. I was to sit and listen – not able to cry when I wanted to, and afraid to laugh too hard when it seemed that this would be acceptable.

I am intentionally painting a very cold and insensitive picture of the way the interviews came to pass. None of the interviews were devoid of emotion, and never did I complete an interview without the feeling that I had, for a brief moment, made a connection with another person, or that every participant had given me a great gift in having shared their story. Yet somehow, no matter what transpired during the previous two to three hours, no matter how much participants told me that they appreciated being heard, I was always left with the same feeling – this was exploitative. This stemmed from my feeling that I was opening old wounds during interviews and participants were left to manage their feelings – alone. It made no difference that I encouraged all participants to call me to discuss the impact of the interview, either in three hours time, or in three years time. I knew that many of them would not. Stacey (1988) argues that there is a risk of exploitation, betrayal and abandonment in feminist-oriented ethnography as the fieldwork inevitably represents an intrusion, and an intervention into a system of relationships that the researcher can leave more freely. As Reinharz writes:

> Researchers take, hit and run ... intrude into the subject's privacy, disrupt their perceptions, utilize false pretences, manipulate the relationship and give nothing in return (Reinharz, 1979: 95).

By simply asking the questions and then leaving, I felt I was exploiting participants. I had fulfilled *my* task so to speak – I had completed another successful interview and on to the next one ... But what of them? Although

I never managed to rid myself of such feelings, focusing on the potential good that could come from the research did help to some degree.

As a researcher, maintaining objectivity in such emotionally charged and sensitive matters was difficult. On the one hand, I needed to establish good rapport to facilitate disclosure, ease the potential discomfort of participants, and show a degree of care and concern to their struggles. I wanted to establish a relationship rather behave in an 'indifferent, disinterested, alienated [way] towards the 'research objects' as positivism requires' (Mies, 1983: 122). On the other hand, over-identifying with participants could compromise an unbiased understanding of the topic. It can also be exploitative in that superficial friendships are created for the purpose of data collection (Wincup, 1999). These contradictory objectives cannot be easily reconciled. They required a delicate balance of interest, self-disclosure, and rapport yet always keeping in mind the goals of the research. The need for reflexivity, a point that Hammersley and Atkinson (1995) make explicitly, is crucial to help resolve such dilemmas inherent in this research.

A Qualitative Inquiry: Using Interviews

A method of inquiry was needed which not only addressed the sensitive nature of the research, but also captured the diverse perspectives and meanings of professional and victim experiences. After careful consideration I chose to employ a qualitative approach for several reasons. First, I felt that the pre-determined, standardized categories and the closed nature of a questionnaire would hinder spontaneous information. The exploratory nature of the research required a more open-ended qualitative approach to allow for serendipitous and unforeseen responses. Second, qualitative research is said to be particularly appropriate for studies attempting to uncover people's *experiences* and the *meaning* they make of those experiences (Rubin & Rubin, 1995; Mason, 1996), which were important aspects of this research. Third, qualitative research can give *intricate details* of phenomena that are difficult to convey with quantitative methods (Strauss & Corbin, 1990). I felt that a qualitative approach would yield a rich, in-depth picture of the experiences of participants.

The scale of a study is also an important factor in determining the research method (Kelly, Burton & Regan, 1994). This study's small scale and the desire to provide a comprehensive look at a previously unexplored area justified the use of qualitative methods. Qualitative research is not concerned with ensuring representativeness or making inferences about the broader population from a selected sample (Kvale, 1996) but seeks to gain rich, in-depth data from a small number of participants (Strauss & Corbin, 1990).

The in-depth interview[2] was chosen as the best means to allow both interviewer and participant time to examine the attitudes, beliefs, meanings, interactions, relationships, and settings, surrounding participants' experiences. I decided to deploy a semi-structured format with police officers and psychiatrists that would facilitate elaboration and exploration but offer some structure of comparability (Jones, 1985). Interviews with victims were characterized by a thematic, biographical approach. Instead of structured questions, there were a range of topics, and themes which I hoped to cover (Mason, 1996). This approach allowed participants to explore the subject freely and unconstrained, being careful not to set the research agenda in advance which may limit the field of inquiry (Fontana & Frey, 1994). It also allowed participants to have a greater voice in the research process (Douglas, 1985; Atkinson, 1998). However, little may be gained by allowing participants to simply 'talk' unencumbered. Guidance was required to help participants to report adequately, and to ensure that the research questions were being addressed (Brenner, Brown & Canter, 1985). This was accomplished through an interview guide, which ensured that four main issues were discussed; participants' personal history and family background, their sexually abusive experiences, disclosures to professionals, and the long-term effects of the sexual abuse experience. All interviews lasted between one and three hours and were audio-taped and later transcribed.

While issues of confidentiality, anonymity and informed consent are crucial to all research involving human subjects, the sensitive nature of this study made these issues particularly important. Prior to involvement in the study, all potential participants were given a summary of the research goals, what would be required of them as participants, and ethical issues of informed consent.[3] It was emphasized that they could refuse to answer any question during the interview, and that at any sign of discomfort, I was prepared to halt the interview. With their permission, the interview would be recorded on audiotape and later transcribed verbatim. Once transcribed, the tapes would be destroyed. I ensured potential participants that all information gathered for the research would remain confidential, anonymous, and used for research purposes only.

Data Collection Sites

The fieldwork for this study was conducted in two urban Canadian cities. Thirty-seven individuals made up the sample; 12 police officers, ten psychiatrists and 15 survivors. The majority of the 37 participants were white, with 8.1 per cent of the sample being from a visible minority (two psychiatrists and one victim). The ages of psychiatrists participants ranged from 34 to 65; the victims ranged in age from ten to 59 years; the police officers ranged in age from 35 to 52.[4]

The selection of interviewees involved purposive sampling, a non-probability sampling method in which a researcher uses his or her own judgement in the selection of sample members, which is largely based on the researcher's knowledge of the population under study, and the nature of their research aims (Babbie, 1986: 176). Snowball sampling, where a sample is collected by incremental contacts (Beck, 1999) was also used. The following section provides an overview of the data collection sites, the selection of the sample, and the characteristics of participants.

Police Officers

Police officers were interviewed from a sexual assault unit of an urban Canadian police force. Fieldwork was conducted within the unit six days per week from September to December 1997. The Sexual Assault Unit was made up of 26 investigators; 23 men and three women. When the unit was initially formed, the police administration decided that they would hire only officers who held the rank of Detective-Sergeant. However, four Detective-Constables were accepted into the unit because of their significant professional experience (20, 29, 30 and 33 years respectively as police officers), as well as their prior work in sexual assault. Officers in the unit differed from those employed in other police units in two important ways. First, they were selected by the police administration because of their level of sensitivity to the issue of sexual assault. Prospective officers were required to undergo a rigorous selection process which included two sets of interviews (including one with a psychologist) and two stages of testing; a written test on conducting sexual assault investigations and a psychological test (a MMPI – Minnesota Multiphasic Personality Inventory). According to a Detective-Lieutenant who was on the hiring committee, the written test was meant to determine the officer's level of investigative expertise, and the MMPI was meant to ascertain the officer's level of sensitivity and suitability to work in the area of sexual assault. Second, unlike police officers in other divisions, once accepted to work in the unit, officers were required to complete a two-week specialized training course on sexual assault.

Interviews Twelve officers were interviewed for the study; ten sexual assault investigators; one Detective-Sergeant who handled the unit intelligence, tactical analysis and statistics, and one Detective-Lieutenant who supervised the investigators. Officers were selected to be interviewed if they had, at some point in their career, investigated at least one case of sexual assault involving a female suspect. Of the 12 participants, ten were male and two were female. Four held the rank of Detective-Constables (DC), eight were Detective-Sergeants (DS) and one was a Detective-Lieutenant (DL). The police participants ranged in age from 35 years old to 52 years old.

Observation within the unit Ample data was gathered through daily observation in the unit. My activities were closely matched with Hammersley and Atkinson's (1995: 1) definition of ethnography which 'involves the ethnographer participating, overtly and covertly, in people's daily lives for an extended period of time, watching what happens, listening to what is said, asking questions – in fact collecting whatever data are available to throw light on the issues that are the focus of the research'. I relied on a less-structured approach to observation which emphasizes studying participant's ideas, attitudes, motives, intentions and behaviour in 'natural' situations and in its cultural context (Foster, 1996).

I adopted the role of 'observer as participant' where the researcher interacts with subjects but does not take on an established role in the group (Jorgensen, 1989). It was fortuitous that I was given a desk in what was unofficially known as the investigator's 'smoking room'. Officers frequently came into this room to smoke, chat and drink coffee and many informative discussions were observed. On these occasions, I had access to the remarks, conversations, complaints and insights of officers which would have been unavailable to me otherwise. These informal talks would sometimes lead to more serious discussions about police daily work. My participation in these discussions varied. Sometimes I would participate, or at least listen attentively. However, the majority of my observations occurred covertly in the course of carrying out other research activities. In most instances, I would jot down notes as events occurred and then wrote more elaborate field notes at the end of the day.

Reviewing police case files Documents can be used as either a resource *for* social research or as a topic *of* social research (Jupp & Norris, 1993; May, 1993; Brookman, 1999). For example, documents such as police sexual assault files can be used to learn about sexual assault. Alternatively they can be used to learn something about the officers who produce and maintain these records (Smith, 1975; Lemert, 1976; Meehan, 1986). In this sense, documents are not neutral artifacts, but reflect a particular social or political context or underlying social meanings (Scott, 1990).

I had initially hoped to use the police case files as a means to learn about the officers and their representations of female suspects. However, the files contained very little police commentary. As such, I decided to use the files as a resource *for* the research rather than a topic *of* research. All (48) cases of sexual assault involving a female suspect that were reported from June 1995 to October 1997 were reviewed. The background features of each case (gender, race and age of the perpetrator and victim, and the victim's statement) were recorded. This information was used during interviews to enhance discussions on officers' investigative work.

Psychiatrists

Psychiatrists were recruited for in-depth interviews from three research sites. Two sites were divisions of psychiatric hospitals and the third site consisted of psychiatrists working in private practice. The sites were targeted because of their specialization in forensic psychiatry[5] and more specifically, sexual offending. To recruit psychiatrist-participants, over 60 letters were sent out to psychiatrists working within the three sites. Letters explained the nature of the research and my interest in interviewing them regarding their perspectives on with female sex offending. Ten psychiatrists were interviewed in all – two psychiatrists specialized in child and adolescent psychiatry and the remaining eight specialized in forensic psychiatry. Three psychiatrists were female and seven were male. They ranged in age from 35 to 60 years. The length of professional experience ranged from four years to 30 years.

Victims of Female Sex Offenders

Victim-participants were recruited in one of two ways; either through referrals from professionals working in the area of child sexual abuse, or through poster advertisements placed in counselling services. I sent letters outlining the research and my desire to recruit survivors to over 20 social workers and psychiatrists working in private practice, and over 40 social service organizations who might have contact with survivors. Many had no clients who had been sexually abused by females. In other cases, professionals declined my request to interview their clients claiming that issues of confidentiality and their client's vulnerability prevented them from providing such referrals. Several professionals agreed to discuss the study with their clients. Their interested clients telephoned me to learn more about the research. Twelve participants were recruited in this way. The three remaining participants were recruited through poster advertisements placed in counselling services. The posters outlined the goals of the research and encouraged those interested to telephone me for further details. Fifteen individuals who self-identified as victims of female sex offenders were interviewed for the study; eight females and seven males. Victim participants ranged in age from ten years to 59 years.

Data Analysis and Interpretation

The analysis of the interviews was informed by a grounded theory approach. Glaser and Strauss (1967), the founders of this approach, chose the term 'grounded theory' in order to express the idea of theory that is generated by (or grounded in) an iterative process involving the continual sampling and analysis of qualitative data. A researcher, with time, builds an understanding of the patterns that exist in the social world under study which is firmly grounded in the concepts and theories of the persons inhabiting and acting in it (Glaser & Strauss, 1967; Charmaz, 1983). When doing grounded theory, researchers systematically develop theory by combining observations of phenomena, abstractions from these observations, and previous research and theory (Gilgun, 1992).

The analysis of qualitative data is a process of finding and making a structure in the data (Jones, 1985; Pidgeon, 1996). As Ritchie and Spencer note:

> The qualitative researcher has to provide some coherence and structure to this cumbersome data set while retaining a hold of the original accounts and observations from which it is derived' (Ritchie & Spencer, 1994: 176).

According to Ritchie and Spencer (1994), there are four main stages to analysing qualitative data; familiarization with the data, identifying and indexing themes within the data, charting and mapping the themes, and finally, interpretation. These stages were closely followed throughout the analysis. Moreover, during the process of data analysis, I tried to adopt a critical outlook, questioning and playing devil's advocate toward my initial findings (Kvale, 1996: 241). To enhance the credibility, plausibility, representativeness, and trustworthiness of the findings, Miles and

Huberman's (1994: 263) techniques of triangulating, weighing the evidence, using extreme cases, looking for negative evidence, replicating a finding, checking out rival explanations, and getting feedback from informants were used.

Study Limitations

Operational definitions chosen for this study, by necessity, limited the findings. Sexual abuse was limited to sexual activities that involved actual physical contact. The study did not examine non-contact forms of sexual abuse such as harassment, being made to view pornography, exhibitionism, voyeurism and so forth as well as their implications. Other forms of child sexual abuse than those operationally defined for the purposes of this study clearly exist and are areas for future research.

The age criteria for defining child sexual abuse required that the child was fourteen years old or younger at the time of the first sexual contact and the female perpetrator was at least five years older. These criteria may have excluded incidents of sexual abuse by females. Indeed, some victims did describe sexually abusive experiences as adults which were not included in the study.

One of the study's greatest limitations lies in its sample size. As a result of the small sample, the data generated from this study cannot be generalized to the wider population of victims and professionals. While a qualitative approach was chosen because it provides important depth and detail from a small number of participants, it fails to provide demonstrable patterns concerning victims' experiences.

Several psychiatrists and victims were recruited through snowball sampling. It has been argued that a limitation of snowball sampling is that researchers may inadvertently collect a sample whose politics and stance may be similar to those providing the contacts. This may have an impact on the representativeness of the sample (Beck, 1999). This is an issue that needs to be taken into consideration in the study's findings.

Victims were solicited from helping professionals and other clinical sources due to the likelihood that they would provide a greater number of participants. However, these data sources may have artificially inflated the number of participants reporting psychological and emotional problems as well as after-effects of the sexual abuse. This sample may therefore not be representative of all victims of child sexual abuse by females. Also, the individuals who revealed themselves as having been sexually abused by females may be more trusting and less likely to be currently using defences of denial, minimization or repression when contrasted with other victims.

They may also be more interested in having others benefit from their participation in research.

Now that I have described the study's methodology, I turn to the first of the three groups under study. The following chapter examines police perspectives on female sex offending.

Notes

1   Survivors were encouraged to choose an interview setting where they would feel most comfortable. Some participants chose to be interviewed at my home to ensure their anonymity and privacy. However, the majority of participants chose to be interviewed in their own home claiming that this provided them with a greater sense of safety and control over the interview process. Regardless of where the interview took place, the informal and casual domestic setting appeared to facilitate rapport and, to some degree, intimacy. Moreover, interviewing survivors at their homes allowed me to gain a greater sense of their lifestyle, their personal circumstances, and the complexities of their situations.

2   Although interviewing was the principal method of data collection, observations and to a limited degree case file analysis were used to gather data on police officers. These two methodological practices are addressed later on in the chapter.

3   One interview was conducted with a ten year old child, under parental consent. The father and step-mother of the child were also interviewed for the study.

4   It is difficult to determine the ways in which race, ethnicity, age, and social class mediated professional and victim perceptions of female sex offenders. Although these factors were taken into consideration during the data analysis they did not appear to be highly significant, perhaps because of the small sample size. Nonetheless, these factors are highly important to understanding the complexities of perceptions of female offenders and any large-scale study would benefit from exploring these relationships further.

5   Forensic psychiatry is defined as a 'subspecialty of psychiatry in which scientific and clinical expertise is applied to legal issues in legal contexts, embracing civil, criminal and correctional or legislative matters' (Heisel, 1996: 73).

4 Police Perspectives on Female Sex Offending

This chapter explores the ways in which a sample of police officers working in an urban Canadian sexual assault unit constructed female sex offenders and their offences, and how they made investigative decisions on their behalf. Because professional discourses and decision-making practices do not exist in a vacuum, we cannot fully understand them without also studying the social context of police work. How police officers think about their work and how they make decisions is said to be influenced by the occupational culture (Fielding, 1988; Holdaway, 1996; Chan, 1997; Crank, 1998; Holdaway, 1999). Therefore, the first part of this chapter examines the police occupational culture and how this culture constructs sexual assault generally, and female sex offending more specifically. The second and third sections of the chapter explore police constructions, portrayals and decision-making practices with regard to female sex offenders. The notion of female sex offending appears to create varying degrees of discomfort for police officers. By adopting a gendered lens, police officers appear to transform sexual offences by women in ways that reflect traditional sexual scripts and culturally acceptable meanings of femininity. This ultimately leads to the denial of women as potential sexual aggressors. In exploring the factors which appear to contribute to and shape the police culture of denial, the analysis highlights the dialectical and interdependent relationship that exists between societal values, institutional values, and individual values, which, reflecting Giddens' notion of the duality of structure, simultaneously construct, sustain and reproduce notions of female sexual passivity and male sexual aggression.

Police Occupational Culture

Police discourse and decision-making practices cannot be understood without also exploring the social context of police work. Systematic observation repeatedly affirms that police actions are dictated by contextual factors rather than individual predisposition (Worden, 1989, 1996; Locke, 1996). This highlights, among other contextual factors, the significance of the working environment. The concept of 'police culture' originally emerged from ethnographic studies of police work, which uncovered informal occupational norms and values operating under the apparently rigid hierarchical structure of police organizations (Cain, 1973; Manning, 1977; Holdaway, 1983). Manning (1977: 143) refers to police culture as the 'core skills, cognitions, and affects' which define 'good police work'. It includes 'accepted practices, rules, principles of conduct that are situationally applied, and generalized rationales and beliefs' (Manning, 1989: 360). Holdaway suggests that the occupational culture is a framework of shared meanings, assumptions and relationships within which officers undertake police work (Holdaway, 1997: 23).

Considerable research has pointed to the importance and power of the police occupational culture (Jones, 1980; Ericson, 1982; Manning, 1989; Shearing & Ericson, 1991; Young, 1991; Chan, 1996, 1997; Crank, 1998). Its structures and content are of relevance to the whole workforce, reaching across all ethnic groups, and indeed, to the public (Holdaway, 1997, 1999). Some researchers have noted that the culture can provide an alternative morality and an identity (Manning, 1977). As Fielding has noted:

> The resilience and solidarity of the [police] occupational culture has long been implicated as a prime force in undermining organizational innovation, with resistance greater the more innovations threaten established working practices (Fielding, 1994: 46).

The Black Police Association in the UK had this to say about police occupational culture and its role in shaping everyday police work during the Macpherson Inquiry into the death of Stephen Lawrence:

> ... we should not underestimate the occupational culture within the police service ... we are all consumed by this culture. Some of us may think we rise above it on some occasions, but, generally, we tend to conform, to the norms of this occupational culture, which we say is all powerful in shaping our views and perceptions of a particular community (Macpherson, 1999: 25).

Similarly, Holdaway (1996), who interviewed ethnic minority police officers who had resigned from the British Police, found the occupational culture of central importance to the formation of officers' ideas and patterns of thinking. One of his informants noted:

Yes, unfortunately, there are some aspects of [police culture] that aren't very savoury but by and large it tends to indoctrinate you, well brainwash. Because the police culture, it applied even to me. I found myself regurgitating and spewing it up at home. It was like I was a third person. I could actually see myself making these comments, thinking, 'Well, that's not quite right'. I found myself doing it. I mean, specifically, I started picking people, putting them into little compartments. I found myself thinking 'Well, that's not quite right', perhaps coming from an ethnic minority myself and having experiences at first hand, I should know better, but I found myself doing it (Holdaway, 1996: 156).

In her critique of the existing theories of police culture, Chan (1996) notes that police culture is often described as monolithic, homogeneous and portrays officers as implicitly passive in the process of acculturation. While the culture may be powerful, it is nevertheless up to individuals to accommodate or resist its influence. In her reconceptualization of police culture, Chan argues that cultural practices result from the interaction between the socio-political context of police work and various dimensions of police organizational knowledge. This perspective is not unlike Giddens' emphasis on incorporating both individual action and structure in any study of social life.

Given the importance of police culture in forming and influencing police discourse and practice, the culture of the sexual assault unit will be examined. However, in keeping with Chan's critique and the need to examine the social context, three aspects of the police occupational culture will be explored. First, I examine the formal structural level of the occupational culture – that of organizational policy and training initiatives and their potential relevance to police discourse and practice. Second, the informal sexual assault culture is explored – the everyday talk and banter of police officers and its relation to the construction of sexual assault. Finally, I trace the use of stereotypical thinking and organizational shorthands among officers in the context of their daily work and how these shorthands contribute to constructions of sex offenders.

Formal Culture: Training, Organizational Policy and the Construction of Sexual Assault

The formal culture, which includes both administrative policies and police training are particularly important as it is said that the way policing is administratively organized, regulated, and the values that are imparted, have an impact on the translation of police cultural values into action

(Fielding, 1994: 51). Moreover, organizational police training is said to have a homogenizing effect on police officers (Fielding & Fielding, 1991).

Sexual assault training in the unit consisted of a two week, eighty hour course, which concentrated on sexual assault investigations. The course was led by a variety of mental health and legal professionals including Crown attorneys, medical doctors, psychologists and social workers who discussed the psychological, legal, medical and emotional aspects of sexual assault. In particular, the course focused on conducting non-leading interviews with children and adults, the legal and investigative aspects of sexual assault, and the 'appropriate' attitude to adopt when interviewing victims. The course concluded with a final exam in which the officers were required to obtain a mark over 70 per cent.

Officers were queried about the content of sexual assault training and its relationship to gender. Training appeared to focus exclusively on sexual assault as a crime committed by males perpetrators against female victims:

Our training focused on male offenders ... because 95 per cent of cases involve male perpetrators (M-Detective-Sergeant3).[1]

[During training] we had crisis workers from hospitals come and talk to us. They discussed sexual assault from the perspective of the victim. For example, when a victim goes to *her* family doctor and discloses that *she's* been a victim of sexual assault and the assault happened in the last 48-72 hours, the doctor is obliged to send *her* for a medical examination (M-Detective-Constable13;[2] emphasis added).

In contrast, sexual assault by females was never mentioned in training:

Female perpetrators were never mentioned. During the training the topic never came up. We were never presented with the possibility that a woman would be the perpetrator (M-DC15).

Like formal training, organizational policies within the unit also appeared to present sexual assault in a particular light. Formal police directives required that during investigations officers attain 'proof' that a sexual assault occurred. What were recognized as 'proof' were elements such as DNA, hair, saliva, or sperm samples to be attained from the victim, or medical evidence of penetration. This highlights the male orientation of the formal investigative system – the criteria for evidence are based on factors present in cases of male sexual perpetration. In cases involving female perpetrators, these elements of proof may not be present or are unobtainable. Sexual assault by females may involve fondling or oral sex, but may not include penetration (digital, or penetration with objects) and searching for DNA evidence from sperm samples is obviously out of the question.

Another example of a sexual assault policy which appears to deny the possibility of female sex offenders concerns the Crime Analysis Report. The Crime Analysis Report is a document to be completed for every sexual assault investigation and is later catalogued in a nation-wide database. Police investigators are required to record specific information about the victim and the suspect. Among a vast array of elements to report, investigators must list the clothing of the victim at the time of the offence. Included in the victim checklist are articles such as 'shirt, skirt, bra, underwear, dress, hose ...' – all very much pointing to the presence of a female victim. In contrast, under the heading of 'physical description of the offender at time of offence' the checklist is absent of any typically 'female' paraphernalia. No 'bra, hose, dress, skirt' are listed. Instead, only typically male/masculine articles such as 'pants, shorts, shirt and socks' are listed. The Crime Analysis Report appears to preclude the possibility of a male victim and a female perpetrator.

Such training initiatives and policies reflect the structural aspects of police culture. They are the 'rules' which both enable and constrain police behaviour. In the following section, we turn away from the formal police culture and instead explore the informal culture of the sexual assault unit.

Informal Culture: Traditional Sexual Scripts in Police Talk and Banter

While the formal administrative culture provides an important source of occupational knowledge, informal talk and banter has long been considered a crucial component for understanding police culture (Fielding, 1988; Shearing & Ericson, 1991; Waegel, 1981; Young, 1991; Chan, 1996; Crank, 1998). The occupational culture is said to 'live' through jokes and storytelling (Holdaway, 1983, 1997). In their routine activities, police use informal verbal exchanges as critical sources of information about customs, procedures, and departmental lore and to create a way of seeing and being. In the constant telling of tales, values are cited and shared which instruct officers on how to see the world and act within it (Chan, 1996). As Meehan suggests:

> In such common conversational activities such as bitching, bantering, complaining, and telling 'combat stories' officers assemble, disseminate and hence create a stock of knowledge about local individuals and situations ... an

oral history of persons, places, and incidents constructed by virtue of the police officer's access to the everyday activities of individuals (Meehan, 1986: 91).

Within the sexual assault unit, informal exchanges and storytelling were frequent. During the course of the day, officers would congregate to drink coffee and tell sexual assault stories which centred around past investigations, memorable arrests, 'stake-outs' on unsuspecting sexual offenders, and odd suspects that they had interrogated. They would also compare notes on current cases under investigation. However, female perpetrators were rarely part of these informal exchanges and were thus invisible within the informal culture. Although the majority of officers had experience with female suspects, they did not appear to feel confident about their knowledge on the issue. Female sex offending was seen as puzzling, bewildering, and an absolute anomaly. Officers could (and did) tell countless stories involving male perpetrators and could also provide in-depth explanations as to why they sexually offended. However, when asked about female perpetrators and why they sexually offended, there was often a long pause for reflection and then: 'I don't know' ... 'I can't answer that question' ... 'I have absolutely no idea'. Officers' initial reaction to a female suspect did vary, yet the majority of officers were surprised or in disbelief when confronted with such a case:

I didn't believe it, I simply didn't believe it ... when [the victim] told me that she [the suspect] would sexually assault him in his bed and while giving him a bath (M-DC1).

I felt like laughing. I mean it was ridiculous. It was like everything was in reverse. The world upside down ... It was surprising (F-DS5).

Through informal verbal exchanges, in the form of light-hearted humour, talk and banter, officers appeared to construct sexual assault in ways that reflected both the content of their training, and broader societal beliefs about female sexual passivity and male sexual aggression. For example, while reading some case material alone in my office, a Lieutenant-Detective/supervisor approached me to inquire how 'things [my research] were going'. He then laughed and said sarcastically:

Hey, how are those dangerous, violent, scary, female rapists who are on our streets sexually assaulting? [sarcastic tone] Ooooh yeah, I'm scared ... I only wish they would sexually assault me ... [laughter]. Yeah baby, tie me up with your garter belt and beat me! (M-Detective-Lieutenant12).[3]

The Lieutenant's comments reflect traditional sexual scripts that males enjoy and seek out all forms of (hetero) sexual contact – even under circumstances of sexual assault, while female sex offending is regarded as harmless, even desirable. Moreover, we see that supervisory officers, who often serve as role models to officers lower in the ranks (Jones, 1980; Fielding, 1988) draw upon and endorse rather than challenge stereotypical gender attitudes.

Male officers not only constructed traditional sexual scripts in their talk and banter, they also enacted them within their daily interactions. This is illustrated in the following comments; one by a female secretary working in the unit and the other by a female detective-sergeant:

The male officers ... get away with a lot here ... stuff that would never be acceptable in other [police] units. Especially the sexual stuff – the sexual jokes and innuendoes, the comments made to us [female secretaries] ... Investigators frequently comment about what I wear. One day, one of them came up to me smiling and said: 'You look gorgeous today. I really like that low-cut top you're wearing' ... [Another day] I was wearing red, and several of the investigators said to me: 'Wow! You look hot in red'. Then they all laughed because I blushed. I was really embarrassed and I didn't know what to say ... Now, I just laugh. I'm used to it now (Female Secretary).

My boss is a real macho. A real macho ... Things will go along nicely and then whoops! certain [gender] distinctions are made ... He doesn't treat me like he treats the other [male] officers. Even my [male police] partner has commented on it. My boss doesn't assign me the good cases. Sometimes he'll put me on a case that requires interviewing a child – a sensitive case. You know, like women are 'supposed' to know how to handle children. Don't get me wrong, I do like working with kids, but somehow I feel as though he's labelled me as some kind of babysitter, not as a sexual assault investigator (F-DS5).

In the first example, within the informal context of their everyday work, the male officers appear to be enacting traditional scripts of males as sexual initiators and females as sexually passive. In the second example, the female officer suggests that she is being 'ghettoized' in particular assignments, and expected to perform in ways that conform to traditional sexual scripts. Duties appear to become informally identified as 'men's work' ('crime fighting') or 'women's work' ('social service work') with areas associated with the feminine being undervalued (Hunt, 1990; Fielding, 1994). Within the context of police relationships, traditional sexual scripts easily find expression.

Within the police unit, informal talk and banter attribute meaning to the structure and hierarchy of relationships. However, they are not phenomena introduced into the occupational culture for the sole purpose of 'gendering' the police force. Informal talk and banter cover a myriad of subjects (Holdaway, 1997). Yet as a stock feature of the occupational culture they provide existing forms that can easily lead to gendered relationships and responses within the workforce.

Through the informal police culture it is possible to see the 'action' component of Giddens' action-structure conceptualization and the enabling nature of police culture. Although officers may be influenced by and draw upon existing institutional 'rules' (regarding gender and its relationship to sexuality) which inform their behaviour, they ultimately have the ability to choose whether or not to enact traditional sexual scripts.

We turn next to the final aspect of police culture under review – the use of organizational shorthands and their relationship to police discourse on sexual assault.

Stereotypical Thinking, Organizational Shorthands and Sexual Assault

Sexual assault investigators were asked if there were 'typical' sexual assault cases that the unit handled. Indeed, organizational shorthands did emerge, particularly with regard to the type of offence, the type of offender, and victim:

> There's a lot of gang raping – street gangs, usually involving fourteen year old girls being raped by three or four gang members. All this happens in schools. There's a lot of grabbing happening in schools and dragging victims to secluded places to fondle or even rape her (M-DS3).

'Typical' sexual offences were perceived to be gang-related. 'Typical' sex offenders were considered male, predatory, and violent. Victims of sexual offences were deemed young, vulnerable females. However, according to the unit statistics, 'gang-rapes' were not typical at all – occurring in less than ten per cent of cases. Moreover, despite the myriad of particulars that made each case of sexual assault highly unique, officers maintained that most sexual assaults were similar, even predictable in nature:

> It's always the same pattern. These guys ... the abusers ... are still using the same way to act, the same things, the same stories. And they use the same modus operandi to target victims or get close to victims (M-DC4).

Investigators appeared to establish and perpetuate 'background expectancies' (Sudnow, 1964) of 'typical' sexual assault cases – the manner in which sexual offences were thought to be committed, the social characteristics of the persons who committed them (symbolic assailants), the characteristics of those who were victimized (symbolic victims), and esteemed cases ('good cases').

Symbolic victims Police officers assumed that victims of sexual assault were unequivocally female. When officers spoke of victims of sexual assault, without exception, they referred to the victim as 'she':

> Obviously it's important and even a priority to be able to identify a suspect, arrest him, and bring him to justice, but really, for me, it's the victim – *she* is the priority (F-DS5; emphasis added).

> This is sexual assault, not a stolen bicycle. There is a human exchange here ... For the victim, well it's [necessary] to show *her* a lot of empathy ... When I meet a victim I tell *her* that I will be there for *her* at every stage [of the investigation]. It's very important to show the victim that you care, that you support *her* (M-DC4; emphasis added).

Here we see how the concept of victimization appears gendered in police discourse. Females are deemed the symbolic victims of sexual assault, while the notion of a male victim was altogether absent from police discourse.

Symbolic assailants In the same manner in which females were perceived as the symbolic victims of sexual assault, males were perceived to be the symbolic assailants. However, even among the male offenders, there was a conceptual continuum in place that differentiated 'real' sexual perpetrators from the rest. One officer explained the idea of a 'real' perpetrator:

> I've had cases of perpetrators – real perpetrators – the guys who drive around in their trucks looking for victims to rape (M-DC4).

What officers conceptualize as a 'real' perpetrator is male, predatory, and sexually assaults a female who is unknown to him. Despite that the majority of sexual assaults involve a victim and suspect who know each other, 'stranger rapes' are what officers believe to be the 'real' cases. Moreover, high levels of violence were seen as 'typical' in cases of male perpetrated sexual assault:

I would say that in most cases, men will use physical violence ... or will use a weapon of some sort. They will hit, will forcibly confine, or tie the victim up ... he wants to show that he is in control, that he is the kingpin and she is absolutely nothing (M-DC1).

In fact, the unit statistics reveal that a minority of sexual assault cases involved a charge of sexual assault with a weapon[4] – making up only 4.5 per cent of the total cases of sexual assault in 1997. Similarly, during the same year, 0.9 per cent of sexual assault cases involved a charge of aggravated sexual assault.[5] What officers conceived as 'typical', was not necessarily so.

With regard to sexuality, males were viewed by officers as 'naturally' sexually aggressive, even animalistic. They were perceived to be unable to control their sexual urges:

For men, sexual assault isn't about reason. These men don't think with their heads, they think with their balls. They have desires and urges and they act on them ... Men are more animal-like. Men can try to control their urges, but their sexuality and their urges are always there (M-DS2).

Good cases   Not all cases in the unit held the same investigative status. While female victims appeared to hold priority status among investigators, cases referred to by officers as 'good cases', gained similar status. Each investigator had twenty to twenty-five cases that she or he would be investigating at one time. Officially, all cases were considered a priority. As a Detective-Lieutenant noted:

We don't prioritize our cases. No case is more important than another. All our cases are priorities (M-DL12).

However, investigators did appear to informally prioritize cases. One officer described a time when none of his cases seemed to be worthy of investigating:

I remember at one point I had a whole slew of cases [to investigate], and I didn't want to deal with any of them. I would look at one and say 'Oh God, not that one!' and I would put it at the bottom of the pile. The problem was that this would happen with each case (M-DS2).

When dealing with sexual assault, without strong physical evidence or a 'credible' story from the victim, it was often times the alleged victim's word against the suspect's, and the 'truth' lay in a fog in the distance.

These ambiguous cases would often be relegated to the bottom of the case hierarchy and the investigator would concentrate on the more pressing or 'interesting' cases. Cases that investigators found exciting or interesting appeared to receive more attention. Officers would frequently refer to an exciting case as a 'good case'. Several features distinguished good cases from the rest. Good cases tended to be non-ambiguous or what investigators referred to as 'real' sexual assaults. They were clear and unequivocal from the outset; the offender was male, the victim was female. There was medical or physical evidence that a sexual assault had taken place. The victim was credible, the suspect was not. There were witnesses present or other 'experts' who could support the victim's claims. All of these elements together embodied proof, and it was proof that investigators needed to have the charge accepted by the Crown attorney and ensure a quick and easy conviction in court. As one investigator described:

> What is a good case? That's when you have a sexual assault – a real one. Most of the time sexual assaults are never clear, never black and white. It's always grey ... [I want] one where you have a crime scene, medical evidence, when you have a credible victim and where you have proof. It's fun to work with that – you go to court and you'll have expert witnesses ... If you have at least three good cases a year that stimulates you and gives you a boost to go on (M-DS2).

The high drama inherent in these cases was also enticing:

> I don't wish anything bad to come to anyone, don't get me wrong – but I want a good case. I want a crime scene, a sexual assault ... I want a victim who's been ... [Another officer interrupts and adds] Yeah ... you want her almost dead. Not dead though, because if she's dead, then the case will go to homicide. You want her almost dead and sexually assaulted (M-DS2; M-DS3).

The stereotypical thinking common to police work may be formed and sustained within a work context that continually demands the immediate summarizing of ambiguous situations (Holdaway, 1997). Stereotypical thinking can lead to processes that facilitate the articulation and amplification of gendered categorizations and responses. Gender may not be a separate, discrete aspect of the occupational culture, but is interconnected with and expressed through organizational shorthands, reflecting the influence of both action and structural components.

Through an examination of formal police policies and training, informal police talk and banter and organizational shorthands, it is possible to understand more fully the social context of police work as it relates to sexual assault. Gendered categorizations and traditional sexual scripts are interwoven with and articulated through the three aspects of police occupational culture. Males were perceived to be sexually aggressive, and the indisputable perpetrators of sexual offences while there appeared to be an implicit denial of women as potential sexual aggressors. From the preceding discussion, it appears that police culture operates as a culture of denial with regard to female sex offending. In fact, the only 'script' available to investigators was that female sexual offending was a non-issue, that is, females were 'incapable' of committing a sexual offence. As one investigator noted:

> A woman doesn't have the capacity to sexually assault ... it's not in their nature, not in their customs (M-DC4).

If there is indeed a denial of women as potential sexual aggressors within police culture as well as among police officers, then it is important to examine how officers speak of and manage cases involving females suspected of sexual offences. The following section elucidates the police discourses, and constructions of female sex offending.

Constructions of Female Sex Offenders

The presence of female sexual offenders challenged traditional sexual scripts and the 'accepted' reality within the formal and informal occupational culture of women as benign victims of sexual assault. The female sex offender thus created an element of disharmony and conflict within the working culture. This conflict appeared to be most effectively abated by enacting the transformation process and renegotiating sexual offences by women. By employing a gendered lens, officers brought her 'aberrant' female behaviour into congruence with traditional sexual scripts and the culturally accepted belief that females do not commit sexual offences. Police officers reconstructed the female sex offender and her offence around two poles of representation; she was recast as either the harmless, benign woman incapable of sexual aggression, or the wanton, unruly woman who is set apart from 'real' femininity. Her gender, her femininity and at times, her 'out of control' sexuality, are treated as central to any explanation of her incongruous acts. This transformation process ultimately worked to sustain the police culture of denial. The following section traces the enactment of the transformation process and more specifically, the two representations officers used to realign female sex offending with traditional sexual scripts.

Rendering Her Harmless

> Sexual assault is the most repugnant crime in the world, the dirtiest crime. It is the most appalling crime and I repeat the most appalling crime (M-DC1).

Within police discourse, there appeared to be three common techniques used to render the female sex offender as 'harmless' (Allen, 1987a). First, although it was recognized that a sexual offence took place, the offender's acts were absolved by affirming that there was no malicious intent to her actions. Second, she was portrayed as not dangerous and posed no threat to the community, despite evidence available to the contrary. Finally, the circumstances surrounding the sexual offence were reconstructed and it was the victim who was held responsible for the incident and not the female perpetrator. By employing these techniques, the female sex offender became the innocuous offender. Her sexually aggressive acts were manipulated, sometimes neutralized, and ultimately transformed. If, as noted in the above quote, sexual assault is perceived to be the most 'repugnant' and the 'dirtiest' crime, officers in the unit systematically 'sanitized' cases involving female perpetrators. This ultimately led to the denial of moral agency and allowed the culture of denial with regard to female sex offending to be upheld.

The female sex offender as 'not meaning any harm' Although officers acknowledged that sexual offences by females had taken place, they frequently provided explanations which exonerated the offender as 'not intending the deed' and 'not meaning any harm'. There is an attempt to redefine her actions not as 'sexual assault', but as behaviour that is more congruous with the sexual script that women do not commit sexual offences. For example, one officer described a case where a thirty-five year old woman was sexually abusing a thirteen year old boy. When asked to share his views on the case, the detective stated:

> [The victim] was young. [The offender] was able to show him things ... It was initiation to sexuality. These women want to teach what they know. Her goal is to educate him about sex, to show him how things work ... It's not done with malice in mind (M-DC1).

In this instance, the offence is not portrayed as a sexual assault, but as an initiation experience or a rite of passage. In turn, the female offender is transformed from a sexual offender into a well-meaning and non-malicious 'teacher' who provided the boy with sexual 'education'.

The following is a summary of a report on a female babysitter who sexually assaulted two infants. It provides an example of how a female detective absolves the offender and her offence by insisting that 'she didn't mean any harm':

Two mothers contacted police to report the sexual assault of their daughters, both age two, by the same female babysitter. In the first case, R.D. [the female suspect] had been babysitting the child for five months. The mother became suspicious when the child refused to have her diaper changed and said to her mother, pointing to her vagina, 'Hurt!   R. touch there'. The child's other babysitter [not the suspect] reported to the mother that the child refused to have her diaper changed and continually pulled the babysitter's hair when she tried to do so. On several occasions, the child put her hands down the babysitter's shirt and tried to caress her breasts. When the babysitter protested, the two year old replied: 'R. want it'. On one occasion, the mother witnessed the child trying to force the handle of a hairbrush inside her vagina.

In the second case, R.D. had been babysitting the child for eight months. The two year old female child complained of pain in her vagina and was in a state of panic every time her diaper was changed. At one point, the mother witnessed the child take her doll, place it on its back, and stick her fingers up between the doll's legs. When the mother asked her what she was doing, she replied: 'R. does that'. Very concerned, the mother took her daughter to a doctor to be examined further. During the examination, the child cried continually and would not let the doctor examine her. She kept repeating 'hurt, pipi'. When the doctor finally examined her, he noticed that the child's genitals were red and there was a scratch and a bacterial infection on the inner labia.

When interviewed about the case the female detective stated:

I don't think that we can really consider this a sexual assault, because [the offender] had psychiatric problems ... I'm not saying that she didn't do it ... It was clear that the sexual abuse happened. The children had vaginal cuts ... But, I sincerely believe that she was not conscious of what she was doing (F-DS5).

Despite the sexual nature of the crime and the injuries sustained by the two infants, according to the detective, this is not a sexual assault. In her 'unconscious' state, the offender is portrayed as not knowing or understanding her actions and is oblivious to the injuries that she has caused. The offender's alleged 'psychiatric problems' appear to relieve her of responsibility and even appeal for a redefinition of the crime itself. Indeed, the issue at hand is the woman's intent:

> When I interviewed her, it was clear that she had hurt the children ... but to say that this woman had sexual intent – that's another story (F-DS5).

The police narrative focuses primarily on the background of the offender and not on the offence:

> I don't think that this woman had criminal intentions. When I met with this woman, she was covered in scars all over her body, she self-mutilated regularly and attempted suicide many times. She was sexually abused by her brothers ... she cried and cried and cried and said that she would never have done anything sexual, that she had been [sexually] abused and knew what it was like ... I don't think that this woman meant any harm (F-DS5).

There is little doubt that previous sexual victimization plays an important role in understanding sexual offending by women (McCarty, 1986; Travin, Cullen and Protter, 1990; Higgs, Canavan and Meyer, 1992; Freel, 1995). However, it seems inappropriate to use such experiences as justifications for subsequent abuse on others. In this case, the offender's own history of abuse works to neutralize her actions.

The female sex offender as not dangerous When a case of sexual assault involved a female perpetrator, there was a general feeling amongst officers that there was no great danger or potential threat to others. In fact, humour characterized much of the informal commentary around female sexual offending. Although the issue of male sexual offending was treated as 'no laughing matter' and immediate steps were taken to assess the male suspects' potential risk to others in the community, any question of a woman's future dangerousness was simply passed over and female sexual offending became a source of great amusement. One female detective noted the reaction of her fellow officers when a case involving a female suspect was reported to the unit:

> You want to know what happens when a case of [sexual assault] comes forward involving a female suspect and a male victim at our office? The entire office breaks out in laughter. Lots of snickering. It's not taken seriously (F-DS6).

During the first week of fieldwork I asked a Detective-Lieutenant if he could provide me with a copy of the unit's formal mission statement to serve as background information. The detective looked astonished and with a very serious voice he shouted:

> You want to know why we're here? Why?   We're here to get those motherfuckers off the street! (M-DL12).

When I probed further, it was clear that these 'motherfuckers' came in the form of male sexual predators who preyed on unsuspecting females. His comment and the serious tone that accompanied it was in contrast to the light-hearted and amused tone of another comment he made several weeks later when the unit received its second report that week of a female suspected of sexual assault. One of the investigators informed the Lieutenant: 'Hey, boss, we got another one! [female suspect]'. The Lieutenant replied with a sarcastic and playful tone:

> Another female sexual offender?   Oooooh, those savages! [laughter]   Watch out! (M-DL12).

The light-hearted and amused tone suggested a lack of fear or alarm about these cases. Women were not, despite evidence available to the contrary, potentially dangerous. Even contemplating the idea that a woman could present a sexual danger to others was perceived as oddly amusing and even desirable by some of the officers:

> If I was kidnapped by three beautiful women and tied up, would I report it [to police]? [laughter] ... well, maybe if they hurt me ... [loud laughter] Imagine, three women attack me and shove a broomstick up my rear. Well, man, you can bet I would complain [loud laughter] (M-DS2).

In another instance, a sexual assault was reported involving two adult women. The suspect was a 44 year old female who had an extensive criminal record including an attempted murder charge and a prior conviction for sexual assault. The victim, a 37 year old female and the ex-partner of the suspect, reported that her ex-lover had sexually assaulted her at knifepoint. During the assault, she alleged that the suspect had used a lighter to burn her face and hands and used a knife to disrobe her and cut her bra straps. After reading the victim's statement a male Detective remarked sarcastically:

> I liked the part where she talks about her bra straps being cut and her being burned and all ... Yeah right! [laughter] God, how can they take that seriously?

... Yeah, watch out for that one! Another dangerous predator on the loose! [laughter] (M-DS3).

Reconstructing the 'assault': blaming the (male) victim The final means of rendering the female sexual offender harmless was in the reconstruction and retelling of the events by investigators. Through complex narratives, the sexual assault was renegotiated and while the actions of the female offender were rendered invisible, the male victim was ultimately held responsible.

The traditional sexual scripts that females cannot and do not commit sexual assault had an important impact on the way female offenders were perceived by police. Although male suspects were automatically viewed with suspicion and outright contempt, female suspects were given the benefit of the doubt by investigators:

> With a woman [suspected of a sexual offence] I would tend to give her the benefit of the doubt. You know, maybe it wasn't true ... because it's so rare ... With guys [suspected sex of sexual offences], I have the tendency to want to beat them over the head with a baseball bat (M-DS3).

In cases of sexual assault involving a female suspect and a male victim, the female suspect appears to be given the benefit of the doubt, and the male victim is often perceived as unreliable or hiding some aspect of the truth. There is a feeling that, beneath it all, he is the guilty party. The elements of the crime are reconstructed and manipulated. In the 'new' version, the female sex offender is rendered harmless and it is the male victim who has either consented to the sexual 'encounter' or was in some way responsible for the outcome of events. The following case illustrates this:

> The victim is a sixteen year old male who delivers groceries for a local shop. At 5:45 p.m. he makes a delivery for the second time that day to a motel room. On the second visit, the forty-one year old female suspect invites the victim in for a drink. The victim accepts and drinks two beers. During the conversation, the female suspect puts her hand between the victim's legs and asks if he will tell the police that she did so. The victim says no, out of fear of her reaction. The female suspect removes the victim's clothing, and touches his penis. At some point, the victim touches the suspect's cat, which makes her very angry. The suspect reacts by grabbing a nearby knife and threatens to castrate the victim. She puts the knife to his penis and shouts, 'Do you want me to cut it off?' A short time later, the victim manages to take hold of the knife and throws it out of reach. The suspect gets very angry and grabs the victim by the neck and attempts to strangle him, causing bruising on his neck. Throughout the incident,

the victim wants to leave the premises, but fears the reaction of the suspect. The victim remained in the room for over two hours. Once the victim was allowed to leave the room he reported the incident to his employer who then called the police.

What is interesting about this case was that it has a very 'masculine' flavour to it. It embodies the kind of sexual assault that investigators associate with male sexual predators or 'real perpetrators', that is, it involved two strangers, the confinement of the victim, a weapon, and the threat of death should the victim not comply. Moreover, in investigative terms, it was a fairly clear-cut case due to physical evidence – a knife was used and injuries were left; there was a crime scene. Although this case has the qualities of a 'good case', it was not considered as such. In fact, discussions surrounding the case were invariably accompanied with great laughter and amusement. One male detective used the case to illustrate that sexual offences involving female perpetrators were intrinsically free of violence:

> Sexual abuse by women will be more subtle and there won't be any violence ... a woman can't be violent ... You know, like the recent case of that woman in the motel. Did you hear about it? [laughter] The woman called for a delivery at her motel and then asked the boy in and offered him a beer! ... [loud laughter] (M-DC4).

The violence perpetrated by the female offender appears to have been erased from memory. When I reminded the officer that the police photos illustrated that an assault causing bodily harm had taken place, he replied:

> Well, those marks on his neck – those could easily have been love bites or hickeys! [laughter] (M-DC4).

The detective's comments subtly transform the events that transpired in the motel room. His 'retelling' of the story throws into question whether a sexual assault, or any offence for that matter, had taken place. The woman is transformed from a violent sexual offender to a harmless woman. At the same time, the male victim is transformed into a willing and consenting partner in the sexual 'encounter'. The possibility that he experienced intense fear and anxiety during and likely following the two hours that he was confined is not considered, nor is the possibility that the sexual touching was unwanted. In the end, the evidence of violence is reinterpreted as 'love bites'.

This section has demonstrated the ways in which the female sex offender was transformed from a potentially dangerous sexual offender to a harmless woman incapable of sexual aggression.

She is Not a 'Real' or 'Normal' Woman

The ideological counterpart to the harmless female sex offender was that these offenders were not 'real' or 'normal' women. The female sex offender's incongruity and departure from 'normal' and acceptable femininity provided the basis from which her story was presented. By casting the female sex offender as 'other' – other than a 'real' or 'normal' woman, her status was once again renegotiated and ultimately transformed. There were three techniques used to transform the offender into not a 'real' or 'normal' woman. First, the female sex offender was construed as an aberrant woman who is set apart from the established codes of female conduct. Second, she was portrayed as an out of control sexual deviant. Finally, she was constructed as devious and manipulative. Investigators created a chasm between 'real', non-offending, 'feminine' women, and the aberrant female sex offender. This worked to uphold the culture of denial and the traditional sexual script that 'real' women do not sexually offend.

The female sex offender as 'aberrant' and 'abnormal' Inasmuch as male sex offenders were perceived as dangerous, female sex offenders were notorious and their notoriety was endemic in their femininity. They became real life representations of the horrors of femininity perverted from its 'natural' course. Indeed, these were not real or normal women at all:

> Just looking at this woman [female suspect], you knew that she was not normal. To leave your two year old child [in the care of] a woman like that? (F-DS5).

> She's perverse. It takes a pretty perverse woman to commit a sexual assault (M-DC4).

Investigators appeared to attribute the female sex offender's incongruous offending behaviour to her lack of femininity. The offender's inability to harness her rage and her uncontrollable sexuality distinguished her from 'real' women. These were examples of women out of control and of femininity gone awry. As such, the offender needed to be regarded with fear and apprehension:

She [the female suspect] seemed to me to be like an enraged bear without a cage. Even the first time I met with this woman, I wondered about her. I had no idea how this woman was going to react. She was never violent with us, except that ... well, let's just say that we had no idea what she was capable of doing (F-DS5).

Investigators also emphasized the 'otherness' of the female sex offender by alluding to her 'masculine' traits to explain her unbridled behaviour:

She was very tall and very strong and had the stature of a very large, strong man. She was capable of any sort of violence (F-DS5).

The type of woman that sexually offends ... is she more masculine than feminine? ... Maybe she's a butch. Maybe she's more inclined to be a man than a woman. Maybe that's what makes her offend (M-DC9).

Sexual offending appears to be conceivable only if it lies within the realm of masculinity. If a woman can be rendered 'masculine' or 'abnormal', it becomes much easier to understand her behaviour. 'Real' women do not commit sexual assault. 'Masculine' or 'perverse' women do.

The female sex offender as the 'out of control' sexual deviant The female sex offender's anomalous actions were implicitly linked to her deviant, rapacious sexuality. These accounts hinge on the well-known idea of a woman's sexuality as her 'master status' – she is the out of control nymphomaniac who is suffering from some form of sexualized 'madness':

This girl [the female suspect] was obsessed with sex. Totally. Completely. She was over-sexed. She told me that she would sometimes spend all day masturbating (M-DC1).

That woman [the female suspect] was a nymphomaniac. A real nymphomaniac. She was sleeping with four different guys regularly (M-DS7).

I suppose the first idea that comes to mind when I think of a female sex offender is a nymphomaniac. That's the portrait I see, the typical case (M-DS10).

These women are perceived as untameable in their defiance of 'real' and restrained femininity. Her sexual licentiousness and her promiscuity combined to explain her behaviour. We can see how the offender's gender and sexuality becomes central to the transformation process. Police officers use her 'out of control sexuality' to realign her behaviour with the traditional sexual scripts of women as sexually insatiable.

The female sex offender as devious and manipulative The final portrayal appeared to turn on the view of the female sex offender as artful and insidious. These offenders were said to compensate for their lack of physical strength by devising covert methods to commit their crimes. Women could indeed become masters of deceit:

> You may find that females may be ... more conniving it her trapping of a victim. She may not always be able to depend on brute force, whereas the male offender can. Females may be more conniving and premeditate a lot more than men do (M-DS3).

Female sex offenders were portrayed as plotting their secret crimes in advance and hiding them behind impassive faces to avoid detection:

> A woman is more likely to hide her crime. Women can hide their crimes better because they are more refined than men. Women are less likely to show their emotions ... It's therefore much more difficult to discover whether it happened or not (M-DC1).

Naylor (1995: 91) has noted that representations of female offenders hinge on portraits of the scheming woman, masking her evil under the appearance of goodness, while playing on the chivalric foolishness of men. The female offender is a heavy-lidded, and sexually powerful temptress and as such, a man must make conscious attempts to extricate himself from her lures. This theme became apparent when investigators were asked whether it was necessary to change their approach when interrogating female suspects. One investigator explained that female suspects frequently used subtle yet devious techniques to try to 'seduce' him in an attempt to have their charges dropped:

> Charm! Women ... oh yeah, they try to use charm. They'll give you this certain look ... They'll wink at you, or say 'Oh, you have beautiful eyes,' or 'what a beautiful tie you're wearing'. It's definitely a mechanism that they'll use (M-DS2).

The same officer believed that a female suspect will try to manipulate the course of the interrogation and turn it in her favour. He devised a well-thought out yet rather unusual strategy to challenge her 'crafty' attempts at eluding criminal charges. He believed that by embracing this approach, he could neutralize her duplicity and obtain a full confession:

> What do you think the first thing a woman will do when she is accused [of sexual assault]? Can you guess? Well, she'll cry. When you're interviewing women do you know what you never do? Never, ever get out a box of tissues and never, ever console her. That's what she wants. But if you console her, she'll never talk. Do you know what will happen if you don't console her like she wants you to? She'll get mad. She gets mad at you, yells and screams at you, and throws things. After that, little by little you talk to her ... Then she'll start crying again. That's when you get out the tissues. After that, she'll tell you everything (M-DS2).

This section has revealed how the female sex offender was transformed into an 'unreal' and 'abnormal' woman. 'Real' and 'feminine' women were set apart from the aberrant and unfeminine female sex offender. In drawing upon traditional sexual scripts, police officers are ultimately sustaining and reproducing the culture of denial.

Understanding Police Constructions

Police constructions can be understood using the framework of the transformation process. The notion of a female sex offender posed a significant challenge to the traditional sexual script of female sexual passivity and harmlessness promulgated within formal and informal police culture. This challenge may have created varying degrees of psychological discomfort and conflict. Perhaps to alleviate the conflict and to help maintain traditional sexual scripts, officers (unwittingly or fully aware) invoked a particular way of seeing sexual assault by females. The enactment of the gendered lens whereby the offender's gender became a central focus in the construction of sexual assault appears to have been used as a tool in this process. The gendered lens worked to distort the reality of female sex offending, bringing this 'unsavoury' reality into alignment with more 'acceptable' cultural representations of women. Once the lens had provided an alternative focus, officers then turned to two sets of traditional sexual scripts to transform the offender and her offence. The first set of scripts, women as sexually harmless and innocuous, appeared to be drawn from both the police occupational culture as well as broader cultural values, whereas, the other set of scripts, women as unruly, as sexually out of control and devious, appeared to be drawn from the broader society. The transformation of female sex offending not only resolved the initial conflict, but also led to the denial of female sex offending by individual officers and ultimately reproduced the police culture of denial. In this sense, police constructions of female sex offending appeared to follow the same transformation process found at the societal level as outlined in chapter two.

The data ultimately reveal how broader structural constraints and organizational 'rules' impact on the everyday life of institutions and thus the everyday sexual scripts of police officers. However, officers were able to actively choose to accept or reject these 'rules' or structural constraints. Officers were also able to choose whether or not to enact the transformation process. The enactment of the duality of structure is apparent in the fact that as police officers drew upon the institutional 'rules' and structural considerations regarding female passivity, docility, or duplicity in order to provide guidance for their own actions, they ultimately reproduced these same structures.

Next, it is important to explore why officers chose these particular representations. It is essential to recognize that officers did not invent these portrayals. Rather, they mirror our most contradictory and 'common-sense' ideas about women. These portrayals reflect a cultural belief system which has historically represented women as sexually passive, harmless, and virtuous on the one hand (the pure woman), and sexually out of control, aberrant, and devious on the other (the whore) (Allen, 1987b; Lunbeck, 1987; Morris, 1987; Welldon, 1988; Birch, 1993; Morris & Wilczynski, 1993; Groneman, 1994; Lloyd, 1995; Naylor, 1995). We can see how in their everyday work, officers drew upon these culturally available representations in their constructions of female sex offending. Without an alternative conceptual framework or narrative through which to understand such cases, the gendered lens and traditional sexual scripts of women as either innocuous or unruly provided an efficient means for officers to explain female sex offending. The infrequency with which officers saw female sex offenders may have produced such extreme explanations for their behaviour.

The fact that these representations were drawn from both the broader societal context as well as from the institutional context highlights the enactment of the dialectical process and the duality of structure. Each carrier of culture appears to influence, maintain and reproduce the other, ultimately upholding traditional sexual scripts and the culture of denial. In this sense, the notion of the duality of structure, the dialectical process and the transformation process provide helpful frameworks to understand police constructions of female sex offending and how and why its denial remains firmly grounded in police culture and practice.

Another possible explanation for relying on these particular representations of female sex offenders may be related to the fact that police organizations have historically been male in spirit and gender (Crank, 1998). For example, as late as 1980, only 3.8 per cent of all municipal officers in the United States were female. In 1994, 9.3 per cent of all municipal officers were female (Martin, 1997). Masculinity is not only a demographic characteristic of the police organization, but also a cultural descriptor. Few occupations have been so fully defined as masculine or been so closely tied to themes and representations of masculinity as policing (Kappeler, Sluder & Alpert, 1994). Fielding (1994) asserts that police canteen culture may be read as an almost pure form of 'hegemonic masculinity' (Connell, 1987) with an emphasis on aggressive physical action, competitiveness, exaggerated heterosexual orientations, misogynistic and patriarchal attitudes towards women and the operation of rigid in-group/out-group distinctions (see also Martin, 1980; Hunt, 1990; Herrington, 1997). The male-oriented culture may contribute to traditional beliefs about women and the denial of women as potential sexual aggressors.

However, the presence of female police officers adds complexity to this issue. Two female police officers were interviewed for the study. One appeared critical of her colleague's responses to female sex offending while the other seemed to renegotiate female sex offending in similar ways to her male colleagues. It is unclear whether women are differentially affected by police culture. Although there is little evidence of a female occupational culture among British police (Fielding, 1994), research has shown that some female officers adopt the culture of masculinity (Martin, 1979; Berg & Budnick, 1986; Brewer, 1991). This could explain the female officer's reliance on traditional sexual scripts and her implicit denial of women's potential for sexually aggressive behaviour. However, the very small sample precludes any clear answers on the issue.

It should also be noted that as a result of police occupational norms and expectations, it may be difficult for individual officers to be openly critical of the culture of denial and readily acknowledge the reality of women as potential sexual aggressors. Sanctions may be associated with deviating from the institutionalized routine. 'The ways things are done' may quickly become 'the way things should be done' (Jenkins, 1996: 128). In this sense, officers may be vilified should they depart from the organizational shorthands concerning female behaviour and the interpretation of that behaviour.

Portrayals of female suspects as innocuous and as unreal women clearly have an impact on the way investigators speak about and perceive female sex offenders. However, it remains unclear whether these perceptions and representations persist during sexual assault investigations. The final section of the chapter examines police investigative practice in relation to female sex offending and the culture of denial.

Police Investigative Policies and Practices

One of the greatest investigative challenges for officers is to determine from the minimal information available to them, who, in terms of the suspect or the victim, is telling the truth. This means conducting interviews with victims, suspects, and witnesses and gathering as much evidence as possible. Once this process is complete the officer is to decide (in conjunction with the Crown prosecutor) whether or not to lay criminal charges. If no charges are laid, it is necessary to classify the case in consonance with pre-defined administrative labels. There are four possible case designations at the conclusion of an investigation. A case classification of 'charges laid' means that the accused has been identified, both the police investigator and the Crown attorney believe that a sexual assault has occurred, and the victim is prepared to testify against the suspect. These cases are then resolved in court. 'No charges laid' means that the investigator has identified the suspect and is convinced that a sexual assault has occurred, however, either the Crown prosecutor believes that there is insufficient evidence to proceed with charges, or the victim has decided to withdraw the complaint. A case file is deemed 'inactive' when nothing at present can be done to advance the investigation however, the case remains open should any new information be revealed. This designation usually means that the suspect was unknown to the victim and has not been identified or the victim has decided that s/he does not want to press charges. Finally, a case is designated 'unfounded' when the sexual assault was believed not to have taken place, and was perceived by investigators to be a fabrication by the victim.

Police Use of Discretion

The process of 'fact-finding' was far from simple and while the aforementioned labels provided 'official guidelines', in practice case designations involved much police discretion. Although organizational policy did play a role in decision-making, detectives appeared to rely upon informal culture, organizational shorthands and even personal feelings to come to a decision about a case. One detective noted:

> How we classify our files is often based on feeling. How we feel about a case, how we feel about a victim and whether we feel she's credible. I'm not saying it's all based on feeling, but a large part of it is ... we have no crystal ball here (M-DS8).

The following comment reveals the degree to which police discretion enters into case designations:

> Ideally, all investigators would classify their cases using the same criteria. Unfortunately, we don't always ... In the case I mentioned earlier, I could have easily classified it as 'no charges laid' ... but [the victim] was not very credible ... I realized that I could make the call easily – that the case was unfounded ... So, I classed it as 'unfounded'. It could also have been classed as 'inactive' in the sense that there was a lack of proof and once we had more proof, the file could be reopened. But, I thought – nah, it's not worth it – it's like running after your own tail. So, I classed it 'unfounded' (M-DC13).

In some instances, officers had different interpretations of what the concept of 'unfounded' actually meant:

> Unfounded means that *we believe* that the sexual assault didn't happen, that it's not true (M-DS2; emphasis added).

> Unfounded ... means that *the victim has called us* up and said: 'Listen, it wasn't true – it didn't happen. I don't want to go to court because it didn't happen' (M-DS10; emphasis added).

In theory, investigators were only to designate a case as unfounded if they could 'prove' that it was in fact a fabrication by the victim:

> If the investigator classifies a file as unfounded, it's because he [sic] can prove it (M-DC4).

In practice however, investigators were often uncertain as to the accuracy of their final decision:

> I recently classed a file unfounded – but I'm not positive that it didn't happen. Is it a real unfounded or a false unfounded? (M-DS2).

These examples illustrate how detectives appeared to use their discretionary powers to determine who and what behaviours warranted criminal charges. 'Truth', 'facts' and 'evidence' are not necessarily 'unearthed' during the course of investigations, but may be constructed by police officers. Detectives can be seen to play a crucial role in the 'making' and 'unmaking' of sexual assault (Ericson, 1982: 134). McConville, Sanders and Leng (1991) indicate that it is 'cop culture' which actually structures police discretion. In this sense, the culture of denial becomes increasingly important when examining cases involving female suspects.

Gender and Decision Making: Classifying Female Sex Offenders

> If you're a female paedophile, you're going to get off. Not because you're not guilty, but because you're a woman (M-DS3).

This comment, although not altogether accurate, can be considered a guide to understanding how cases involving female sex offenders were managed within the sexual assault unit. The collective set of decisions taken by investigators appeared to be influenced by the belief that females did not and could not commit sexual offences. Cases involving female suspects were more likely to be deemed unfounded than cases involving male suspects. Traditional sexual scripts and the gendered lens appeared to guide imageries for action in the treatment of female sex offenders.

As noted in chapter one, statistics from official agencies reveal very small numbers of sexual offences involving female perpetrators. This unit was no exception. Between June 1995 and September 1997, only 35 cases of sexual assaults involving female perpetrators were reported to the sexual assault unit. However, it is interesting to note that of those 35 cases, 22 (62.8 per cent) were classified as 'unfounded' by investigators. In contrast, 2565 cases involving male perpetrators were reported during the same time frame. Of those 2565 cases, 605 (23.6 per cent) of them were deemed 'unfounded'. Cases involving female suspects were nearly three times more likely to be designated as unfounded than cases involving male suspects. It may be helpful to examine decision-making practices in more detail to provide an explanation for this discrepancy.

The Influence of Police Culture on Decision-Making Practices

The earlier discussion of formal police culture highlighted not only the way in which formal policies reflected a male-oriented investigative system, but also the absence of women as potential offenders, as evidenced in the

Crime Analysis Report. It is important to establish the implications of this male–oriented system for decision-making practices – particularly in relation to cases involving female suspects. As a result of the formal policies, it may be easier for investigators to label a case involving a female suspect as 'unfounded' simply because 'proof' in the form that is needed (DNA, sperm samples, evidence of penetration etc.) was difficult, if not impossible to obtain. As these detectives noted:

> With cases of female suspects, I suppose that as an investigator you always ask yourself the question 'how am I going to prove it?' (M-DS10).

> If you've been sexually abused by a woman, you'd better have some damn good proof ... Your credibility is going to have to be really good ... A lot of evidence for sexual assault are things like penetration, sperm, DNA. They are male oriented ... it's more difficult to prove an assault by a female. Victims have to make their case in some other way (M-DS3).

Officers reported being constrained by overburdened caseloads and therefore may not have the time or the resources to find alternative means of proving such cases. Perhaps more importantly, there appeared to be very little organizational support to employ 'alternative' investigative means. Detectives are expected to use the framework provided for them by administrative policies. In cases of female sex offenders, 'making the case in some other way' may not be feasible.

The informal police culture and traditional sexual scripts also appeared to influence officers' investigative decisions regarding female sex offenders. For example, one detective who was trying to account for the greater number of unfounded cases relating to female suspects asked a colleague why he had recently classified a case involving a female as unfounded. His fellow officer provided this response:

> You want to know why it was unfounded? The case was unfounded because she [the suspect] was damn hot! [attractive] (M-DS11).

The offender's femininity and in this instance, her physical attractiveness, is the central theme from which the narrative is told. It sustains the view that 'real' women, that is, women who are feminine and attractive do not commit sexual offences. It also demonstrates the extent to which extra-legal factors, namely a suspect's physical appearance as well as the organizational shorthand that 'typical' sex offenders are male, influence the decision-making practices of investigators. Moreover, deeming the case unfounded did not appear to be based on the evidence of the case, but instead upon traditional sexual scripts of women as passive sexual recipients and as objects of the male (officer's) gaze.

The denial of women as potential sexual aggressors was evidenced in the informal decision-making practices of another officer. This officer was discussing a case in which a fourteen year old girl alleged that she had been sexually abused by two different perpetrators – an uncle, and a female babysitter. While the officer laid charges against the male suspect, he did not in the case of the female suspect. He provided this explanation:

> I believed [the victim] about her uncle sexually abusing her. But the female babysitter? She was exaggerating or fabricating or even transposing another case of sexual abuse. Sometimes victims will transpose – in the sense that they'll say 'oh, a stranger assaulted me' because they are too embarrassed to say that they were assaulted by a relative. I think that's what she was doing (M-DC4).

The victim is perceived to have fabricated the offence because she was 'too embarrassed' to reveal the identity of the 'real' (male) perpetrator. The gender of the offender appears to be of central importance in the process of decision-making.

It is significant to note that prior to investigating a case involving a female suspect, officers often presumed that such cases were unfounded fabrications. For example, one female detective mentioned that in cases where a mother was suspected of sexually abusing her child and it was the father who had reported the incident, her first inclination was to believe that the father was making the complaint to denounce and incriminate the mother as a result of a pending child custody battle:

> At first when I see cases [of sexual abuse by a mother], I guess I would think this is a case of parents fighting over the custody of the child. That's often the question you ask yourself. Is it a case of [the father] taking revenge [on the mother]? (F-DS5).

It appeared difficult for police officers to envision a mother as a sexual offender:

> We see women as mothers, as caretakers. We put women on a pedestal, and with good reason. The woman is the mother of the family – that's the image that we have of her (M-DC4).

The detectives' comments turn on the traditional script that all women are 'naturally' maternal, and protective. To imagine a mother harming her child, particularly in a sexual way, seems so incomprehensible that a father who reports abuse by his wife must be contriving a plan to discredit her.

One officer explained that victims of female sex offenders should expect that their cases will be deemed unfounded:

> If you're stupid enough to press charges [against a female perpetrator], you had better be prepared to be crucified. You'd better have some damn good proof ... Your credibility is going to have to be really good. You are going to have to build your case really well ... Otherwise, you're case is going to be unfounded (M-DS3).

This chapter has revealed the way in which female sex offending is viewed, assessed and understood within traditional gendered narratives and through a gendered lens. The female sex offender's femininity is constantly under scrutiny and becomes central to the meaning of the offence. For police officers, it appears to mean something different to be sexually abused by a female – it is often judged to be less serious and less harmful. Since the meaning of the abuse differed, so too were the responses to the abuse. In her study of organizational responses to male and female delinquency, Gelsthorpe (1989) noted that the notion of 'sexist bias' becomes complicated once it is placed in an administrative and organizational context. She writes:

> 'Sexist ideology' is not a discrete phenomenon, but a mixture of personal views, professional policies and practices which are continually 'shaped' by the exigencies of practice and organizational constraints (Gelsthorpe, 1989: 135).

I would add that broader cultural values also appear contribute to professional policies and practices, pointing to the dialectical nature in the transmission of culture.

I began this chapter by analysing three fundamental aspects of police culture to understand the social context of police work. The analysis pointed to the police culture's reliance on traditional sexual scripts and the implicit denial of women as potential sexual aggressors. The second and third sections of the chapter demonstrated the ways in which officers enacted the transformation process by relying upon a gendered lens to transform and ultimately deny sexual offences by women. The dialectical process appeared essential to the maintenance and perpetuation of the police culture of denial. Both institutional values as well as broader societal beliefs concerning gender, crime and sexuality influenced and, in turn, were influenced by individual police officers, which worked to simultaneously construct, sustain and reproduce traditional sexual scripts and the police culture of denial. In the next chapter, I turn to another professional group – psychiatrists – to examine how they construct, articulate and understand the phenomenon of female sex offending.

Notes

1   Hereafter DS (Detective-Sergeant) – 'M' refers to a male participant; 'F' refers to a female participant.
2   Hereafter DC (Detective-Constable).
3   Hereafter DL (Detective-Lieutenant).
4   Section 272 of the Canadian Criminal Code (CCC) defines *Sexual assault with a weapon, threats to a third party or causing bodily harm* as 'Every one who, in committing a sexual assault;
     (a) carries, uses or threatens to use a weapon or an imitation thereof,
     (b) threatens to cause bodily harm to a person other than the complainant,
     (c) causes bodily harm to the complainant, or
     (d) is a party to the offence with any other person
     is guilty of an indictable offence ... '.
5   *Aggravated sexual assault* is defined in Section 273 (1) of the CCC as 'Everyone who commits an aggravated sexual assault who, in committing a sexual assault, wounds, maims, disfigures or endangers the life of the complainant ... '.

5 Psychiatrists' Perspectives on Female Sex Offending

This chapter explores psychiatrists' perspectives on female sex offending. It begins by tracing the social context of psychiatric work, analyzes the occupational culture and how this culture constructs sexual offending. The chapter then examines psychiatrists' constructions and representations of female sex offenders. The analysis reveals the ways in which psychiatrists employ a gendered lens when assessing cases involving a female perpetrator and ultimately transform and deny sexual offences by women. Once in place, this denial appears to be maintained and reproduced through the dialectical process whereby the three carriers of culture simultaneously construct, articulate and reproduce the culture of denial with regard to female sex offending. Giddens' concept of the duality of structure becomes relevant to understanding the complex relationships within the dialectical process.

The Occupational Culture of Psychiatry

Psychiatric discourse cannot be fully understood without first examining the social context in which psychiatrists work. Compared to the multiplicity of studies on police culture, less attention has been paid to the occupational culture of psychiatry. This may be due, in part, to the difficulty discerning an identifiable 'culture' within psychiatry. Many psychiatrists work in private clinical settings and have few organizational ties. Also, the different sub-specialties within psychiatry (ranging from child psychiatry, to neuropsychiatry, to forensic psychiatry etc.) as well as the lack of consensus regarding aetiologies, treatment, or therapeutic approaches (Daniels, 1972; Bucher & Stelling, 1977) places the discipline within a context of considerable diversity. Matters are further complicated by the fact that each existing psychiatric organization may have different ideological values and outlooks. However, while the culture of psychiatry may be less unified and more complex than that of the police, it may be possible to uncover its foundations.

As in my analysis of police culture, I examine three core elements of the occupational culture of psychiatry and its relation to sexual offending. First, I explore the *formal* occupational culture, which includes formal training initiatives and the Diagnostic and Statistical Manual of Mental Disorders, fourth edition (DSM-IV). I examine their potential relevance to psychiatric discourse and practice. Second, I trace the *informal* culture of psychiatry – the everyday talk of psychiatrists and its relationship to constructions of sexual offending. Third, I discuss the use of stereotypical thinking and organizational shorthands in the daily work of psychiatrists and the influence such shorthands may have on constructions of sexual offending.

Formal Culture: Training, DSM-IV, and the Construction of Sexual Assault

The formal culture of psychiatry can be said to include two important elements; formal training and the DSM-IV. By analysing these elements of the formal culture, it may be possible to uncover the social context of psychiatrists' work.

Psychiatric training, which occurs most intensely during a student's psychiatric residency period, is believed to incorporate psychiatric values, traditions, attitudes and styles (Bucher & Stelling, 1977; Langsley, 1987). Before examining psychiatric training in relation to sexual assault, I look briefly at psychiatric training in a broad sense. In Canada, psychiatrists are physicians who have completed, in sequence, four years of undergraduate university education, three to four years of medical school (depending on the programme), one year of internship (usually in a hospital), and at least three years of clinical psychiatric training called a residency. Legally, only physicians who have finished psychiatric residencies may call themselves psychiatrists.

Psychiatric training is highly important because of its later impact on psychiatrists. In their longitudinal study examining the impact of education programs and socialization on psychiatrist trainees, Bucher and Stelling (1977) found that formal training had a significant impact on trainees' later perspectives and career paths. They compared trainees in a psychiatric residency grounded in a psychoanalytic approach with trainees in a more generalized 'state' program oriented to work in state mental hospitals. The orientations of residents and the careers they anticipated were congruent with their experiences during residency. The psychoanalytically trained group had a psychoanalytic approach and sought jobs in the realm of psychoanalysis, while the state graduates had eclectic approaches and there was more diversity represented in the careers they projected. Bucher and Stelling conclude that outcomes of socialization are, in large part, determined by the nature of the organization's culture and educational training program.

The current approach to psychiatric training consists largely of first-hand clinical experience, individual supervision, and seminars (Langsley, 1987: 65). Psychiatric residents are given a caseload, which is likely to include patients experiencing a variety of psychiatric difficulties. These patients are assessed, diagnosed and treated by the resident on an ongoing basis. As a result of the belief that psychiatric examination, interviewing, problem-solving, and decision-making are best taught through interaction (Yager, 1982a; Langsley, 1987: 67), residents meet with a supervisor (a certified psychiatrist) to discuss their cases and any difficulties they may be encountering. It is expected that the supervisor will provide further guidance, insight, clarification, and validation (Redlich, 1982; Yager, 1982a). Alongside the clinical work, residents attend seminars in diverse areas of clinical psychiatry ranging from how to treat paraphilias, to psychopharmacology, to the origins of schizophrenia. Through these diverse training initiatives, the student is said to develop judgement, problem-solving abilities, creative modes of thinking, and skills to identify medical assumptions and evaluate them critically (Eaton, 1980; Schoettle, Cantwell & Yager, 1982; Yager, 1982b).

The issue of sexual abuse did not emerge as a significant social issue until the mid 1970s. As such, psychiatrists who received their psychiatric training prior to this period were not provided with education or training in sexual abuse. This generation of psychiatrists informed me that they learned about sexual abuse largely through independent study, the emerging clinical literature, and from working directly with survivors of sexual abuse. More recent graduates in psychiatry did receive training in the area of sexual offending. They reported that the curriculum focused exclusively on sexual offending by males. In contrast, none of the psychiatrists who received sexual abuse training had been educated with regard to sexual abuse by females:

Never! [laughter] No, I never learned about female sex offenders ... (F-Psychiatrist7).

I never learned about women [as sexual offenders] ... I talked to my daughter who just finished her psychiatric training and got her degree a year ago. I asked her if she learned about women. She said no. She learned no more than I did apparently! ... They are not teaching this stuff in the schools ... So women are still a bit of a mystery (M-Psychiatrist2).

Once again we find that sexual offending is presented in formal psychiatric training within a particular light. The exclusive focus on male perpetration highlights the role of the institution of psychiatry in reproducing the traditional sexual script of male sexual aggression while failing to provide its trainees with the *possibility* that women can commit sexual offences.

While formal educational training is clearly important to the process of becoming a psychiatrist, the DSM-IV is also a fundamental aspect of the formal culture. The manual is published by the American Psychiatric Association (APA) and is said to embody the groundwork of the system of taxonomy found in physical medicine (Ussher, 1991). The purpose of the DSM-IV is 'to provide clear descriptions of diagnostic categories in order to enable clinicians ... to diagnose, communicate about, study, and treat people with various mental disorders'[1] (APA, 1994: xxvii). The manual is 886 pages long, has 16 major diagnostic categories and describes almost 400 separate mental disorders. According to psychiatric theory, mental disorders, whatever the cause, can be properly diagnosed and treated through the categories provided by the manual. These categories are said to be objective and equally applicable to any patient regardless of race, class or sex. Diagnostic procedures are said to dictate appropriate treatment under the impartial medical direction of the psychiatrist (Penfold & Walker, 1984: 12).

Since its inception, the manual has been transformed from an obscure desk reference – a peripheral clinical tool – into an omnipresent compendium known as the 'psychiatric bible' (Kutchins & Kirk, 1997). The manual has become the centre of attention in psychiatry (Kirk & Kutchins, 1992: 12). Moreover, it is now a significant part of the psychiatric curriculum with residents learning how to use the manual during educational training (Maxmen, 1985). The DSM-IV is relied upon by the vast majority of psychiatrists internationally to assist in clinical assessments (APA, 1994). Because of its pervasive use as a diagnostic tool, the manual can be considered a powerful device in shaping psychiatrists' perspectives on human behaviour and diagnostic decisions.

It is important to recognize that as a diagnostic tool, the DSM-IV is considered by many to be quite controversial (Caplan, 1995; Kutchins & Kirk, 1997). Many authors have claimed that the current manual, as well as its predecessors, reflect a gender bias (Russell, 1995; Busfield, 1996; Becker, 1997; Allison & Roberts, 1998) and that women appear to be more likely than men to be diagnosed with particular mental disorders such as

Borderline Personality Disorder, Histrionic Personality Disorder, Dissociative Identity Disorder and other mood disorders (Nolen-Hoeksema, 1990; Seeman, 1995; Garb, 1996; Sleek, 1996; King, Koopman & Millis, 1999). Authors have also suggested that the manual reflects cultural biases (Fernando, 1988; Pilgrim & Rogers, 1993; Busfield, 1996) and that ethnic minorities, particularly blacks, appear be more likely to be diagnosed with a mental disorder than whites (Sillen, 1979; Rack, 1982; Fernando, 1988; Loring & Powell, 1988; Cope, 1989; Pipe et al., 1991; Browne, 1993; Coleman & Baker, 1994; Garb, 1996; King et al., 1999).

To understand how the DSM-IV constructs sexual offending, it is helpful to examine its definition of sexual disorders. The manual describes a Paraphilia as:

... recurrent, intense, sexually arousing fantasies, sexual urges, generally involving;
   1) non-human objects,
   2) the suffering humiliation of oneself or one's partner, or
   3) children or other non-consenting persons,
that occur over a period of at least six months ... They include Exhibitionism ... Fetishism ... Frotteurism ... Pedophilia ...Sexual Masochism ... Sexual Sadism ... Transvestism ... and Voyeurism ... The behaviour, sexual urges, or fantasies cause clinically significant distress or impairment in social, occupational or other important areas of functioning (APA, 1994: 522-3).

Paraphilias appear to be presented as primarily a male problem. For example, an addendum to the section on Paraphilias reads:

Except for Sexual Masochism ... Paraphilias are almost never diagnosed in females (APA, 1994: 524).

This addendum suggests that female sex offending is peripheral, even inconsequential to discussions on sex offending. Within the DSM-IV, paedophilia is defined as follows:

... recurrent, intense and sexually arousing fantasies, sexual urges or behaviours involving sexual activity with a prepubescent child or children (generally age 13 or younger) ... which cause distress or impairment in social occupational or other important areas or functioning ... The person [with paedophilia] is at least 16 years and at least five years older than the child or children (APA, 1994: 528).

The manual notes that paedophiles may adopt sophisticated measures to help them access child victims. Several examples are given including the following:

> [Individuals with paedophilia] ... develop complicated techniques for obtaining access to children, which may include, *winning the trust of the child's mother*, [or] *marrying a woman with an attractive child* ... (APA, 1994: 528, emphasis added).

'Winning the trust of the child's mother' portrays women, particularly mothers, as the caregivers and protectors of children, and not the potential paedophiles. Similarly, 'marrying a *woman*' in order to access a child presupposes that paedophiles are male. The gendered language implicitly ignores the *possibility* that a female paedophile could employ similar techniques to access children. If the DSM-IV reflects the official psychiatric discourse on clinical diagnosis, females are rendered invisible as potential perpetrators. It is possible to see how the manual sustains and reinforces traditional sexual scripts of female sexual passivity and harmlessness.

Perhaps some would argue that female sex offending is rare and that the DSM's 'gendering' of paraphilias reflects the available empirical evidence on sexual disorders. However, the relationship between empirical evidence and the DSM needs to be explored further. It may be that traditional sexual scripts and broader cultural notions of female sexual passivity may be a factor in the DSM's portrayal of sexual offending.

Psychiatrists have long declared that the development of the DSM has been based on rigourous scientific inquiry and testing. For example, in an article concerning the development of the DSM-III, Bayer and Spitzer characterized it in the following manner:

> The adoption of DSM-III by the American Psychiatric Association (APA) has been viewed as marking a significant achievement for psychiatry. Not only did the new manual represent an advance toward *the fulfillment of scientific aspirations* of the profession, but it indicated an emergent consensus over procedures that would eliminate the disarray that has characterized psychiatric diagnosis (Bayer & Spitzer, 1985: 187; emphasis added).

Similarly, Gerald Klerman, the highest ranking American psychiatrist in the federal government at the time that DSM-III was developed and published, was even more adamant about the scientific rigour of DSM. At a national convention in 1992, Klerman stated:

In my opinion, the development of DSM-III represents a fateful point in the history of the American psychiatric profession ... its use represents a *significant reaffirmation on the part of American psychiatry to its medical identity and its commitment to scientific study* (Klerman, 1994: 539; emphasis added).

Despite the insistence on scientific rigour and objectivity, it is difficult to ignore the fact that there have been four different diagnostic systems since 1979, each time claiming that the resulting manual and its expanded list of disorders are based on scientific research. With each change, mental disorders are created, eliminated or radically redefined. Although the professionals who formulated these various diagnoses presented their arguments in the language of science, some researchers have suggested that the actual influence of empirical data has been negligible (Kutchins & Kirk, 1997). Caplan (1995) has declared that the DSM is 'shockingly unscientific' as do Allison and Roberts (1998: xxvii). Brown (1990) suggests that psychiatry cannot explain why some of its diagnostic categories appear and disappear, because these categories are based not on medical knowledge, but on social and political factors. Kirk and Kutchins (1992), Armstrong (1993), Kutchins and Kirk (1997), and Curra (2000) argue that revisions to the DSM can seldom be explained by advances in science but can often be explained by the shifting fortunes of various powerful factions within the APA.

The rise and fall of homosexuality within the diagnostic manual provides a strong example of how *cultural values* and not scientific evidence appear to guide the creation and elimination of diagnostic categories. A separate diagnosis of homosexuality first appeared when the original DSM was revised in 1968. The new edition, DSM-II, listed homosexuality as one of the sexual deviations. It was defined as follows:

> 302 Sexual deviations. This category is for individuals whose sexual interests are directed primarily towards objects other than people of the opposite sex, toward sexual acts not usually associated with coitus, or toward coitus performed under bizarre circumstances as in necrophilia, pedophilia, sexual sadism and fetishism. Even though many find their practices distasteful, they remain unable to substitute normal sexual behavior for them (APA, 1968: 44).

Several years later with the development of the DSM-III, homosexuality was dropped as a sexual deviation and modified as 'Ego-dystonic Homosexuality', a diagnosis directed at those troubled by their homosexual impulses. In 1987, after years of fierce lobbying by the gay community, the APA omitted Ego-dystonic Homosexuality as a pathological condition in the DSM-III-R.

Through the shifting status of homosexuality in the DSM, it is possible to see how definitions of mental disorders are revealed to be particularly susceptible to *external pressures* and *cultural values* in a way not easily matched by physical disorders like influenza or cancer. The homosexuality controversy illustrates that science is often not central to the decision to include or exclude a diagnosis from DSM and was not about research findings (Kutchins & Kirk, 1997). Instead, the homosexuality controversy concerned a twenty year debate about beliefs and values concerning (hetero) sexuality. Psychiatry as an institution appears to draw upon and reflect broader societal meanings of gender and sexuality in their practices, highlighting the dialectic between society and its institutions.

Arguably, this same process can be said to hold true of the DSM's categorizations of sexual offending. Perhaps the invisibility of women as potential sexual offenders within the DSM-IV is a reflection of psychiatry's reliance on traditional sexual scripts and broader cultural notions of females as sexually passive and harmless. I am not arguing that female sex offending is a hidden problem reaching epidemic proportions and being ignored by the psychiatric community. What I am arguing is that the construction of sex offending within the DSM appears to preclude the *possibility* of women as potential sexual aggressors, which may be based on traditional sexual scripts.

Psychiatric training initiatives and the DSM-IV are highly important as they reflect the structural aspects of psychiatry. They represent the 'rules' which both enable and constrain psychiatric decision-making and help us to further understand the occupational culture.

Next, I turn to the informal culture of psychiatry and how psychiatrists construct sexual offending in their daily talk.

Informal Culture: The Construction of Sexual Offending in Everyday Talk

Although formal training and the DSM-IV are likely to provide important sources of occupational knowledge, everyday talk is also important to understanding the culture of psychiatry. For example, research has uncovered that many psychiatrist trainees place greater emphasis on the information gathered from informal conversations with colleagues than they do from their supervisors (Bucher & Stelling, 1977).

The boundaries marking the informal culture of psychiatry were far less discernible than that of informal police culture. While informal police culture was highly perceptible and largely unified, the informal culture of psychiatry appeared more discrete and diverse. Given that psychiatrists conducted their work in a variety of institutional and clinical settings (hospitals, out-patient clinics, government agencies, and private practice) and frequently in conjunction with other professionals (social workers, psychologists etc.), it was difficult to establish the parameters of a discernible informal *psychiatric* culture. Although such informal cultures are likely to exist, identifying the culture may require long-term observation which was beyond the scope of this study. Nevertheless, one psychiatric institution where I conducted fieldwork, which I will refer to as 'Institution B', appeared to have a relatively cohesive and discernible set of informal values and beliefs. The following discussion highlights the ways in which psychiatrists within this institution constructed female sex offending in their everyday informal talk.

When psychiatrists in Institution B spoke of female sex offending there appeared to be an implicit denial of the issue. Echoing traditional sexual scripts of female sexual passivity, one psychiatrist stated:

> Women are not erotically attracted to children. That's my feeling and that's certainly the feeling here [at Institution B]. That is how we view it (M-Psychiatrist5).

Psychiatrists within Institution B also appeared to informally relegate cases of female sex offending to a second-class standing compared to male sex offending. For example, one recently graduated female forensic psychiatrist reported that none of the more senior (male) psychiatrists were interested in following cases of female sex offenders. The female psychiatrist was thus informed by her supervisor that cases involving a female sex offender would be referred to her:

> One of the reasons that I got into [female sex offending] was because none of the other psychiatrists here wanted to see the female patients ... I think some of my fellow psychiatrists just weren't interested ... They didn't want to follow them (F-Psychiatrist8).

The fact that the relatively inexperienced psychiatrist who had the least amount of seniority was the main clinician responsible for such cases highlights two things. First, it underscores the general attitude at Institution B toward cases of female sex offending – they are not perceived as trying cases that need a great deal of expertise. Second, it demonstrates that female sex offending held a relatively low status within the psychiatric repertoire. It appeared to be marginalized within the informal culture of psychiatry, with few psychiatrists wanting to work with female sex offenders.

Perhaps echoing her institution's informal belief that female sex offenders were clinical non-sequiturs and relatively uninteresting, the female psychiatrist expressed her discontent to being assigned these cases. In her view, this population did not require her expertise:

> Most of the female sex offenders are referred to me ... I was getting quite discouraged for a while because I ended up seeing these [female] patients that I felt were not requiring my forensic expertise (F-Psychiatrist8).

This psychiatrist's discontent with her caseload illustrates how beliefs are informally cited, shared and reproduced among psychiatrists. It underscores how informal verbal exchanges provide crucial institutionally-based knowledge. Also, we see how one newly recruited female psychiatrist adopts the informal cultural view that female sex offending is largely unchallenging and peripheral. The dialectical process once again becomes apparent whereby the institutional culture, in this case the informal culture of psychiatry, may work to influence the ideologies of individual psychiatrists.

A final example pointing to the insignificance of female sex offending within the informal culture of Institution B was the pervasive belief that although there was no educational training provided in the area of female sex offending, it was not an issue that required further attention. As one female psychiatrist indicated:

> I haven't felt the need to learn more about [female sex offending] ... I don't see that it's such a big need that it has to be incorporated in the education. I don't think it needs to be addressed (F-Psychiatrist7).

The indifference and marginalization of female sex offending is important. Within the informal occupational culture, psychiatrists appear to be constructing and sustaining sexual assault in ways that follow both formal psychiatric training and broader traditional sexual scripts, implicitly denying women's potential for sexual violence, and aggression.

Stereotypical Thinking, Organizational Shorthands and Sexual Assault

As found in chapter three, a close examination of the use of organizational shorthands can provide information on patterns of professional thinking, discourse and decision-making practices. This section traces the use of organizational shorthands in the daily work of psychiatrists elucidating the ways in which these shorthands may contribute to constructions of female sex offenders.

Organizational shorthands emerged when psychiatrists were queried about the nature of male and female sexuality. There appeared to be an agreed upon, 'typical' manner in which sexuality, and following that, sexual assault was perceived by psychiatrists. Female sexuality was perceived to be *markedly different* from male sexuality:

The sexuality of a female ... is not the same as the sexuality of the male (M-Psychiatrist1).

Women's sexuality is quite different from men's ... women's arousal rate is quite different than male sexual arousal (F-Psychiatrist7).

Reflecting traditional sexual scripts, psychiatrists appeared to attribute sexual aggression with males and sexually passivity and sexual disinterest with females. This section discusses these organizational shorthands in greater detail.

Males as sexually aggressive Males were viewed by all of the psychiatrists as sexually aggressive and as having a greater intensity of sexual feelings than females. As these psychiatrists noted:

Men are [sexually] aggressive and women are not (F-Psychiatrist7).

Males experience a much greater intensity of sexual feelings ... [They have a] greater need to act on them than females do. They're simply more likely to act that out than females (F-Psychiatrist4).

Another psychiatrist commented:

The male is much more singular. The [sexual] stimulus creates a response ... The [sexual] object of choice is portrayed either visually or through auditory stimulation, and then bingo! – a response. I think that with a female there is much more emotion in the overlaying context that has to come into play for that response to occur (M-Psychiatrist11).

These examples reveal that female sexuality is perceived to be less urgent, and more complex involving emotion and an array of contextual factors. In contrast, male sexuality is perceived to be definitive and intense, with clear and explicit stimuli and responses.

The belief that males enjoy all forms of (hetero) sexual contact and 'are ready, willing and eager for as much sex as they can get' (Tiefer, 1989: 451) was also present in psychiatric discourse. One psychiatrist light-heartedly noted that if an adult female engaged in sexual contact with a boy without his consent, the boy would inevitably enjoy the experience:

> I'm sure [the boy] would 'get a rise' – quite literally – out of the touching! [by an adult female] [laughter] (M-Psychiatrist1).

Psychiatrists appear to invoke traditional sexual scripts regarding gender and sexuality. Males were perceived by psychiatrists to be highly sexually aggressive and as enjoying (hetero) sexual contact, regardless of the circumstances.

Females as sexually passive   Psychiatrists seemed to construct female sexuality in direct opposition to male sexuality. Take, for example, the comments of this psychiatrist:

> Females ... cannot be particularly [sexually] aggressive ... They are the passive recipients (F-Psychiatrist7).

Sexuality and sexual desire was perceived to be less significant in the lives of females. While male sexuality was perceived to be raging and imperious, female sexuality was considered inconsequential. Unlike men, it was believed that women could easily ignore their sexual urges:

> I think it's a difference [between males and females]. Most women can ignore their sexual urges if they haven't got an adequate sexual outlet (F-Psychiatrist4).

Once again, we see the influence of traditional sexual scripts in psychiatrist's constructions of gender and sexuality.

Symbolic assailants   As was seen with police officers, there appeared to be an agreed upon, 'typical' manner in which psychiatrists believed that sexual offences were committed and the social characteristics of those who regularly committed them. Again, we find that males are viewed as the symbolic sexual assailants. Here is one male psychiatrist's view of a 'typical' sexual offender:

If there is a category of an offender that is persistent, it's the sex offender. On average, he won't stop. When he develops [sexual] urges, he gets on a roll and he doesn't stop. In fact, he [sexually offends] more often. He starts doing two [sexual assaults] a year and then four a year and then it becomes one a month and two a month until he's doing so many that he gets caught (M-Psychiatrist12).

A sexual offender was perceived to be male and reflecting male sexuality to an extreme he is predatory, indefatigable, and at the mercy of his sexual urges.

By examining *formal* psychiatric culture including training and the DSM-IV, *informal* psychiatric talk and *organizational shorthands*, it is possible to understand more fully how gendered categorizations and traditional sexual scripts are interwoven with and articulated through the three aspects of the occupational culture of psychiatry. Males were perceived to be sexually aggressive, predatory and at the mercy of their sexual urges, while females were perceived to be sexually passive, disinterested and, as offenders, clinical non-sequiturs. Similar to police officers, there appeared to be a *denial* of women as potential sexual aggressors within psychiatric culture. As these psychiatrists noted:

I can assure you that there are no female paedophiles on the police [sexual assault] database. You should definitely take my word on that ... women are not erotically attracted to children (M-Psychiatrist5).

I don't believe that women are inclined to engage in that kind of behaviour [sexual offending] (M-Psychiatrist2).

If there is indeed a culture of denial with regard to female sex offending within psychiatry, then it is important to examine how psychiatrists speak of and manage cases involving female sexual offenders. The following section elucidates psychiatrists' discourses, and constructions of female sex offending.

Constructions of Female Sex Offenders

The notion of a female sex offender appeared to challenge both traditional sexual scripts and the formal and informal culture of psychiatry and thus created a source of conflict. In an attempt to allay the conflict, psychiatrists appeared to transform sexual offences by women. Psychiatrists' use of the gendered lens becomes apparent – the offender's gender, her femininity, or lack thereof, became the central feature in psychiatrists' appraisal of the case, not the crime that she was thought to have committed. The gendered lens worked to distort the reality of the female sex offender's actions and brought her 'aberrant' female behaviour into congruence with traditional sexual scripts. Interestingly, psychiatrists constructed the female sex offender around similar poles of representation to that of police officers: she was cast as either the harmless, benign woman incapable of sexual aggression, or the aberrant woman who is set apart from 'normal' femininity.

Rendering Her Harmless

Psychiatrists' explanations of female sex offending frequently transformed a woman's sexually abusive acts, ultimately rendering her harmless in much the same way as police officers. There appeared to be two ways in which the offender's acts were transformed and ultimately absolved. First, in contrast to the male sex offender, the female sex offender was perceived to be harmless, posing little danger or threat to the community, despite evidence available to the contrary. Second, the female sex offender was reconstructed as a benign victim who sexually offended not of her own volition, but as a result of factors external to her and beyond her control. By employing these techniques the offender's agency, intentionality, and potential for sexual harm were neutralized, allowing traditional narratives concerning women's virtuousness and sexual passivity to remain firmly in place. The transformation process ultimately worked to uphold psychiatry's culture of denial in regard to female sex offending.

The female sex offender as not dangerous When a case involved a female perpetrator there appeared to be a general feeling among psychiatrists that compared to male sex offenders, female sex offenders posed little danger or threat to the larger community:

> [Male sex offenders] seem to be more impulsive and more dangerous. They don't seem to care about the consequences ... [Female sex offender's] are quite different ... not as dangerous (F-Psychiatrist7).

Even contemplating the idea of a dangerous and sexually aggressive female appeared perplexing to some psychiatrists. For example, one male psychiatrist seemed puzzled as to how a female could pose a sexual danger or instil fear in a male. He stated:

'Well, what's he [the male victim] *afraid of*?' (M-Psychiatrist2).

When a female offender engaged in very serious acts of sexual violence, she still was not perceived to be dangerous. For example, one psychiatrist discussed a case in which a woman had been implicated in a violent sexual assault. He noted:

Despite the rather horrendous events that took place ... and the events that she [the offender] actually participated in, I do not see her as being a danger now or ever again to society (M- Psychiatrist1).

An exonerative and sympathetic tone appeared alongside descriptions of convicted female sex offenders. As this female psychiatrist stated:

I seem to feel a lot of sympathy for [female sex offenders] ... There was one [case] where a major [sexual abuse] investigation went on. It was a [paedophile] ring. The woman [offender] didn't play *much* of a role in it. I felt very sorry for her (F-Psychiatrist7).

The sympathetic tone implies a generalized harmlessness and lack of dangerousness to these offenders and their actions. It also reveals the way in which psychiatrists transform the offender and realign her actions with traditional sexual scripts of women as docile and harmless.

Discussions of male sex offenders frequently turned to their impulsive and dangerous sexual urges which needed to be curtailed. Several psychiatrists mentioned the need for drug therapies to reduce the male offender's sex drive:

Treatment for male sexual offenders would be different [than for female sex offenders]. I believe [male sex offenders] need to be treated with sex-drive suppressing drugs (F-Psychiatrist7).

In contrast, discussions of the female offender's libido appeared to be absent from psychiatric discourse. During a discussion with a psychiatrist about drug therapies, I inquired whether the sex-drive reducing drugs were also used for female sex offenders:

[Sex-drive reducing drugs] might work in females, because they diminish libido, but I've never known anybody who used it. But it's an interesting point. I've never heard of anybody using the anti-hormone therapies in women. It's never been a focus of attention (M-Psychiatrist3).

Female sex offenders appeared peripheral to discussions on drug therapies. Perhaps as a result of the pervasive view of women as sexually passive and having low sex drives, female sex offenders were perceived as not posing enough of a 'danger' to warrant such attention.

There was a belief that treatment was not necessary for female sex offenders. As an example, one psychiatrist discussed her views on the 'treatment' of a convicted female offender who was involved in a long-standing paedophile ring:

> She didn't really feel that she needed any help and I really didn't feel that she needed any help other than help to move away from those people [in the paedophile ring] ... In regard to treatment, there's not much for [female sex offenders] to learn (F-Psychiatrist7).

Portrayals of female sex offenders as not in need of treatment and not dangerous were invoked despite having knowledge that the offender had been convicted of serious and sometimes violent sexual offences.

The Female Sex Offender as Victim

The other means to transform female sex offending and render the offender as harmless was to claim that she offended not of her own volition, but instead was a victim of circumstance or a victim of a coercive male partner.

A victim of circumstance In appealing to the idea that the female sex offender was a victim of circumstance, psychiatrists' narratives on female sex offending tended to focus not on what the female perpetrator had done, but instead upon factors acting upon her:

> It's [the female offender's] partner and the substance abuse ... it's her intellectual limitation (F-Psychiatrist7).

> I believe that ... women may *find themselves* being used by men to act out their aggressive things ... mothers have *found themselves* getting [sexually] involved with their children as opposed to other unrelated people (F-Psychiatrist4; emphasis added).

The language being used here is interesting. The offenders do not appear to be active or responsible for their actions. They do not make relationships, or consciously commit sexual assault, but merely *'find themselves'* in situations involving sexual assault. They are victims of circumstance.

Another psychiatrist cited an offender's 'Borderline Personality' as an essential factor in explaining her sexually aggressive behaviour:

Another case I had was a pretty seriously disturbed Borderline Personality. *By virtue of the personality many things became sexualized* with a sexual acting out behaviour (M-Psychiatrist11; emphasis added).

Interestingly, there is no mention of the offender at all – only a case of a 'pretty seriously disturbed Borderline Personality', which becomes an entity in and of itself. It is the 'Borderline Personality', not the offender, who appears to be responsible for the sexual offence. In this way, the female sex offender is denied moral agency and is transformed into a victim of circumstance.

Other factors seemingly beyond the offender's control were also used as explanations. One psychiatrist noted:

One woman I [assessed] digitally penetrated five children under her care in her daycare. Was she aroused by these children? No. Her marriage was bad, she was frustrated ... (M-Psychiatrist5).

This time, it is the offender's failed marriage and subsequent frustration that are said to be factors influencing her offending behaviour. There is no intrinsic motivation for the offence, such as an erotic attraction to children. On the contrary – elements *external* to her are responsible for her actions.

One psychiatrist noted that during case conferences, her colleagues appeared uncomfortable discussing female sex offenders. She noted, however, that their discomfort would dissipate because she would consistently present female offenders as victims of difficult personal circumstances:

I think a lot of [my colleagues] were more offended and more grossed out by females doing this [sexual assault] than they were by males – partly because they don't think of females as being sexual predators ... *but I would've given them a framework which would have conveyed the female as a victim of disturbing situations that she had to contend with* (F-Psychiatrist4; emphasis added).

In many cases the offender may be a victim of 'disturbing situations'. However, prior to any knowledge of the case, the female sex offender is *presumed* to be and is presented as a victim of disturbing situations. Portraying her as a victim of circumstance appears to make her behaviour more understandable, conforming to traditional sexual scripts that women under 'normal' circumstances do not commit sexual offences.

The focus on a woman's difficult personal circumstances appears to be in contrast to discourse on male sex offenders which instead tended to focus on the male offender's behaviour and actions:

> [Male offenders] have an urge and they like to have a ... partner who is easily controlled. That's why they pick younger females (M-Psychiatrist1).

Male offenders '*have an urge*' and '*pick*' younger females. Their actions appear to be calculated and with conscious volition.

The construction of female sex offenders as victims of circumstance reveals not only a denial of her intentionality, agency, and offending behaviour, and a transformation of her actions and motivations, but also demonstrates the extent to which psychiatrists appear to invoke traditional sexual scripts of female passivity in their understandings of sexual offending.

A victim of a coercive male partner   Psychiatrists also appeared to transform sexual offences by females by claiming that she was a victim of a coercive male partner. It is important to note that many women are threatened and coerced by male partners into participating in acts of sexual violence and abuse (McCarty, 1986; Matthews et al., 1989; Wolfers, 1993; Saradjian, 1996). However, there appears to be occasions where psychiatrists presume that a woman's participation in sexual abuse is male-coerced *prior* to obtaining a full picture of the events, sometimes in spite of evidence pointing to the contrary. For example, one psychiatrist considered that a female sex offender was, *by definition*, a victim of a coercive male. In fact, he used the term 'female sex offender' synonymously with 'compliant victim of a male perpetrator':

> The best definition of a female sex offender that I've seen is ... a category called 'compliant victim' [of a male perpetrator] ... (M-Psychiatrist5).

Although not part of my direct fieldwork, the high profile Canadian case involving Paul Bernardo and Karla Homolka demonstrates that even when there is evidence to the contrary, psychiatrists appear to render female accomplices of male sex offenders as harmless victims of the male. The case demonstrates the way in which psychiatrists transform sexual offences by women, simultaneously invoking, sustaining and reproducing traditional sexual scripts and psychiatry's culture of denial with regard to female sex offending and thus supports some of my own claims and assertions which are grounded in the data.

Paul Bernardo was a serial rapist who sexually assaulted 13 women in a suburb of Toronto over an eight year period. Prior to being apprehended by police in 1993, he abducted, confined and murdered two of his victims. Karla Homolka was Bernardo's wife and accomplice in several of the assaults, including a sexual assault on her own sister, Tammy. Below are the facts of the case as documented in a report to the Attorney General of Ontario:

Tammy Homolka

According to Homolka's testimony, Bernardo told Homolka that he wanted to have sexual relations with her fifteen year old sister Tammy. Homolka reported that she was opposed to the idea, but later agreed because of death threats Bernardo made against her and her family. To prepare for the sexual assault, Homolka obtained Halothane, an anaesthetic for animals, and Halcion, a powerful sleeping pill, from the animal clinic where she worked as a veterinary assistant. Following a family dinner on December 23, 1990, Bernardo put Halcion in Tammy's drink and Homolka served it to Tammy. Once asleep, Homolka applied a cloth soaked in Halothane and held it to Tammy's face while Bernardo sexually assaulted her. Homolka then performed cunnilingus on her sister. The sexual assault was videotaped by the couple. Shortly after the assault, Tammy vomited and began to choke. They noticed that she had stopped breathing. Homolka called for an ambulance and she and Bernardo quickly dressed Tammy, disposed of the Halcion in the toilet and hid the remaining Halothane. The ambulance arrived and took Tammy to the hospital, but she did not survive. The determined cause of death was asphyxiation on her vomit. Her death was ruled accidental and the investigation was closed. Neither Homolka or Bernardo were ever charged in Tammy's death (Galligan, 1996).

Jane Doe[2]

In 1991, Jane Doe was fifteen years old. She had known Homolka for two years, having met her at a pet shop where they both worked. On two occasions Homolka invited Jane to her home with the knowledge that Bernardo intended to have sexual relations with her. In the first instance, Homolka, without Bernardo's knowledge, invited Jane to her home and drugged and anaethetized her in much the same manner as was done to Tammy Homolka five months earlier. She then telephoned Bernardo, telling him to 'come home, because she had a present for him'. Jane was sexually assaulted by both Bernardo and Homolka. The assaults were videotaped by the couple. Jane had no recollection of the assaults and it only came to light when videotapes were recovered and Homolka conceded that the unconscious, unidentified girl in the videotape was Jane Doe (Galligan, 1996).

Leslie Mahaffy

In June of 1991, two weeks before marrying Homolka, Bernardo abducted fourteen year old Leslie Mahaffy. Leslie was sequestered in the couple's home for two days. The young girl was repeated raped by Bernardo while Homolka looked on and captured it on video. Bernardo filmed Homolka performing cunnilingus on Leslie. On her second night of confinement, Leslie was strangled. Her body was then dismembered, its parts encased in concrete and discarded in a nearby lake (Galligan, 1996).

Kristen French

In April, 1992 Bernardo and Homolka began to make plans to abduct another victim. The plan was for Homolka to approach a young girl while driving and ask her for directions. As sixteen year old Kristen French was coming home from school, they put their plan into effect. They drove to a church parking lot and Homolka enticed Kristen to the car on the pretext of asking directions. Kristen was grabbed by Bernardo and pulled into the car and held down by Homolka. Kristen was taken to the couple's home where Homolka closed all the blinds, and collected and hid all the telephones in the house. During her three day confinement, Kristen was repeatedly beaten by Bernardo and sexually assaulted by both Bernardo and Homolka. Bernardo and Homolka took turns operating the video camera while the other sexually assaulted Kristen. Kristen was ultimately strangled by Bernardo. The offenders washed her body to remove traces of evidence. Homolka cut Kristen's hair to preclude the possibility of carpet or other fibres being found in her hair. Her naked body was then dumped in a ditch (Galligan, 1996).

The videotapes, which acted as crucial evidence against both Bernardo and Homolka, were not recovered immediately. During the initial police search of the couple's home, a single videotape was recovered. The videotape depicted Homolka committing a sexual assault upon the nude body of an unconscious and unrecognizable female (later identified as Jane Doe). Despite this evidence, police assumed that Homolka played an insignificant role in the offences. As a police investigator noted to Homolka early in the investigation: 'We're not here to get you, we need you to get him. You're innocent. You're the victim' (Pearson, 1997: 36).

Desperate to convict Bernardo, the Crown negotiated a plea bargain with Homolka. In return for testifying against Bernardo, she received immunity for her role in the drugging and sexual assault of Jane Doe, and a twelve year manslaughter sentence for her involvement in the abduction, sexual assault and murder of Leslie Mahaffy and Kristen French. Homolka had no criminal trial, nor was she ever charged with sexual assault.

The Homolka/Bernardo case was discussed with the majority of psychiatrists during interviews. When questioned about the case, many of the psychiatrists did not perceive Homolka to be a sex offender, but instead a victim of Paul Bernardo:

> [Homolka] was a victim ... She was under [Bernardo's] thrall ... She was a naive, simple, innocent, helpless child ... She was not strong and she was simply dominated by him and afraid of him ... This was a very strong and powerful man. This was not a strong girl in my opinion ... She had everything to make her a good follower (M-Psychiatrist2).

> I don't see [Homolka] as a sex offender. I see her as a victim, a battered wife, a victim of post-traumatic stress. I see her mainly as having done something because she was told to ... [Bernardo] totally dominated her. She had no choice (M-Psychiatrist1).

However, there appears to be evidence that throws into question the idea of Homolka as a victim. For example, in a letter written to a friend six weeks after the death of her sister Tammy, Homolka's voice and tone does not indicate a bereaved or victimized woman. Instead, it reveals an outspoken woman more preoccupied with money and her upcoming wedding, than with the death of her sister:

> Dear Deb: Fuck my parents. First they took away half of the wedding money, then they kicked us out [of their house]. My father doesn't even want us to have a wedding anymore. Screw that. We're having a good time. If my father wants to sit at home and be miserable, he's welcome to. He's only worked a day since Tammy died, he's wallowing in his own misery and fucking me [over] (Excerpt from letter presented in court).

Videotapes (recovered only after Homolka had negotiated her plea bargain) show a conversation between the couple three weeks after Tammy's death. Homolka tells Bernardo:

> I loved it when you fucked my little sister ... I want you to do it again [sexually assault an adolescent girl] ... Do you think we can do that? Do you wanna do it fifty times more? Do it every week then? (Pearson, 1997: 192).

This evidence throws into question the following psychiatrists' comments:

> But then you see, you have this person [Homolka] who was virtually brainwashed by [Bernardo]. She was controlled by him ... Karla was manipulated into being a participant in what eventuated in the death of a much loved sister (M-Psychiatrist2).

The psychiatric discourse seems to disregard her role in the sexual assault and death of her sister. She is perpetually moved by the agency of Bernardo, rather than her own. She is transformed into a dominated and dependent victim.

The sexual assault of Jane Doe also challenges the idea of Homolka as a victim. It was Homolka who initiated these sexual assaults – she invited Jane Doe to her home knowing that Bernardo would sexually assault her. Homolka's own admissions not only challenge her status as a victim of Bernardo, but also bring forth the possibility that she may have been more involved in the sexual assaults and murders than presumed. When questioned by police about the events leading up to Kristen French's murder, Homolka shared the following with police:

> I said [to Bernardo], well, we have to go to my parents' for Easter dinner. [Bernardo] said, well, why don't we just not go? And I said well, I don't think it would look very good. I mean, we're supposed to go to my parents' for Easter dinner and we don't go ... How is it going to look if this girl's missing and we have no alibi? We haven't gone anywhere, we haven't done anything. And [Bernardo] said, Well, I guess you're right ... He wanted to keep [Kristen] for longer and I didn't want to. Like, I was going to work – I didn't want to go to work knowing that this girl was in my house and she could escape so easily ... So I didn't suggest to him that we kill her on Sunday, but I knew she had to ... be gone (Fifth Estate, Canadian Broadcasting Corporation, 1998).

Much of the incriminating evidence against Homolka (letters she had written to Bernardo and to friends and videotapes of her sexually assaulting) were only recovered *after* Homolka's psychiatric assessments had been carried out and her plea bargain had been negotiated. The fact that many psychiatrists and other professionals deemed her a victim of Bernardo at the early stages of the investigation demonstrates their reliance on traditional sexual scripts of women as sexually passive victims. It was *presumed* that Homolka's participation in the offences was a result of Bernardo's coercion and abuse. It was only when the incriminating evidence was made public that her alleged victimization was disputed.

Homolka's role and status as an offender is complex and the thin line separating her perpetration from her victimization is indeed blurred. Perhaps the 'truth' lies somewhere in the middle. However, the case illustrates that many psychiatrists have difficulty perceiving a woman as a sexual offender and efforts are made to mute and transform her sexually abusive acts.

Over the last twenty years, much effort has been made to raise the profile of women as the victims of domestic violence and abuse (Lloyd, 1995).

However, by *over*emphasizing women as victims, there is the risk of depriving women of their moral agency (Birch, 1993; Lloyd, 1995; Shaw, 1995; Ballinger, 1996). By realigning the offender's behaviour within the margins of victimhood, whether a victim of circumstance or a victim of a male partner, the female sex offender and her offence were more easily placed in accordance with traditional scripts regarding gender and sexuality.

This section has demonstrated the way in which psychiatrists transformed female sex offenders from violent sexually abusive women into benign victims of circumstance or a victim of a coercive male partner. In doing so, psychiatrists appear to be exemplifying the notion of the duality of structure whereby they simultaneously articulate and reproduce the culture of denial with regard to female sex offending.

She is Not a 'Real' or 'Normal' Woman

To psychiatrists, much like police officers, the ideological counterpart to the harmless female sex offender was that these offenders were not 'real' or 'normal' women. The female sex offender's incongruity and departure from 'acceptable' femininity provided the basis from which her story was presented. Psychiatrists transformed sexual offences by women in two ways. First, she was portrayed as an aberrant and abnormal woman who is set apart from the established codes of female conduct. Second, she was portrayed as mentally disturbed with her alleged pathology separating her from 'normal' womanhood. Both portrayals worked to uphold traditional sexual scripts that 'real' women do not sexually offend.

The female sex offender as 'aberrant' and 'abnormal' To psychiatrists, committing a sexual offence did not reflect an act of a 'normal' woman. Their sexually aggressive acts appeared to put them outside the boundaries of appropriate female behaviour:

This girl was bizarre ... she's scary (F-Psychiatrist7).

She was a very sick woman (F-Psychiatrist8).

For some psychiatrists, the 'abnormality' of the female sex offender was evidenced by her displays of 'out of control' aggression and rage:

> Clearly this was a pretty seriously disturbed woman ... She was emotionally very poorly controlled – intense reactions, aggressive episodes, and anger control [problems] (M-Psychiatrist11).

As was seen among police officers, an offender's odd behaviour was sometimes explained by reference to her 'masculine' traits. For example, two psychiatrists discussed a female sex offender that they had both treated. In this particular case, the female sex offender was considering a sex-change operation. Although peripheral to the sexual offences she committed, the psychiatrists continually referred to her desire for a sex change, and to her masculine style and appearance in their discussion of the case:

> She was a would-be transsexual. At one point she applied for a sex change operation ... Before she had the operation, she decided that she didn't want it. She was on male hormones for a considerable amount of time ... She had taken enough male hormones to masculinize her looks ... (M-Psychiatrist12).

> She's scary ... There were a lot of problems with her sexual identity to begin with ... She wanted to undergo a sex change. She was arrested as a man at one point ... (F-Psychiatrist7).

The offender's desire to be male and her failure to conform to the feminine was used, at least in part, to explain her anomalous female behaviour. Constructing the offender as masculine operates to 'explain' and transform her actions. It appears to resolve the contradictions around femininity and her unfeminine acts.

The female sex offender as psychotic What also appeared to set the female sex offender apart from real or 'normal' women was her mental state. Her offending behaviour was believed not to be the result of a sexual deviancy, or a quest for power as is often held to be the case with male sex offenders. Instead, her actions were said to stem from an underlying mental disorder, namely psychosis.

According to the DSM-IV the term psychotic refers to 'delusions, any prominent hallucinations, disorganized speech, or disorganized or catatonic behaviour' (APA, 1994: 273). A psychotic state is one in which thought and emotion are so impaired that the person appears unable to perceive reality (Saradjian, 1996: 152). The literature on psychosis among female sex offenders is contradictory. Earlier studies suggested that these women were suffering from psychosis. Mayer (1983: 21) stated that in the case of mother-daughter incest the mother is often 'extremely disturbed, manifesting ... psychotic behaviour'. Meiselman (1978) noted that mothers who molest their sons may have serious mental disturbances. However, Margolin (1987), Travin et al. (1990), and Ramsay-Klawsnik (1990) have warned against generalizing from these early case studies, as it is often the most disturbed women who come to the attention of the authorities. Saradjian (1996) argues that some women perpetrators are often judged to be psychotic on the basis of the sexual acts that they commit rather than any considered psychiatric examination.

Other studies have not found female sex offenders to be psychotic (Wolfe, 1985; Marvasti, 1986). Grier, Clark and Stoner (1993) compared the personality traits and clinical factors of eleven incarcerated female sex offenders with eleven non-sex offenders and found no significant mean differences in the two groups. Davin et al. (1999), who administered an MMPI-2 to a sample of 46 female sex offenders found that those who had co-offended with male offenders showed little emotional or psychological disturbance. In fact, the co-offenders in her study scored within normal limits on the clinical, supplementary and content scales.

Psychiatrists in this study claimed that the majority of female sex offenders committed their offences as a result of psychosis:

> Most of the female sexual offenders that I've seen have been mentally ill in a fairly obvious way. They wouldn't do what they did if they weren't acutely psychotic. Most are psychotic (M-Psychiatrist12).

> I think female sex offenders are more likely to be mentally ill than the males ... Some of them seem to flip in and out of psychosis ... They are quite severely disturbed at least, if not formally psychotic (M-Psychiatrist3).

It is important to note that when queried about the mental state of male sex offenders, mental illness was not a significant issue:

> In male sex offenders I don't see illness as a major part at all (F-Psychiatrist7).

> Psychotic illnesses? No ... I haven't seen any psychosis in male sex offenders (M-Psychiatrist1).

> I'd say nine out of ten male sex offenders that I've dealt with there is no issue of mental illness (M-Psychiatrist12).

Although there is little doubt that some female sex offenders are psychotic (Saradjian, 1996), it is of interest to understand why female offenders are more likely than male offenders to be deemed psychotic by these psychiatrists. There is evidence to suggest that female sex offenders may be diagnosed as psychotic on the basis of the sexual acts they commit, rather than on any psychiatric assessment. For example, one psychiatrist reported that he had 'never *seen* [assessed] a female sex offender' in his clinical practice. However, this did not deter him from claiming that female sex offenders are more likely to suffer from psychosis. His reasoning reveals his reliance on traditional sexual scripts of women as sexually passive and harmless:

> My suspicion would be that yes, it is more likely that female sex offenders would suffer from psychosis, because [sexual offending] is just not typically female behaviour. They would have to be quite warped and possibly psychotic to do something like that (M-Psychiatrist1).

The psychiatrist's 'diagnosis' appears not to have been based on past clinical experience or concrete evidence of an offender's delusions or hallucinations. Instead, it is the female sex offender's departure from traditional sexual scripts and 'typical' femininity that has earned her the diagnosis. Committing a sexual offence is such a flagrant deviation from 'normal', 'feminine' behaviour that the only way to make sense of it is to label it 'psychotic'. Indeed, *real* women do not sexually offend – only 'warped' and 'psychotic' women do.

The fact that the psychiatrist suggested that female sex offenders were likely to be psychotic without any previous clinical experience with this population is significant. It demonstrates that although diagnoses are held to be based on stringent clinical evidence (APA, 1994), in practice, labels such as 'psychotic' may be a reflection of traditional sexual scripts or the ideological underpinnings of individual psychiatrists.

Female behaviour deemed 'bizarre' or perplexing by psychiatrists, may also be designated as 'psychotic'. While discussing a case of a female sex offender, one psychiatrist noted:

> I could never really figure [the female sex offender] out completely ... This girl was bizarre. Her whole demeanour, the way she had her hair done, she was quite bizarre ... Although I cannot specifically say that she had this delusion or that hallucination, her behaviour was so bizarre, the only way I could control it was through big doses of anti-psychotics (F-Psychiatrist7).

The psychiatrist's affirmation that she 'could never really figure her out completely' illustrates the precarious nature of the diagnostic label. The offender did not display symptoms of delusions or hallucinations and therefore may not have conformed explicitly to the diagnostic criteria of a Psychotic Disorder. However, her 'bizarre' character, which was evidenced by her offence, her demeanour, and even her hairstyle, appears to justify the diagnosis of 'psychotic', warranting treatment with anti-psychotic medication. This example suggests that behaviour that challenges traditional sexual scripts, not clinical evidence, may, at times, give rise to a psychiatric label.

The issue of control is also interesting. The psychiatrist's statement 'the only way I could control her was through big doses of anti-psychotics' implies that the offender was 'out of control'. It appears that her aberrant behaviour was what rendered her as such. In attempting to 'tame' and 'normalize' the offender through medication, the psychiatrist is marking the limits and boundaries of 'normal' and 'acceptable' female behaviour.

These examples reveal that because the female sex offender behaves in a deviant manner, violating traditional sexual scripts concerning 'appropriate' female behaviour, she is said to be suffering from psychosis. As Sarajian has noted in relation to female sex offenders:

No state of altered consciousness such as these women experience can be said to be the *cause* of the women sexually abusing children. This is a construction made in order to help distance ourselves ... from women who carry out these unspeakable acts (Sarajian, 1996: 3).

By transforming the offender into an unruly and psychotic woman, traditional sexual scripts and the culture of denial are once again affirmed and the known 'truths' about women remain in place.

Understanding Psychiatrists' Constructions

To account for psychiatrists' transformations of sexual offences by women as well as the culture of denial that seemed to pervade psychiatric discourse, the issue of discomfort appears to be important. Psychiatrists expressed varying degrees of discomfort with regard to the issue of sexual assault by females. These psychiatrists noted:

Psychiatrists feel uncomfortable dealing with female sex offenders ... a lot of [my colleagues] are more offended and more grossed out by females doing this [sexual assault] than they were by males – partly because they don't think of females as being sexual predators (F-Psychiatrist4).

Some psychiatrists have seen a few [female sex offenders] throughout their career, but ... they don't want to deal with it ... Some clinicians feel uncomfortable in dealing with them (F-Psychiatrist8).

It is possible that transforming and ultimately denying the female sex offender and her offence becomes an efficient means for psychiatrists to alleviate the discomfort.

Like police officers, psychiatrists appeared to employ a gendered lens to assist in the transformation process. The gendered lens provided an alternative gaze from which to view the offender. The lens worked to distort the reality of her offending behaviour, aligning her actions with more socially acceptable notions of female behaviour. Once the lens was in place, psychiatrists looked to two sets of traditional sexual scripts which helped to further transform the offender and her offence. The first set of scripts were based on the notions of women as sexually harmless, and as victims whereas the second set of scripts depicted women as unruly, aberrant, and mentally disordered. Both sets of scripts appear to have been drawn from the occupational culture of psychiatry, as well as broader cultural constructions of gender, crime and sexuality. Appealing to the gendered lens and to traditional sexual scripts enabled psychiatrists to resolve the initial conflict, maintain the security of their worldview, and ultimately reproduce the culture of denial with regard to female sex offending. Psychiatrists' constructions of female sex offending appeared to follow the same transformation process that was found among police officers as well as at the societal level.

Next, it is important to examine why psychiatrists constructed female sex offending in the ways that they did. As was noted in relation to police officers, psychiatrists did not invent these portrayals. Instead, they reflect a cultural belief system which has frequently represented women within these thematic constructs. Themes of women as harmless, as prototypical victims, as abnormal, or as mentally disordered have had a consistent presence within the context of broader culture (see for example Chesler, 1972; Bunker Rohrbaugh, 1981; Allen, 1987b; Showalter, 1987; Ussher, 1991; Elshtain, 1993; Pilgrim & Rogers, 1993; Lloyd, 1995; Russell, 1995; Ballinger, 1996; Busfield, 1996). It is possible to see how psychiatrists appear to draw upon these culturally available representations in their constructions of female sex offending. Once again, without an alternative narrative or a way of conceptualizing female sex offending, these traditional scripts of provided an effective means to understand and negotiate such cases.

The fact that these representations were drawn from both wider societal beliefs as well as from the institutional context of psychiatry underscores the importance of the dialectical process in explaining how the culture of denial is maintained and perpetuated. It is possible to see how the three carriers of culture are interconnected and simultaneously construct, and reproduce traditional sexual scripts and the culture of denial with regard to female sex offending.

Like police officers, psychiatrists' constructions of female sex offending illustrate many of Giddens' conceptualizations. First, there is evidence that psychiatrists are both influenced and constrained by the existing structural considerations of society and the institutional 'rules' of psychiatry concerning 'appropriate' behaviour for women. Second, individual psychiatrists were active and knowledgeable agents who were able to choose to embrace and reject the broader societal and organizational 'rules'. They could also choose whether or not to enact the transformation process. In terms of the duality of structure, by drawing upon societal and institutional 'rules' concerning gender and sexuality as guidance for their behaviour, they ultimately reproduced them. The dialectical process, the transformation process, and Giddens' concept of the duality of structure, offer a helpful model to understand psychiatrists' constructions and to discern how and why denial persists within psychiatric culture and practice.

Another possibility is that psychiatrists turned to these representations as a result of the male dominated nature of both medicine in general and psychiatry in particular. While women have historically been healers and provided medical care, men have long controlled the medical profession (Luchetti, 1998). In fact, efforts were made to actively and effectively exclude women from medicine until recent times (Walsh, 1977; Penfold & Walker, 1984; Bickel, 1996). For example, in Canada no woman was allowed to study medicine until the 1880s. Many Canadian university medical faculties did not open its doors to female students until 1945 (Duffin, 1996). However, as a consequence of second-wave feminism, increasing numbers of women began to apply and be accepted into medical schools in the mid-1970s (Dickstein, 1996). While more women may be entering medicine, evidence suggests that they are often segregated within particular fields of medicine such as pediatrics and obstetrics and those requiring interpersonal skills because of their perceived capacity for compassion (Jones, 1996).

The discipline of psychiatry is said to be informed by its roots in physical medicine (Ussher, 1991). It is therefore not surprising that women have also struggled for professional ascendancy within psychiatry. In the mid-1980s, women were said to make up less than ten per cent of psychiatrists in North America (Penfold & Walker, 1984). While more women are entering psychiatry as a career (Crimlisk & Welch, 1996), in many countries they are still under-represented in senior positions, particularly in academic psychiatry (Kastrup & Petersson, 1986; Leibenluft et al., 1993). Psychiatry has been described by some psychiatrists as a sexist, paternalistic, and authoritarian profession, which has contributed to the subjugation of women (Levine & Kamin, 1974; Penfold & Walker, 1984). Feminist writers have argued that psychiatric theories and practices have presented the male as a prototype, legitimized women's second class status, validated dominant-subordinate relationships between men and women, and reflected descriptions and prescriptions based on archetypal images (Chesler, 1972; Penfold & Walker, 1984). The male-oriented culture as well as the historical exclusion, absence, and invisibility of female psychiatrists may contribute to traditional beliefs about women within the culture of psychiatry. This may, in turn, encourage the enactment of traditional sexual scripts and the denial of women as potential sexual aggressors. The power and influence of this culture is evident in the fact that the two female psychiatrists interviewed for this study also appeared to transform sexual offences by women, and reproduced traditional sexual scripts and the culture of denial.

This chapter has explored the importance of the transformation process, particularly the gender lens, in psychiatrists' perceptions, understandings and explanations of sexual assault by females. The offender's gender and her femininity are fundamental to the meaning and interpretation of the offence. As was the case with police officers, it appears to mean something different to be sexually abused by a female – it is often judged to be inconsequential, with the offender being perceived more as a victim or as suffering from psychosis. Since the meaning of the abuse differed, so too were the responses to the abuse. The common response was to transform sexual offences by women to align them with more culturally acceptable meanings of gender, crime and sexuality. The analysis of psychiatrists' constructions and the prevalence of denial among them reveal the *possibility* that female sex offenders may be overlooked and disregarded by psychiatrists. However, as was noted in the previous chapter, the notion of 'sexist bias' within the institutional context are complex and cannot be understood as an isolated phenomenon among individual psychiatrists as they are but one element in a complex dialectic involving both institutional and broader societal values.

This chapter began by analysing three fundamental aspects of the culture of psychiatry to understand the social context in which psychiatrists work. Analysis of the interviews reveals the professional culture's reliance on traditional sexual scripts and the implicit denial of women as potential sexual aggressors. The chapter's second section revealed that broader societal beliefs, as well as the values imparted during formal training, informal talk and banter, and through organizational shorthands appeared to influence psychiatrist's constructions of female sex offenders. Psychiatrists appeared to neutralize and transform female sex offending. By employing the gendered lens and transforming the offender and her offence around two poles of representation as either innocuous or unruly, psychiatrists simultaneously constructed, sustained, and reproduced traditional sexual scripts and the culture of denial with regard to female sex offending. The dialectical and transformation processes and Giddens' notion of the duality of structure are helpful in understanding the complex relationships with regard to the organizational context of psychiatry and perceptions of female sex offenders. In the next chapter, attention is turned away from professionals and instead explores the perspectives and experiences of victims of female sex offenders.

Notes

1   The DSM-IV defines a mental disorder as 'a clinically significant behavioural or psychological syndrome or pattern that occurs in an individual and that is associated with present distress..or disability..or with a significantly increased risk of suffering death, pain, disability, or an important loss of freedom' (APA, 1994: xxi).

2   Jane Doe was the name that police gave to the victim in order to protect her identity.

6 Victims' Perspectives on Female Sex Offending

The following chapter explores victim perspectives on female sex offending. The chapter begins by outlining the demographic characteristics of the sample of survivors and the ways in which they experienced women as sexually abusive. It then traces how participants negotiated the abuse experience both as children and later as adults. In exploring the life histories and perspectives of victims, we will see how their experiences of sexual abuse not only appear to defy traditional sexual scripts, but also how victims transform the sexual abuse experience in ways that are reminiscent of police officers and psychiatrists. The chapter then examines the reported impact of the sexual abuse. It also addresses survivors' experiences and perceptions of professional responses to their disclosures of sexual abuse by females.

The Experience of Sexual Abuse by Females

Demographic Characteristics of the Sample

Fifteen victims of child sexual abuse by females were interviewed for the study; eight females and seven males. Participants ranged in age from ten years to 59 years. The majority of victims were adults who were recalling childhood abuse. Fourteen participants (93 per cent) were White, and one (seven per cent) was Aboriginal.

Victim-Perpetrator Relationship

Childhood sexual interactions were reported with a variety of female perpetrators. Ten participants (67 per cent) reported sexual abuse by a female relative, while four participants (27 per cent) reported being abused by an unrelated female. Of those who reported sexual abuse by a relative, seven of the participants (47 per cent) reported sexual abuse by their mothers. Two participants (13 per cent) reported sexual abuse by both their grandmother and their mother. One participant (7 per cent) reported abuse by both his mother and his sister. Of those reporting sexual abuse by an unrelated females, three participants (20 per cent) reported abuse by a female babysitter, while one participant (seven per cent) reported being abused by several nuns at her local church. One participant reported being abused by both a family member (sister) and an unrelated female (neighbour).

The contradictory literature in this area makes it difficult to determine whether the relationships in this sample reflect those in other studies. Some authors have found the majority of female sex offenders to be unrelated to the children with whom they have contact (Petrovich & Templar, 1984; Fehrenbach & Monastersky, 1988; Shrier & Johnson, 1988; Allen, 1991). Others have found that females are more often related to their victims (Wolfe, 1985; O'Connor, 1987; Finkelhor et al., 1988; Rowan et al., 1990).

All fifteen of the participants reported an experience of ongoing sexual abuse by a lone female (without the presence of a co-perpetrator and not under duress or coercion from another individual). Although two participants (13 per cent) reported sexual interactions within a group context involving both male and female perpetrators, they also reported separate instances of lone female abuse. Within these group contexts, none of the participants reported that the abuse by females was done under duress or coercion by males. In fact, when the notion of coercion was proposed, many participants found the idea preposterous:

> My mother? Coerced? [Laughter]. My mother was certainly not coerced. Certainly not. I'm almost positive that my mother took money from the men who she let [sexually] assault me (Laura[1]).

Four participants (27 per cent) reported sexual abuse by both their mother and their father. In all four cases, the sexual abuse was carried out by the mother and father separately. In fact, some participants were unsure whether one parent was aware of the ongoing abuse by the other parent. The predominance of lone female perpetrators contradicts the available data on female sex offenders which has found that most women sexually assault in concert with a male and/or under his coercion (McCarty, 1986; Faller, 1987; Mathews et al., 1989; Rowan et al., 1990).

Age of Onset, Duration and Frequency of Abuse

The literature has reported a variety of ages of children against whom females offend ranging from as young as one week (Chasnoff et al., 1986) to sixteen years (Wolfe, 1985). In this study, the average age of onset of the sexual abuse by females was five years, ranging from age three to age nine. The sexual abuse ended, on average, at 12 years, ranging from age five to age 16. The average duration of the sexual abuse was seven years ranging from three to 11 years. In terms of frequency, five participants (33 per cent) reported being sexually abused more than once per week, four participants (27 per cent) reported being abused once per week; four participants (27 per cent) reported being abused once per month. Two participants (13 per cent) reported a single incident of sexual abuse.

Characteristics of the Sexual Abuse

Sexual interactions reported between children and older females represent a wide variety of activities (Davin et al., 1999). The literature on female offenders has documented acts such as fondling, oral stimulation, and intercourse (Petrovich & Templar, 1984; Wolfe, 1985; McCarty, 1986; Faller, 1987; Fehrenbach & Monastersky, 1988; Rowan et al., 1990; Allen, 1991; Mayer, 1992). The sexual activities experienced by participants were divided into three levels of severity based on models proposed by Russell (1984) and Saradjian (1996). Taken from Saradjian (1996), sexually abusive behaviours by women were divided into three levels of severity: severe, moderate, and mild. Behaviours that comprised severe, moderate and mild sexual abuse were taken from Russell's (1984) study of female sexual abuse victims of male perpetrators. *Severe sexual abuse* comprised intercourse, vaginal and/or anal penetration (with objects or fingers), cunnilingus, fellatio, or the forced performance of any of these acts with a third party. *Moderate sexual abuse* consisted of genital contact and fondling (without penetration) as well as simulated intercourse. *Mild sexual abuse* included acts such as kissing in a sexual way, and sexual invitations or requests. Nine participants (60 per cent) reported severe sexual abuse. The remaining six participants (40 per cent) reported moderate sexual abuse. Although participants reported experiencing acts considered mild abuse, none of the participants experienced *only* mild sexual abuse (see Table 6.1 below).

Severe Sexual Abuse

Intercourse Three male participants (20 per cent) reported being forced to engage in vaginal intercourse:

> With my sister, the abuse involved cunnilingus, and intercourse ... I would perform cunnilingus and then we would have intercourse. I can remember that I was six and she was eleven. It's only in hindsight that I realize that my father had been working her over for some time. But the intercourse continued between my sister and I until I was fourteen and she was nineteen (Jacob).

> I was eight and a half. I remember that [the babysitter] asked me to come into the bedroom with her ... That day she told me to lay on top of her and she put my penis in her. That was the first time that that happened (Charles).

Table 6.1 Victim Data

Name	Duration (age)	Relationship with Perpetrator	Type of abuse*
Al	5 – 16	Mother	GFC
Alexandra	9	Babysitter	SI
Anna	6 – 16	g-mother + mother	AP CP GFC VP
Carmen	4 – 12	Mother	AP GFP K OS
Charles	6 – 10	Babysitter	GFC I OS
Danielle	4 – 14	Mother	AP BS GFC GFP OS SI VP
David	3 – 6	babysitter	GFC GFP OS
Dominique	4 – 8	mother	GFP K SI
Jacob	3 – 14	mother sister	GFP I OS
Kyra	7 – 14	clergy	AP CP GFP OS VP
Laura	6 – 11	g-mother + mother	AP CP OS VP
Mark	3 – 5	neighbour sister	GFP
Matt	6 – 12	mother	GFC GFP
Patrick	3 – 5	mother	I K GFP OS
Vanessa	3 – 14	mother	GFC GFP

* AP Anal Penetration   K Kissing
  CP Child Prostitution   OS Oral Sex
  GFC Genital Fondling by Child   SI Simulated Intercourse
  GFP Genital Fondling by Perpetrator   VP Vaginal Penetration with
  I Intercourse   fingers and objects

Vaginal penetration with objects and/or fingers Four of the eight female participants reported being vaginally penetrated with fingers or objects. Laura reported being sexually abused by her grandmother from age six to age eleven and then at age seven by her older sister:

My grandmother did a variety of things. Not just to me, she did them to my older sister and she did them to my brother as well. She would take our clothes off, and tie us up on tables. She would stick things in our bodies ... She would say: 'You've got to get up on the table and lie there' ... I would tell her it was hurting and she would say 'well, it won't hurt for long'. She would stick her fingers inside of me and I remember how much that hurt ... When I was six, she tied me to a chair and inserted a very sharp stick in my vagina. If I were to move, I would cause myself to bleed ... She left me there for hours ... That was just part of what she did to show me that she was in control ... Later on, my sister would try to do what my grandmother had done to her. She would have me lie down and she would want to stick things in my body (Laura).

Other participants reported similar incidents:

[My mother] would do these vaginal 'exams' on me. She used to 'examine' me and insert objects in my vagina. My grandmother would do the same thing. She would shove things inside me and it hurt (Anna).

Anal penetration Five participants (33 per cent) reported anal penetration which, for some of the participants, centred on the abusive use of enemas or suppositories. Several authors have noted the use of enemas by female sex offenders (Evert, 1987; Kasl, 1990; Rosencrans, 1997; Mitchell and Morse, 1998). There are few legitimate medical reasons for enemas (Herman-Giddens & Berson, 1994) and this can easily be experienced by a child as sexual abuse. Authors report that enemas may be used by the perpetrator to obtain sexual gratification (Herman-Giddens & Berson, 1994) or power and dominance (Evert, 1987). Two participants explain:

The brutality with my mother all had to do with the rectum. She was brutal. She got into suppositories ... She would invade me with suppositories or her finger, any time she wanted – it was just about every day when I was little. I can't remember it not happening, so my guess is that this happened right away ... it [was] violating, degrading, humiliating (Carmen).

If I didn't have a bowel movement by ten in the morning, [my mother] would sodomize me with something, usually soap. She would take a knife and cut a shard of soap off of a soap bar. The edges were very sharp and it was quite painful (Vanessa).

Oral sex Eight participants (four males, four females) (53 per cent) reported that they were forced to engage in oral-genital contact. Seven of the eight participants reported being forced to perform cunnilingus on the perpetrator. In three cases, the perpetrator performed cunnilingus or fellatio on the victim. The following male victims describe their experiences:

> I was about five years old and my mother was bathing me. After I got out of the bath she was drying me off ... and she started to fellate me. I said to her 'no mummy'. She stopped and then she continued to do it again. I said no again and she acknowledged 'Yes, mummy shouldn't do that'. But all I can remember is that I sank into an abyss after that ... the part I can remember most was the hair rustling on my thighs ... I have memories of cunnilingus. Having to do cunnilingus on her (Patrick).

> With my mother, there would be a lot of oral sex. She would have me perform cunnilingus. I'm floored when I try to think what was in her mind. It's a difficult area. I remember just gagging from loss of breath, being ill, and having her sit on my face and laugh (Jacob).

> I had to give her [female babysitter] oral sex ... I have this memory of me trying to stop and her insisting that I keep on doing it ... I was really disgusted ... I just couldn't do it. The oral sex is more vague and a feeling like I was somewhere else ... In my adult life, I've always had a problem with oral sex (David).

Child prostitution Three participants (20 per cent) reported that the female perpetrator aided, abetted and even procured male sexual offenders to abuse them:

> I have an image of my grandmother holding me down while I was raped by a man (Anna).

> My mother met people who were paedophiles ... I suspect that they paid her. She would be in the same room while these men did what they wanted with her female children. My sister and me were part of what she offered to these men. She would be in the room when they were having sexual contact with us. As far as I'm concerned, she was an abuser because of that ... I remember lying there when these things were happening to me and watching her. She was sitting on the couch having a cigarette and watching what was happening ... I was frightened and I kept crying out for her and she never helped. So I stopped crying out. The one time I remember calling out to her, she just looked at me and laughed. After that, I would never ever call out to her. I was completely cut off during these assaults, but I certainly remember seeing her sitting there

smoking a cigarette and watching me with this look of satisfaction on her face —
like she got me (Laura).

Moderate Sexual Abuse

Simulated intercourse Three participants (20 per cent) reported having to
engage in simulated intercourse which involved genital to genital contact.
For Danielle and Dominique, the simulated intercourse was with their
mother:

> The last time I had sex with my mother was when I was fourteen. We almost got
> caught by my sister (Danielle).

> She had sex with me. She was on top of me with no underwear ... She started to
> move her body on top of mine. She moved her sex on my sex. It lasted fifteen
> minutes. She would say things like 'you're beautiful, I love you, this is good'
> (Dominique).

Alexandra reported that at the age of ten she was forced by her female
babysitter to simulate intercourse with her seven year old brother. Although
Alexandra self-identifies as a victim of sibling incest, Alexandra believes
that she was 'raped' by the female babysitter:

> Michelle [female babysitter] forced us to perform sex with each other, in a
> variety of positions ... The incest stigmata and trauma was there in the extreme
> — the guilt, the shame, the confusion. Yet I can derive no psychological benefit
> from turning to the perpetrator because [my brother] was a victim as well ... we
> were raped by Michelle ... [she] physically [held] me down on top of [my
> brother] when I expressed my reluctance. My reluctance was based on a fear of
> hurting him. I was physically bigger and taller than him, I really thought I would
> crush him underneath me ... So there was that fear, and when I expressed that
> fear, I was held down physically. But mainly her role was as a deceiver to
> suggest that we do this and it would be a great idea ... Everything that I
> suggested against it — like 'Well, mommy and daddy say that only adults do that
> etc.' was countered with an argument. I don't think it was a spur of the moment
> experiment. She had to have given it some thought. She always had an easy
> answer. I was fairly bright kid but I had zero experience. So I was easily fooled
> ... by her experience and her being in control — [she was] the babysitter
> (Alexandra).

Genital fondling Genital fondling, where the victim was forced to touch
the genitals of the perpetrator or vice versa, was the most common form of

sexual abuse reported. Thirteen victims (87 per cent) reported genital fondling:

> I remember that my mother used to make me do these vaginal exams on her. I would have to examine her vagina to see if everything was okay, that everything was normal ... I had to do what she said. I thought that if I didn't, she would kill me ... I would end up dead ... I was still 'examining' my mother when I was older – up until I was sixteen (Anna).

> The sexual abuse was done when she came over to babysit us. It involved a lot of fondling. Fondling her breasts, her genitals, her vagina. The touching evolved to sucking her breasts and moved on to oral sex (David).

> I remember at eight years old a lot of times waking up in the middle of the night and having [my mother] there with a flashlight poking me. I remember that she would touch me all over ... She would have my pyjama bottoms right down and I had no idea what was going on. I would wake up in a daze. She would say to me 'oh, I'm checking for worms'. That was supposed to be acceptable ... I remember a lot of touching with her hands. She would be 'checking' my bum and then she would 'check' my front. She would always check my pelvic area ... I was really frightened and had this awkward feeling of – what does this mean? Some nights because I actually woke up, I knew some of what was happening. Other times, I could never figure out how my pyjama bottoms got off ... I felt totally ashamed ... She was still doing that when I was twelve (Matt).

Dominique, a ten year old participant, described sexual abuse by her mother from age four until age eight, when she was removed from her mother's care by social services as a result of neglect and a lack of supervision. Dominique disclosed the sexual abuse to her father much later. At the time of the interview, Dominique was living with her father and step-mother and sexual assault charges were pending against her mother:

> My mom was abusing me sexually. She would touch me on my vagina. And she touched my breasts. She touched me a lot ... All the time that I lived with her ... When she was touching me I thought that it was normal ... She said that she liked touching me, and that she loved me ... It happened in the kitchen. She would lie me down on the kitchen table. She touched me and told me to touch her. It also happened in her bedroom (Dominique).

Three participants reported that the genital fondling would occur while the perpetrator was bathing. In these instances, the perpetrator would call in the victim and ask that he or she 'wash' them. The confusion, shame and disgust that accompanied the experience are illustrated by Al:

At the age of five, she was in the bathtub and she called me into the bathroom ... She wanted me to wash her body. She had me wash her breasts, and her clitoris and vagina. The odd thing was that she had me wash [her] and she was having an orgasm and I thought she was going through a lot of pain. I didn't know what it was ... This went on for so many years, constantly washing her ... Even when I was sixteen, [after her bath] I would dry her off, put a towel around her and give her her night gown, bra or panties. I thought that this was normal ... This was an ongoing routine for a long time. The older I got, the more she wanted me to wash. It's disgusting when I think about it, enough to make you sick. It seemed like every single night I was constantly washing my mother in the bath, it was sick ... (Al).

Mild Sexual Abuse

Kissing Three victims who reported sexual abuse by their mothers reported inappropriate and sexual kissing:

My mom kissed me on the mouth and she put her tongue in my mouth. It was disgusting. She smelled of cigarettes (Dominique).

I was sixteen [when] my mother got remarried. On her wedding night, I got drunk and I totally passed out. On her wedding night she is looking after her drunk, passed out son − isn't that ironic? She's sitting by my bed ... I'm so drunk and she leans over to kiss me. We started French kissing. I think about that and I think ... what kind of crazy stuff is going on here? (Patrick).

Grooming for compliance and preventing disclosure Grooming is the process by which sexual abusers ensure the compliance of their victim in order to engage in sexual interaction and maintain secrecy. Saradjian (1996) has noted that women use similar tactics to men in grooming the child for compliance. Grooming may be less necessary for younger children because they do not know any other form of treatment. For older children however, perpetrators may rely on the child's dependency on them to prevent disclosure. Some female perpetrators use threats or severe violence so that the children are terrified of the consequences of the sexual abuse being discovered (Saradjian, 1996). Five participants (33 per cent) reported that they were threatened by the perpetrator(s) to maintain secrecy. The threats were directed at participants as well as their family:

If I told, I was dead. If I told, my mother would die, my father would die, my sister would die and any of the [foster] babies that we had living with us at the time would die ... They threatened to drown me in a nearby lake (Kyra).

In the early days, [I was told by my parents] 'Don't tell anyone you little bastard' and a couple of good slaps. That was really confusing for me because I had no one to tell to begin with and I didn't know that it was bad. Later on, it was already deeply entrenched in my mind that you don't talk about this ... From my parents, there were threats of extreme violence. Real sick stuff like putting their cigarettes out on me (Jacob).

For one participant, the threats were so powerful that the fear of disclosure remained with her in adulthood:

No, I never ever told anybody. I was terrified. I was threatened by my mother. She told me that bad things happen to bad little girls who don't do what they're told. I thought that if I said anything ... I would be dead. I still think that. I'm sitting here talking to you and to be honest, I'm terrified that if I talk about this, someone is going to come after me and hurt me for talking about it. So I just don't talk about it (Anna).

Physical Violence and Sexual Abuse

Three participants (20 per cent) reported that physical violence was often an integral part of the sexual abuse, occurring during or after the sexual abuse:

That's often how the sexual abuse started. She got mad at me. She would get angry and then it would turn into something sexual. [One incident] started because I wouldn't eat my dinner ... She took my clothes off ... She was touching me and sticking stuff inside me. Then she made me put my hand up inside her and I didn't want to do that. I was only about four. It was degrading and hurtful. And the beatings ... She would sexually abuse me and then beat me. When [the sexual abuse] was done, I wanted her to hug me. Instead, she shoved me right up against the wall and started to hit and kick me ... Sometimes she would put me into the bathtub and then she would hold my head under the water ... She would try to choke me sometimes too – she said that I initiated [the sexual abuse] and I wanted it ... I was the bad person (Danielle).

I don't remember ever being affectionately touched by her. It was either rage, where she would be slapping me or attacking me, or some kind of sexual perversion. The undercurrents to the sexual activities, there was always violence associated with that stuff ... It would be before the sexual abuse, sometimes after. Usually not during, because I couldn't endure the pain (Jacob).

The data reveals that participants experienced a broad range of sexually abusive acts, predominantly at the hands of a lone female perpetrator, frequently the participant's mother. Factors such as age at which the sexual abuse begins, the severity of the acts, their relatively long duration, the prevalence of mother-child incest, and the presence of multiple perpetrators are important. Early onset, severity of abuse, long duration, a close relationship between the victim and the perpetrator, and multiple perpetrators have been noted as predictors of later disturbance (Browne & Finkelhor, 1986; Mendel, 1995). The presence of these factors could be seen to play a role in the later difficulties experienced by participants and which precipitated seeking treatment.

What is striking about the participants' experiences of sexual abuse by females is that they are in stark contrast to the perceptions and portrayals of female sex offending by the professionals interviewed for this study. Police officers and psychiatrists viewed women as sexually passive and harmless, yet participants experienced women as sexually abusive with the majority of participants experiencing severe sexual abuse as well as physical abuse. This is an important finding. Contrary to traditional sexual scripts and broader cultural and institutional views, women appear to be capable of invasive and serious forms of sexual abuse. Moreover, there were few instances of women acting in concert with a co-perpetrator and, according to survivors' recollections, no instances of male coercion. The professional assumptions that female sex offenders are likely to act as an accomplice to a male perpetrator, especially under his coercion, is thus thrown into question.

Negotiating the Past: Transforming the Sexual Abuse Experience

The ways in which victims of female perpetrators negotiate the experience of sexual abuse, both as children and as adults is an important area of inquiry as it helps to shed light on childhood understandings of sexual abuse and whether or not with time perceptions of sexual abuse change. This section outlines how participants construct and negotiate the sexual abuse both as children and as adults. It reveals the ways in which adult victims sometimes employ a gendered lens and transform the sexual abuse experience, aligning it with traditional sexual scripts of women as sexually passive and harmless. Reflecting the duality of structure, victims, much like police officers and psychiatrists, appear to draw upon, enact, and reproduce the culture of denial in regard to female sex offending.

Participants reported that as children they attempted to cope with the sexual abuse experience through fantasy, dissociation or repression. Such coping mechanisms have been noted in the literature on victims of child sexual abuse (Browne & Finkelhor, 1986; Sgroi & Sargent, 1993; Rosencrans, 1997). Carmen reported daydreaming and using fantasy as a means of escape while Laura remembers dissociating:

> I daydreamed. I had a castle. I created my own world. I would go to these places before and after she would sexually abuse me. Not during because I had too much to do. I couldn't cry, and I had to be polite. I had to perform (Carmen).

> I tried not to think what was happening to me at the time. While it was happening, I would look out a window and watch something out there – I felt a connection with nature. I just dissociated (Laura).

Alexandra, who experienced a single incident of abuse, reported repressing the experience:

> Afterwards, it wasn't discussed. [I] got up the next day and went to school. I don't think I even woke up with it in my head. I doubt it made it twelve hours in my mind before it was shut off (Alexandra).

None of the participants perceived the sexual interactions as 'abusive' as children. Instead, it was perceived to be a 'normal' part of their lives:

> I never saw what was happening to me as sexual abuse. It was normal ... I hated it, but it was just one of those things that I had to do (Anna).

> Because I was involved for so long, I got to thinking that it was pretty normal and that it was my lot in life (Kyra).

> I thought that [sexual abuse] is what all parents did. This is what families do. This is normal (Matt).

In fact, the routine nature of the sexual abuse led some participants to pick up cues and signals of when, and by whom, they would be sexually abused. As Jacob noted:

> The abuse was very ritualized so it did happen in similar places, at similar times and there were routines built into it. There were signals so that I would know ahead of time. On drinking night, when my dad would be at the tavern, my mother would be the perpetrator. On bingo night, my father would be the perpetrator. As we get older, my sister would be the perpetrator (Jacob).

Transforming the Experience

Given that these children were all very young when the sexual abuse began (the average age of onset being five years old) it is not particularly surprising that they did not perceive the interactions as abusive. Most did not know any other form of treatment. As adults, however, the majority of participants continued to have difficulty perceiving the sexual interactions as 'abusive'. Participants would frequently recount highly disturbing childhood experiences of abuse and following that minimize it or question whether it was truly 'abusive'. For example, David, who from age three to six years old was forced to fondle, and perform cunnilingus on his female babysitter did not believe that his experience was 'abusive' and wondered whether it warranted admission into a therapy group:

> It wasn't dramatic because there was no violence involved and there was no penetration ... It was more subtle and done in a sneaky, seducing way. Do I really qualify to be in this [therapy] group? (David).

Similarly, Al, who was forced to bathe his step-mother, wash her breasts, vagina, and clitoris and bring her to orgasm, questioned whether he had experienced sexual abuse:

> I don't know if it's really sexual abuse actually ... She came to climaxes ... it was traumatizing ... I question it though (Al).

In much the same way as did the professionals in this study, adult participants tended to minimize, transform and ultimately deny the sexual abuse that was perpetrated against them. Like police officers and psychiatrists, survivors' attempts to transform their experiences appear to be related to the discomfort that female sex offending evoked. For example, the idealization of women and the pervasive sexual script that women do not abuse made it particularly difficult for Kyra to come to terms with her experience. She began to question her memories of sexual abuse by females, believing that it must have been a male abusing her because women do not commit sexual offences:

> When I started to begin to even whisper the fact that there may have been a female that abused me – it was like 'no way!' I thought to myself – I must really have this wrong. I kept thinking where was the male in there? He had to be doing something ... There is a lot of shame around that ... Men can be monsters, but women can't ... It was definitely harder to come to terms with (Kyra).

In a similar vein, those who were sexually abused by their mothers found it difficult to come to terms with the fact that their mother, the person who is 'supposed' to be nurturing and protecting, could sexually abuse them:

> It's more of a difficult issue to confront because it's your mother. Your mother is supposed to nurture you. My mother never did that (Carmen).

From these comments, we can see how female sex offending creates varying degrees of discomfort for survivors. This discomfort appeared to be (temporarily) abated by transforming the offender and her offence. With a gendered lens in place, survivors (either consciously or unconsciously) distorted the reality of female sex offending and realigned the offender's behaviour with traditional sexual scripts and culturally acceptable notions of female sexual passivity and male sexual aggression. For example, David and Jacob, whose sexual abuse began at the age of three and six years old respectively, attempted to (re)define their sexual interactions with adult females not as sexual abuse, but as an early initiation to sexuality:

> I never really saw the sexual activities between my sister and me, my mother and me ... in the context of abuse ... Those were supposed to be man-like things, those were supposed to be acceptable ... I had a hard time accepting that as abuse because it was just sex ... I tried to see it more like I had gained sexual experience sooner than other guys. In that context I could frame it not as abuse. It was sex with a woman. Getting fucked in the ass by my cousin or my father – that's another story. That I knew was abuse. That's abuse. That was pretty damn clear (Jacob).

> I was a little boy, but I knew how women and men worked and operated. I think that had the perpetrator been a man, I would have seen it as more abnormal than a woman ... Touching a man sexually as a child would have made me feel a lot more uncomfortable than touching a woman sexually. I think when I was older and I was trying to rationalize what was happening, I thought well, men are supposed to have sex with women. What happened to me was just an example of it ... I used that as an excuse ... I've told myself sometimes, you know, she was a woman. Just look at it as having started [sexual activity] early ... that you had an early experience (David).

These comments illustrate the difficulty in conceptualizing sexual abuse by women and the ways in which survivors actively attempt to transform their experiences by drawing upon traditional sexual scripts of males as sexually aggressive and enjoying or profiting from all forms of heterosexual contact (regardless of the circumstances). It also highlights the real-life enactment of the duality of structure whereby individuals rely upon broader structures and societal 'rules' with regard to 'appropriate' female behaviour and in doing so, reproduce these rules.

Other survivors also appeared to transform the sexual abuse from an uncomfortable and frightening experience, to one that was more harmless, benign, conforming to traditional sexual scripts. For example, as an adult, Anna, who was forced to conduct vaginal 'examinations' on her mother, came to view the experience not as sexual abuse, but as a 'medical exam':

> I never really felt it was abuse. It was a medical exam ... It was me who made something out of it other than what it really was (Anna).

Patrick and Al came to view their experiences not within the context of sexual abuse, but within the context of a mother's traditional role as caretaker:

> I rationalized my mother fellating me after my bath ... I looked at other animals and saw mother cats cleaning their kittens. I said to myself 'well it must be something that happens. It's a part of nature'. That's how I looked at it for years (Patrick).

> I didn't look at it as abuse. It was always in the bathtub (Al).

There appeared to be other factors besides the gender of the perpetrator that made it difficult for survivors to perceive their experience as 'abusive'. The absence of violence, the victim-perpetrator relationship, the fact that the abuse was often committed under the guise of nurturing, experiencing pleasure from the sexual interaction, and holding themselves, not the perpetrator, accountable for the abuse appeared to facilitate survivors' ability to transform their experiences.

Lack of violence The absence of physical violence coupled by the more subtle nature of the sexual abuse prevented many participants from seeing themselves as victims and perceiving the experience as abusive:

> I didn't see myself as a victim of sexual abuse. What made it hard to accept was that there were no physical signs of abuse or violence. There was coercion involved, but that coercion didn't leave any physical traces on me ... It's not like I got raped or I got mugged on the street or I got beaten up ... It was never really done in a dramatic, violent way ... so that makes it all the more confusing (David).

All of my mother's abuse was under the guise of love, so it's harder to sort out and harder to get through. My dad is so clear. He rapes you. He's so clearly violent and insane ... in some ways, I'm almost thankful for my dad. It's so cut and dry. You know it's abuse (Patrick).

Nurturing Many participants noted that the sexual interaction with the perpetrator was often coupled with or followed by periods of nurturing and affection. The presence of nurturing was highly confusing for participants and, in many cases, contributed to their inability to perceive the experience as abusive:

With my grandmother, even though she was so horrible to me as a child, she was the only one that would nurture me. She would sexually abuse me one minute, beat me afterwards and then hold me and hug me the next minute ... After sexually abusing me she would often untie me and hold me and rock me in a chair ... There was incredible confusion around her giving me this love and, at the same time, being such a brutally violent person (Laura).

Pleasure It has been documented that victims of sexual assault, despite having overall feelings of fear, and disgust, may experience physical pleasure during the sexual abuse (Sarrel & Masters, 1982; Mendel, 1995; Rosencrans, 1997). Coming to terms with this was a great struggle for several of the participants:

The most difficult part for me now is that my body responded ... I really liked the oral sex with my mother ... It's very difficult because no one wants to admit – 'Yeah, I wanted to have sex with my mother'. I wanted to have sex with my mother. She was my lover (Danielle).

Experiencing physical pleasure not only brought about feelings of shame. It contributed to victims' belief that the experience was not abusive and the older female could not be considered an 'abuser'. Many participants viewed themselves as accomplices, not victims:

I enjoyed some aspects of the sexual abuse. Because I enjoyed it, I felt as though I was an accomplice. I was just as guilty as her, if not guiltier (David).

One of the hardest things for me to come to terms with is the fact that having sex with my sister felt good. I don't think that early on I grasped the implications of what we were doing. Later on, as I started to understand our relationship and the moral implications, it became a source of material that I could use to reinforce some core beliefs that I had about my own worth. Basically, I was a bad person, because only a bad person could like having sex with his sister ... I feel more responsible for the sexual abuse with my mother and my sister. It's more difficult for me to talk about that incest. I'm still trying to sort out that I did something and I liked it ... Coming to terms with the fact that I enjoyed it – I could get ill just thinking about it (Jacob).

Responsibility and self-blame   Self-blame is a recognized after-effect of sexual abuse (Dimock, 1988; Myers, 1989; Lew, 1990; Dhaliwal et al., 1996). Victims often reflect back on the experience, focus on what they could have done to ward off the inappropriate contact, and ultimately hold themselves responsible for the abuse. As adults, many of the participants continued to blame themselves:

I'm to blame. It was my fault (Danielle).

Sometimes I blame myself for not having said no, fuck you, or stopping it ... I should have at least put up a fight ... Why didn't I protest? (David).

I blame myself ... I think it's my fault. Things could have been different if I could have just been a little bit more polite ... if I wouldn't have started up that trouble and gone to the police. I guess I could have prevented it somehow (Al).

Feelings of self-blame are likely to add to the difficulty in perceiving the experience as abusive.

Perhaps because of the challenge it poses to both traditional sexual scripts and broader cultural ideas concerning gender and sexuality, sexual abuse by a female appears to add complexity to participants' ability to negotiate the experience and evokes varying degrees of discomfort. However, transforming and denying the experience appears to preserve the worldview of women as docile, harmless, and nurturing, and appears to allay the discomfort experienced by survivors. As such, just as repression, fantasy and dissociation were effective mechanisms to cope with the sexual abuse as children, the transformation process involving the gendered lens appears to be an equally effective way to cope with the experience as adults.

The preceding sections have highlighted three crucial issues. First, contrary to popular and professional beliefs, women appear to be capable of serious and invasive forms of sexual and physical abuse. Second, the transformation process and culture of denial which was found among professional groups also appears to exist within the realm of survivors. Third, the section shows once again the importance of the dialectical process and the duality of structure mentioned in previous chapters. Survivors, who are at the *individual level* of the dialectic, appeared to draw upon and articulate wider cultural meanings of gender, crime and sexuality in the negotiation of their experiences and ultimately reproduce them. By re-negotiating sexual abuse by women, and transforming the offender and her offence as harmless and benign, they too are contributing to the reproduction and perpetuation of traditional sexual scripts and the culture of denial.

The Long-Term Effects of the Sexual Abuse

Research on the effects of female perpetrated sexual abuse is contradictory. Some research has suggested that abuse by females may be less damaging than abuse by males, particularly when the victim is male (Browne & Finkelhor, 1986; Condy et al., 1987). However, males may be less likely to reveal emotional vulnerability, particularly those resulting from their own victimization experiences (Nasjleti, 1980; Dimock, 1988; Bolton et al., 1989; Holmes, Offen & Waller, 1997). Other research has found that sexual abuse by females can be damaging. Sgroi and Sargent (1993) found that victims who had been abused by both males and females reported that the sexual abuse by a mother or sister was the most shameful and damaging form of childhood victimization they had suffered. In Rosencrans' (1997) sample of 93 female survivors of mother-daughter incest, 100 per cent reported that the sexual abuse by their mothers was damaging. In fact, 44 per cent reported that it was 'the most damaging experience of their lives'. Fromuth and Burkhart (1987) found significant negative consequences associated with sexual abuse by an older female on a male victim, despite the fact that these experiences tended not to be perceived as abusive.

In the following section I outline participants' reports of the long-term effects of the sexual abuse. Given that the majority of participants were accessed through out-patient therapists or posters placed in counselling services, participants can be considered a 'clinical sample'. As such, participants may have been more likely to be experiencing adverse effects of the sexual abuse. The majority of participants (80 per cent) were receiving therapy related to the after-effects of the female sexual abuse at the time of the interview.

All but one participant reported that the female sexual abuse was damaging. Charles was the only participant to report not feeling damaged by the experience: 'I don't think the sexual abuse did anything really wrong to me'.[2] The remainder of participants reported that the sexual abuse by females was highly damaging and difficult to recover from:

I'm constantly haunted by [the sexual abuse]. It's not something that just goes away, and I don't know how to put it behind me. That's what I'm trying to do. It's constantly remembering all the beatings, the washing, the sucking ... There is not a day that goes by that I haven't experienced depression, anxiety, fears. These are part of my daily existence (Al).

It seems reasonable to anticipate interactive and cumulative effects for those who experienced abuse by multiple perpetrators. However, it is important to note that all of the nine victims who were sexually abused by both men and women believed that the sexual abuse by female perpetrators was more harmful and more damaging than the sexual abuse by male perpetrators. For example, Laura, whose father attempted sexual intercourse with her at age five and had intercourse and oral sex with her until the age of eleven, believed that his actions were the least invasive of all the sexual abuse that she experienced. She felt that her mother's abuse, which was to aid and abet the sexual abuse of her by strangers, was far more traumatic:

The [sexual abuse] done by my father was the least invasive ... The abuse by the females had far more of an effect on me than he did ... When looking at the big picture and the layers of hurt ... out of all that happened to me, what my mother did was the absolute worst ... far worse than what my father had done (Laura).

Alexandra, who experienced sexual abuse by both a male and a female, insisted that female perpetrated sexual abuse incited a greater sense of betrayal:

There is a deeper sense of betrayal [with a female perpetrator]. It's like there's no safe place. How can a woman face a world that belittles and condemns us because we're women, face that world and struggle within it and still turn her hand against her own sex? That's a bitter betrayal (Alexandra).

The following section outlines the emotional and behavioural responses and after-effects of the sexual abuse that were most frequently reported by participants. Responses to the sexual abuse included substance abuse, self-injury, suicidal ideation and attempts, depression, and rage. Other after-effects included problematic relationships with women, self-concept and identity problems, and difficulties with sexuality.

The sexual abuse by females cannot be seen as the single *cause* of the responses or after-effects, as other life experiences and circumstances are likely to be factors as well. Moreover, for those abused by both men and women, it is difficult to isolate the singular effects of sexual abuse by females. However, the female sexual abuse can, at the very least, be considered an influencing factor. Indeed, it was the participants themselves who attributed the after-effects to the sexual abuse by females.

Substance Abuse

Substance abuse is said to be a coping strategy among victims of child sexual abuse to help repress memories of the abuse (Hunter, 1990) and to cope with emotions such as a sense of powerlessness, lower self-esteem, and the inability to trust others (Rohsenow, Corbett & Devine, 1988). Mullen et al. (1996) found that female victims reporting child sexual abuse had a greater chance of drinking at hazardous levels than female victims who reported emotional or physical abuse. Cavaiola and Schiff (1989) found, in a residential treatment centre for chemically dependent adolescents, that sexually abused subjects (male and female) had a significantly younger age for beginning use of either alcohol or drugs than their control groups drawn from the same treatment centre and local high schools. Several authors have documented substance abuse among their samples of victims of sexual abuse by females (Krug, 1989; Rosencrans, 1997).

Eight (five men, three women) of the 14 adult participants (57 per cent) reported that they have, or have had, what they considered to be a serious problem with substance abuse which they related to the sexual abuse. All eight participants reported abusing alcohol. In addition to alcohol, two male participants reported a past addiction to heroin and two female participants reported a past addiction to prescription drugs. The abuse of substances began at a very early age (as early as age six), and continued into adulthood. The participants reported that the alcohol and drugs were efficient means to silence their rage and numb the pain that came from being sexually abused:

> I started drinking and taking drugs when I was twelve. That helped the pain go away ... No one would believe me about all of the physical and sexual abuse, so when I took the drugs and alcohol, I didn't even have to believe it myself. It made it easier to deal with ... I buried [the sexual abuse] with booze and drugs (Al).

Two participants reported that their avoidance of drugs and alcohol was directly related to being sexually abused. Vanessa explained:

I never had a problem with [drugs or alcohol] and I think that that is a direct result of the sexual abuse – I have to be in control. I just can't imagine being drunk or impaired because then I wouldn't have control over my body and I have to (Vanessa).

Self-Injury

Self-injury has been described as tattooing one's rage on one's skin – or a means by which some individuals speak about social, political and personal experiences (Babiker & Arnold, 1997). Babiker and Arnold (1997: 37) suggest that individuals may turn to self-injury as a means of self-expression and coping with distress. There is very little clear epidemiological information on the incidence and prevalence of self-injury. Estimates of the problem vary widely with one review reporting rates from 400 to 1400 per 100 000 population per year (Favazza & Rosenthal, 1993). It has been suggested that at least one in 600 people injure themselves sufficiently to need hospital treatment (Tantam & Whittaker, 1992). Moreover, there is considerable under-reporting with many people hiding self-injury from their families and never coming to the attention of health practitioners (Walsh & Rosen, 1988; Babiker & Arnold, 1997). Self-injurious behaviour, whether in the form of slashing, cutting, or burning oneself, has been documented as a response to childhood sexual abuse (de Young, 1982; Heney, 1990; Longdon, 1993; Mitchell & Morse, 1998). Studies on victims of female sex offenders have reported self-injury in their samples (Mitchell & Morse, 1998).

Five participants (three females, two males) in this study (33 per cent) reported engaging in self-injurious behaviour which ranged from cutting or burning themselves, to breaking their hands by punching walls. Other participants reported hurting themselves sexually:

When I talk about the sexual abuse by my mother ... I'm so embarrassed ... I feel so bad ... I often want to turn on myself ... I harm myself sexually. When I was being sexual with myself I would be very rough and hurtful. I used to stick things up inside me ... My mother used to stick things in me. I'm sure it's related to that (Danielle).

[When I was dealing with the sexual abuse, there were times] when I was really considering cutting my dick off. Really hurting myself. I went through a stage when hurting myself was really appealing and I didn't want to have a penis. I didn't want to be sexual ... I battle with self-inflicted wounds ... It's really attractive to me sometimes to want to smash my face in. It gets so that I won't go into the kitchen because there are knives there and I can't trust what might happen ... I don't care if it hurts. I used to do that with sex. I remember having sex until I was bleeding (Jacob).

Suicide

Suicidal tendencies have been found more frequently in sexual abuse victims than the general population (Briere & Zaidi, 1989; Briere, 1992). Brown and Anderson (1991) found that 88 per cent of males sexually abused as children were suicidal in comparison to 57 per cent of non-victims of sexual abuse. Briere et al. (1988) found that both male and female adults sexually abused in childhood were significantly more likely to have attempted suicide than those not sexually abused (55 per cent vs. 23 per cent). Several authors have noted suicidal tendencies among victims of female sexual abuse (Margolis, 1984; Mayer, 1992; Bachmann, Moggi & Stirnemann-Lewis, 1994; Rosencrans, 1997).

In this study, 11 (five males, six females) participants (73 per cent) reported that they have struggled with suicidal ideation throughout their lives. Six of the 11 participants (three males, three females) reported having attempted suicide. Although it is likely that other life factors and difficulties contributed to the suicidal ideation and attempts, it is significant that such a great number of participants contemplated or attempted suicide:

I was very suicidal in those days [when I was a church Minister] ... I had this obsessive fantasy of going to the pulpit and blowing out my brains across the altar. That was the anger — that was my statement on life — fuck you! (Patrick).

I've attempted suicide quite a few times. I believe the first attempt was when I was fifteen years old. I cut my wrists ... I've attempted to gas myself, I've taken multiple overdoses ... My last suicide attempt I was three days in a coma. I took an overdose of pills ... That was two years ago (Mark).

It's connected to all of the abuse. It left me with feelings of ... suicidal wishes. When I was around fourteen or fifteen I wanted to kill myself. I took twenty aspirin! (laughter) but of course it didn't work (Vanessa).

Depression

Depression has been linked with child sexual abuse (Watkins & Bentovim, 1992). Studies finding adults sexually abused as children to be more depressed than non-victims include Burnam et al. (1988), based on self-reported lifetime depression (18 per cent vs. five per cent), Stein et al. (1988), based on the DSM-III-R Major Depression disorder diagnosis (13 per cent vs. two per cent), and Hunter (1991), based on the MMPI-Depression subscale. Depression as an after-effect of sexual abuse has also been noted in the literature on female perpetration (Goodwin & DiVasto, 1979; Krug, 1989; Hunter, 1990; Mayer, 1992; Longdon, 1993).

Nine (five males, four females) participants (60 per cent) reported experiencing depression related to the sexual abuse. Five of the nine participants (56 per cent) were on anti-depressive medication at the time of interview. Both Mark and Kyra were hospitalized for depression:

> I suffer from suicidal depression ... I've been in and out of hospital since I was nineteen with [depressive] breakdowns. I would work for a few years and break down and work for a few years and break down again ... then I finally started talking about the abuse (Mark).

> It was terrible having these memories [of sexual abuse] ... I've been hospitalized ... three times for depression. Sometimes the memories of all this stuff would become so overwhelming that I just wasn't able to function (Kyra).

Rage

Dhaliwal et al. (1996) assert that anger is a coping strategy to deal with sexual abuse. Using the Trauma Symptom Checklist (TSC-33), Briere et al. (1988) found both sexually abused men and women manifested greater anger than their non-abused controls. They also observed that abused men were the most angry group, followed by abused women, and then the control group. Olson (1990) found that a significantly higher proportion of male survivors who were clients of a mental health clinic reported having a problem of rage than did non-survivor clients (89 per cent vs. 44 per cent). Studies on survivors of female sexual abuse have noted rage among their participants (Fromuth & Burkhart, 1987; Krug, 1989). In this study, five participants (four males, one female) (33 per cent) reported intense rage directed towards the women who abused them and had fantasies of harming them:

> I think that I still have so much rage ... What I want to do, and it satisfies me yet it scares me half to death, is slice [my mother's] throat and cut her tongue out, cut her eyes out and stab her until there is no life left in her. That is the frightening part (Al).

> I had this murderous rage. I used to want to kill my mother and I used to have fantasies about it. I had dreams about murdering her (Vanessa).

I was in such a rage ... The worst fantasy that I had was to ... beat the hell out of [my mother], rape, sodomize her and then say to her 'Now you live with what I did, because that's what you did. See if it will drive you insane. I guarantee, that what I just did, will drive you insane'. It was sort of like tit for tat − now you live with it (Patrick).

Relationships with Women

Uncontrolled clinical reports with male and female victims of sexual abuse agree that there is often severe difficulty in maintaining sustained and meaningful relationships following a sexually abusive experience (Russell, 1975, 1986; Dimock, 1988; Krug, 1989; Koss & Harvey, 1991). Maltz and Holman (1987), Carlson (1990), Mayer (1992) and Borden and Laterz (1993) have suggested that sexual abuse by women may later result in a mistrust and strained relationships with women. In this study, 14 (seven males, seven females) of the 15 participants (93 per cent) reported a strong mistrust of women as a result of the sexual abuse:

The sexual abuse has damaged me in that I cannot fully trust a woman. It's sort of a contradiction because I'm married with a woman, but I don't fully trust her ... Something inside tells me she's going to leave me and she's going to take my kids from me ... I feel a sense of doom ... (Al).

The sexual abuse made me never trust people. I am very frightened of girls and women (Charles).

The sexual abuse affected my relationships with women all of my life. I could not trust women. I trusted men even though men abused me as well. What was done to me by my mother and grandmother was so insidious that I just couldn't feel comfortable with a woman (Laura).

The mistrust of women was sometimes related to a woman's sexuality. Several participants reported a fear of female sexuality:

I fear sexuality in other women. If I see a woman who is very overtly sexual, I feel very uncomfortable (Anna).

Because of his fear of female sexuality, in order to maintain friendships with women, David reported separating a woman's sexuality from the rest of her:

I'm paranoid about women getting at me [sexually] ... I developed this strategy to deal with female [friends]. Seeing women as sexual beings would bring feelings of distrust, so I ... separate their sexual aspects [from the rest of them]. If I ... have female friends, what will be easier for me to do is [to think to myself] 'She's a person'. She's a woman, yes, but I kind of take away [her] sexuality ... if I integrate the two it makes it more threatening (David).

Two male participants and one female participant reported feelings of wanting to retaliate against women in order to regain a sense of power and control. These feelings often surfaced in violent sexual fantasies:

I [had sexual] fantasies and they were an angry way of gaining control ... taking revenge on women ... a way of getting back at women ... Sometimes I get really angry. When I get at this angry stage, I just hate women ... Because I was abused by a woman ... I get these feelings where I want to fuck all the women that I can ... I'll be in charge and I'll be in control this time ... I especially get that feeling if a woman looks at me and she has that look of being turned on ... I get this feeling like 'Oh yeah? Well, I'm going to fuck you!' (David).

When I was thirty years old, I was so angry. At that time, it was coming out violently. I was working as a United Church minister and having these violent sexual fantasies towards women. I knew it was related to what my mother had done (Patrick).

I would say that in my [sexual] fantasies, I was abusive towards women. For about ten years, a lot of my [sexual] fantasies were about power, control and dominating women ... It was the only way that I could have an orgasm (Vanessa).

The above participants reported having violent sexual fantasies toward women, yet none of them acted upon them. However, one participant did act out his fantasies and began to expose himself to young girls:

I escalated into exposing myself to young girls. I wanted to feel some kind of control, some kind of power ... I wanted to hurt or shock [girls] ... That would fulfil a desire to want them to feel the same pain that I felt. I think the desire to have power and control over women is because I'm angry at them and I want them to feel the hurt that I felt [when sexually abused] (Matt).

Self-Concept and Identity

This study reveals the difficulty that female participants had with their sense of identity and self-concept. Five of the seven female participants (71 per cent) reported negating their female identity as children and feared growing into a woman:

> Probably the first thing that really becomes clear to me when I'm able to look back on the experience, is that I did not want to grow to be a woman. I wanted desperately to be a boy. I was sure ... that if I tried hard enough, I could change into a boy ... I felt that if I dressed like a boy, if I acted like a boy, if I played the very rough violent sports with the boys ... I wouldn't become a woman (Alexandra).

> I never wanted to grow up and be a woman ... I was a tomboy. I wore t-shirts, jeans. I did tomboy things. I was angry about turning into a girl. I tried to delay and postpone becoming a woman ... I hid being female (Anna).

In retrospect, the female participants believe that their childhood and adolescent negation of femininity was related to the sexual abuse, and particularly to their abuser. They did not want to turn into their abuser:

> At the time I didn't know what motivated [my desire not to be a girl]. I felt that it was just like 'Oh, I don't want to be a girl because girls are sissies' ... Now, I think my motivation was ... that I did not want to grow up to assume the form of my abuser (Alexandra).

> I didn't want to be a woman because I didn't want to be like my mom (Anna).

Several female participants continued to deny their femininity in adulthood. Alexandra reported that she continues to dress and carry herself in a way that emulates, if not a male form, at least a neutral one. To her, females are dangerous and potential sexual abusers and she would be safest to others and to herself, if she was not female:

> [Even now] I don't even want to have a distinguishably female form ... I just want to lose it all in fat ... I wear bulky clothing, I wear lumber jackets, I dress in men's clothes. I'll do anything to be, if not male, at least neutral ... Someone in [my therapy] group called me 'femme' – very affectionately, not meaning anything wrong by it. I got quite incensed ... I demanded that she take it back ... That image wasn't acceptable. I would be safest and be safe for other people if I'm not female ... Being a woman is a large part of my identity and it's my biggest struggle (Alexandra).

Male participants did not appear to experience as much difficulty with their identity and self-concept as a result of the sexual abuse. However, it was still an issue of concern. Three of the eight male participants (38 per cent) reported that following the sexual abuse, they felt as though they had 'failed' as men. The idea that they were 'victims' of sexual abuse caused much distress:

> I felt like I was a victim, and for a man to be a victim is an embarrassment ... A real man is not a victim, a real man is always in charge, always resists and is always in control. A man who is a victim is a failure. In that respect, I felt like I had to hide the fact that I was a victim (David).

> I can't stand being called a victim. I loathe it ... When I focus on the idea of myself as a victim, I want to kill myself. I just want to die. I feel incredibly damaged. Beyond repair. This happened to me, yes, but please don't call me a victim or a survivor (Jacob).

What was even more distressing, however, was the fact that they were victimized by a woman – a 'weaker' gender. This appeared to cause much humiliation and threw into question their sense of masculinity:

> I was not only a victim, but a victim of a woman – a weaker gender ... It makes you a much lesser man. I was asking myself what kind of man was I. I didn't feel very comfortable with my manliness. I didn't feel like a man (David).

> For me to be a victim ... and to be a victim of [my mother], I just have so much trouble accepting that. It messes with this pseudo-self that I built up. This false sense of pride ... Because I'm a male, I should have been able to control women. As a man, I'm supposed to be the powerful one and the actions of women are not supposed to affect me. I'm always supposed to have the upper hand (Jacob).

To compensate for feelings of 'unmanliness', Jacob believed that at a young age, he became 'hyper-masculine'. He reported that as a child, he engaged in highly aggressive sports. Later on, he became involved in trafficking narcotics and organized crime, which he believes, gave him a sense of masculinity and self-esteem:

> I studied martial arts, I boxed competitively. I was a really tough kid ... I would fight anyone. I didn't care ... By the age of twelve, I was already trafficking and pulling break and enters. The older guys would set up jobs for me ... I was always afraid, but I would do it anyway ... I felt good and worthwhile while I was doing it ... It was this machismo, this pseudo-esteem. My role models at that time were carrying guns, and were really tough ... The classic wise-guy ... I didn't get caught until I was sixteen ... Then I started going to jail – big fucking deal ... I was excited about it. I could show my medal. I remember when I got my first sentence – two charges and I got two years for each. I felt like I had

graduated. I felt like it was a good thing. It was like the first time I got stabbed. I can take it. It was this distorted idea of what it means to be a man (Jacob).

Jacob also gained a sense of esteem and pride through sexual activity with sexually inexperienced girls:

> I took pride in the fact that I knew how to perform cunnilingus and could turn on these young girls when I was young and was experimenting. I was already fully sexualized and I could make them crazy with this stuff. There was a sense of pride (Jacob).

However, the feelings of self-esteem attained through these means were often short lived. In the end, the constant reminder that he was a victim of sexual abuse by his mother shattered his sense of esteem:

> The problem with all of these rationales that I would build up is that they have big holes. I want to be the powerful one – this sort of psychological mastery. This whole inflated thing develops. But then I have one thought – I was a victim of my mother. That deflates it. It's not built on anything solid. It's just an illusion. I could tell myself these things and maybe win a few points by performing cunnilingus on this young girl who is not very experienced, but then the thought enters my mind of where I learned that. Then it all falls apart (Jacob).

Sexuality

Researchers have found that men and women who have been sexually abused by females may experience later difficulties with sexuality and intimacy (Fritz et al., 1981; Sarrel & Masters, 1982; Johnson & Shrier, 1987; Mayer, 1992). In this study, all participants, except Dominique who was ten years old at the time of interview, reported varying degrees of fear and discomfort with sex and sexual intimacy:

> I always had a fear of sex ... I haven't had sex in eight years ... ever since I've been dealing with the sexual abuse by my mom. It's very difficult ... I feel dirty (Danielle).

> As far as making love, it's really hard. I can't make love because I feel dirty ... There was a point where [my wife] wanted a lot of sex and I couldn't do it ... I felt dirty and really disgusted. After sex, I would take a bath and scrub down my skin (Al).

Sex often brought back memories of the sexual abuse:

> Sex is sometimes very difficult ... we have to stop and I can't go through with it ... I have flashbacks of the abuse ... I still have problems being on top with my husband ... It seems to be the position that I remember the most [in regard to the sexual abuse] and I just freeze up (Alexandra).

Fear of Abusing Children

The fear of sexually abusing children was prevalent among adult participants in this study. In fact, only two (female) adult participants did not report experiencing this fear. For those participants who had children of their own (60 per cent of participants), they were particularly worried about sexually abusing them:

> I worried that I would abuse my daughter. I think that this started when she started to develop into a woman (Anna).

The fear of abusing their children was so strong that several participants reported spending less time with their children or avoided being alone with them:

> I know that my sexual stuff has really warped my ability to parent my daughter. I'm afraid to be alone with my daughter. It's probably one of the most troubling components of my adult life. You know, I'm good with her. But still, I'm afraid. I'm very afraid. It makes me spend less time with her than I think I normally would (Jacob).

Mark was so afraid of sexually abusing his infant daughter that he would wait in another room while she was in the bath:

> I was so paranoid about that [sexually abusing]. I would make [my daughter] get in the bathtub by herself. I would sit in the living room and she would keep the bathroom door open and I would make her keep splashing the water – 'Splash the water! Let's hear you splash the water so daddy knows you're okay!' I would not walk into the room with her naked. That's how paranoid I was about that (Mark).

Participants were so concerned about sexually abusing children, that four (one male, three females) (27 per cent) consciously chose not to have children. For example, Alexandra who was 23 at the time of the interview had a tubal ligation which would prevent her from ever having children:

I think the abuse by [the female perpetrator] is much more instrumental in my decision to sterilize myself. I had a tubal ligation in September of last year. It's irreversible. I'm twenty-three and I have no children. Right now, I'm not saying I regret it ... But in the future, I may come to regret this decision ... The heart of my concerns at the time were I don't ever want to get pregnant and do to my children what [the female perpetrator] did to me ... I think the original abuse of trust by a woman who was in a caretaking role really has caused me to doubt myself a lot ... Overall, I'm happy with [the tubal ligation]. I'm just wondering ten years from now ... how will I be evaluating [the perpetrator's] role in that decision?

Alexandra, who reported that she was also sexually abused by a male, insisted that her fear and doubts about sexually abusing children was related more strongly to the abuse by a female:

I often think, and I resent it bitterly, that this doubt will always be with me and will deprive me for my lifetime of being able to have children. And it's a doubt and a fear that I do not think would have been felt so strong after the male had abused me. It's the destruction of a safe mothering role which is supposed to be sacrosanct in our society. It is the breakdown of that, that is so much more debilitating (Alexandra).

Sexual Victimization of Others

Several authors have noted that many who have themselves been sexually victimized may replicate their victimization with others (Groth, 1979; Petrovich & Templar, 1984; Condy et al., 1987; Travin et al., 1990; Higgs et al., 1992). Five participants (33 per cent), (two males, three females) reported having sexually abused children at some point in their lives. The two males were charged and convicted. The sexual abuse by the three females was never reported:

On two separate occasions a social worker caught Dominique in the toilet touching the genitals of two different little girls ... With her peers there is always a lot of physical contact and kisses ... We've had other parents very politely tell us that they didn't want their child to play with her. Whenever she plays with other children if she isn't supervised she'll kiss the children on the mouth and try to touch them. One little girl who was playing with her went crying to her mother because Dominique was trying to touch her and kiss her all over ... When we tried to explain to Dominique that she couldn't do that to other little girls, she began to do it with little boys ... She sees no boundaries (Dominique's step-mother).

By the time I was twelve, all of the [sexual abuse] started to cause me a lot of problems. I started acting out sexually. I used to sneak up on my younger sister and grab her breasts ... Twice I got in trouble at school for touching girls ... When I was fourteen, I sexually abused my nine year old sister ... [As an adult] I sexually assaulted two of my nieces and two girls who weren't related to me. I went to jail on two occasions ... The sexual abuse of my victims was oral sex and fondling ... That is exactly what I did with my babysitter. All the sexual stuff that I did with the babysitter really got me into trouble. But it's still no excuse for what I did (Charles).

The vast majority of participants reported the sexual abuse by females was damaging. The data reveal a broad range of responses and effects relating to the sexual abuse which were persistent, often debilitating, and touching diverse areas of the participants' lives. There did appear to be some differences in the responses of males and females, particularly in the area of identity, and the expression of rage. These differences reflect other research findings indicating that male victims of childhood sexual abuse are more likely than females to develop externalized, aggressive characteristics in adulthood (Bolton et al., 1989). However, on the whole, there were marked similarities in the ways in which male and female victims reported being affected by the abuse. Difficult relationships with women, depression, self-injury, fear of abusing children, and difficulty with sexuality were reported close to equally among male and female participants.

The long-term negative effects reported by victims challenge traditional sexual scripts and professional portrayals of women as sexually harmless and inconsequential. In fact, for most participants it was the negative after-effects of the sexual abuse that prompted them to seek professional help. The damaging effects of sexual abuse by women reveal the failure of traditional sexual scripts to account for the reality of female sexual aggression.

Victims' Experiences with Disclosure to Professionals

Victims' experiences of professional intervention have been a neglected area of study. This section explores victims' experiences of disclosure to professionals and how these experiences relate to the culture of denial with regard to female sex offending.

Only two participants (13 per cent) disclosed the sexual abuse as children. Dominique disclosed the abuse to her father at age eight, after being removed by social services from her mother's care (as a result of neglect). Al disclosed the sexual abuse to social workers and to the police once at age six and again during his adolescence, none of which resulted in any formal professional intervention. Al reported that when his mother learned that he had gone to the police to report her, she beat him severely. This prevented any further disclosures.

As adults, participants reported having great difficulty talking about the sexual abuse by females:

> It's more difficult for me to talk about the [female perpetrated] incest. It was really really hard to come forward and say that I was sexually abused by a woman. Those were hard times for me (Jacob).

Some participants believed that it was less 'acceptable' to discuss sexual abuse by females:

> It's been definitely more difficult to deal with the female abuse. I think it's because it's more acceptable to talk about males abusing. That's more the norm. People talk about males sexually abusing females. You don't often hear about females abusing males or females (Kyra).

Because of the discomfort and shame around disclosure of female sexual abuse, participants who had been abused by both men and women and sought therapy would first disclose sexual abuse by males. It was only when they had been in therapy for a significant amount of time and trusted their therapist that they began to reveal the sexual abuse by females. This is consistent with findings of earlier studies on victims of female perpetrated abuse (Goodwin & DiVasto, 1979; Sgroi & Sargent, 1993):

> It's difficult to deal with the female abuse ... It was definitely harder ... I brought up the male abuse before I brought up the female abuse. The female abuse has only come up in the last year (Kyra).
>
> I started having memories about my mother. But every time that I would talk about it in therapy I would always stop and back away. It was easier to talk about my dad. I haven't talked about [the sexual abuse by my mother] in five years with my therapist. That's how much I avoid the stuff about my mother. For some reason, that's more difficult (Danielle).

Despite the difficulty with disclosures, all of the participants had, at some point in their lives, disclosed the female sexual abuse to a professional in an attempt to receive counselling. The following section explores how participants perceived professional responses to their disclosures.

Professionals' Responses to Disclosures: Affirming the Culture of Denial

> If you're stupid enough to press charges [against a female perpetrator], you had better be prepared to be crucified (M-Detective-Sergeant3).

This portion of the chapter traces victims' perceptions of professional responses to their disclosures. It highlights the ways in which the culture of denial found among police officers and psychiatrists in this study also appeared to be prevalent among the professionals from which victims sought help.

Nine participants (60 per cent) reported experiencing at least one negative professional response to their disclosure.[3] Because some participants disclosed the abuse to more than one professional and experienced several negative responses, in total, the sample of fifteen reported fourteen negative responses. The professionals consulted included police officers, child protection workers, psychologists, psychiatrists, and other qualified clinical therapists.[4]

Negative responses to disclosures included discomfort with the subject, shock, denial, and disbelief. According to participants, the reactions of professionals were linked to the gender of the sexual perpetrator. It is important to note that all but one of the reported negative experiences with professionals occurred later than 1989, and as recently as 1997, the year the interviews were conducted. This time frame is said to be a period which reflected a cultural and professional awareness of child sexual abuse. In fact, the issue was even creating a sense of 'panic' among professionals and the general public (Bell, 1988; Deer, 1988; Coward, 1993; La Fontaine, 1997). When examining professional responses, it appears that the social panic is/was being directed at male sexual offending while female sexual offending remains steeped in the culture of denial.

Professional Discomfort and Resistance

Six participants reported that upon disclosing sexual abuse by a woman, the professional expressed marked discomfort and resistance to discussing the issue further:

> I remember telling my therapist in one session: 'I remember my mother fellating me in the bathtub'. I started to get really emotional. My therapist tried to change

the subject. He was obviously very nervous about it. He didn't want to hear about it (Patrick).

When I first got into this material, I felt terribly indebted to the women's movement for bringing these issues [of sexual abuse] out. However, it seemed to be conditional. When I wanted to deal with my own stuff [female sexual abusers], these same women who were so helpful and validating when it came to talking about men as perpetrators, were absolutely repulsed when I raised the subject of women as perpetrators. I couldn't believe the resistance. Talking about that just wasn't okay (Jacob).

Shock from Professionals

Upon learning that the sexual perpetrator was female, two participants reported that the professionals were visibly shocked. In 1997, Dominique's father[5] made numerous attempts to convince a child protection worker that Dominique, who was eight years old at the time, had been sexually abused for many years under her mother's care. After more than a year of trying to convince authorities, the child protection worker finally acknowledged that Dominique had been sexually abused. However, according to Dominique's father, she was shocked that the perpetrator was female:

The social worker was shocked that it was a woman [perpetrator]. She kept saying 'Oh, I can't believe it, I just can't believe it' or 'this is unbelievable!' Those are the kinds of expressions that we heard from her very often. She had a really nervous laugh too. You could tell she was uncomfortable (Dominique's father).

In 1991, after becoming disillusioned by a male psychiatrist who she felt was reluctant to address the issue of sexual abuse by a female perpetrator, Alexandra began to search for another psychiatrist. She decided that perhaps she should try seeing a woman this time. Alexandra saw a young female psychiatrist who specialized in sexual abuse who was recommended to her by her family doctor. She describes her meeting with the psychiatrist:

I went to a [second] psychiatrist ... a woman in her thirties ... A woman who is a psychiatrist and is supposed to be trained in all the various workings of humanity as a whole ... When I told her that the abuse was perpetrated by a 'Michelle', she expressed surprise. 'A woman?' she said. 'Yes, a woman'. Now this obviously leaves a lot of linguistical confusion, so she says, 'Oh, do you mean a female?' 'Yes! I was sexually abused by a female. I hope you don't greet this with surprise'. But she did. Then she told me that that was a *special need* that was not covered by her psychiatric practice. So I basically told her where she could put her *special need*, how hard, and in what position by degrees, and left her office. I was startled, confused, hurt and very angry to have a person who is supposed to be a healing professional, who cannot afford to be naive, express shock that a woman is capable of sexual abuse. Not only was she not able to help me, which is her decision – it's her practice – she had no resources at all that she could recommend. That infuriated me. I really saw that as neglect ... I found that attitude repeated again and again (Alexandra).

Professional Dismissal

Four participants reported that professionals tended to dismiss the abuse by a female as insignificant and inconsequential. For example, during a very stressful period in 1989, David, who was initially weary about seeing a professional, took a risk and made an appointment with a male psychologist:

> I felt very nervous but I thought, well, he's a psychologist, he should know what he's doing. When I told him about the sexual abuse [which occurred from age three to six], he didn't really seem to grasp it. He asked me how I felt when I was being sexually abused. I told him that some of the abuse I enjoyed and that's part of the guilt I was carrying ... If I enjoyed it, I am an accomplice and I felt really ashamed and dirty for it. When I told him that, he laughed. He laughed like 'you dirty dog!' He basically implied that because I'm Catholic, I'm feeling very guilty about having sex so young. I was really scared of being there and he was laughing at something I was saying ... I went to see him a second time. He said, 'I don't understand what your problem is ... You don't have a problem. I looked through the literature but I don't know what's affecting you' ... I don't think that he saw [the sexual abuse] as a problem. I don't think that he saw her as a perpetrator (David).

Similarly, Jacob joined several therapy groups for survivors of sexual abuse. Jacob reported that the groups, which were facilitated by women, were supportive of his disclosures of sexual abuse by males. However, they frequently dismissed his accounts of sexual abuse by his mother and sister:

> Oh God, the reaction of these groups when I would talk about the sexual abuse by my mother was 'we don't want to talk about that, we don't want to hear about that'. Basically, I would be shut down. They would tell me that 'I wasn't staying on top of things' or 'I was changing the subject'. They said things like 'Well just how bad could that have been?' These were really horrible experiences. This happened over a period of a couple of years. It was ongoing. I would go to different groups, but I would get the same reaction (Jacob).

Professional Disbelief

Three participants reported the outright refusal of professionals to believe allegations of sexual abuse by a female perpetrator. Once again, Dominique's father shares his experience of trying to get the help of a youth protection agency for his daughter:

> It took an enormous amount of time for the Department of Youth Protection and the social worker to believe that Dominique was being sexually abused by her mother. At the beginning, the social worker didn't believe us at all. I was seen as the bad guy. I was as guilty as Dominique's mother [the perpetrator] ... Whenever I would mention the sexual abuse, it was as though I was only doing it to be malicious to my ex-wife, to somehow take revenge on her ... If I had said that it was her uncle [who was sexually abusing her] perhaps the reaction would have been different ... I'm certain it would have been ... I can't believe what I had to go through for social services to believe me and more importantly, to believe Dominique (Dominique's father).

Other participants had similar experiences:

> It's not believed. Professionals don't believe you ... they think you're fantasizing – I've had that happen... Who are you going to report [the abuse] to? [The police] would laugh at you. Honest to God. It's a joke. I wouldn't even consider it. No way. There's nobody you can turn to (Mark).

The professional responses of discomfort, shock, dismissal and disbelief were perceived to be negative reactions by participants. These professional responses were markedly similar to the responses of psychiatrists and police officers interviewed for this study, confirming the widespread discomfort and culture of denial that female sex offending appears to invoke. Now that we have ascertained victims' perceptions of professional responses, it is important to ascertain the impact that these responses had on them.

Consequences of Professional Responses

There is a small but growing body of literature describing the damaging effects that negative professional interventions can have on victims of child sexual abuse. These damaging effects are often referred to as 'iatrogenic effects' or 'iatrogenic trauma' (Schultz, 1982; Cooper, 1990). Studies have proposed that the reaction of adults in general, and professionals in particular who deal with children who have been sexually abused, have an effect on the amount of trauma the child experiences from the sexual abuse (Testa et al., 1992; Roesler, 1994; Coffey et al., 1996). Some authors have gone as far as to insist that if professional intervention in cases of child sexual abuse is not done properly, professional intervention could be as damaging, or even *more* damaging than the sexual abuse itself (Kelley, 1990). This is because strong negative reactions make the abusive experience take on a new significance, intensify the immediate impact, and may increase the long-term sequelae.

Adults who disclose sexual abuse may have similar experiences to children. Inappropriate responses to disclosures including responses of discomfort, shock, or denial may increase the long-term sequelae (Longdon, 1993; Sgroi & Sargent, 1993). Adult victims who dare to disclose sexual abuse after years of silence may be devastated when they are not believed or when their experiences are trivialized by professionals. When victims in this study were questioned as to how the negative professional responses affected them, all but one participant declared the negative responses had a damaging impact. The one participant who reported not being negatively affected was Anne. She reported that her therapist was uncomfortable with the fact that the abuse was perpetrated by a female and passed her on to another therapist. The therapists' discomfort did not bother her because she was surprised that she had been believed at all:

> Well, actually, her reaction didn't make me feel bad. You see, to me, it was surprising that someone thought that I wasn't making it up or lying, or being crazy (Anne).

The remaining participants reported experiencing varying degrees of iatrogenic trauma. In most cases, the negative professional response intensified their feelings of rage and sense of isolation. According to participants, the negative professional responses fuelled their anger, self-blame, and caused them to question and sometimes deny that the sexual abuse was 'problematic'. Others reported an increased distrust of professionals.

Anger

Both Kyra and Dominique's step-mother described feeling intense anger as a result of not having their story believed by professionals:

I was enraged. [Professionals] didn't believe us. They showed us no respect at all (Dominique's step-mother).

It makes me angry that [professionals] have blinders on and they don't want to accept that women can be just as evil, and even more so sometimes, as men (Kyra).

For Jacob, the professional resistance by several women therapists not only intensified his anger, but also fuelled his mistrust of women:

I'm fucking angry about this. Because [professionals] really fucked with my mind. I'm really angry about it. These were pros who are highly regarded in the area of sexual abuse – really high profile people. [The responses of these female therapists] fuels my conflict and feeds my anger. My anger that you can't trust women. They're all manipulative cunts (Jacob).

Self-Blame

As a result of the police refusal to believe that his step-mother was sexually and physically abusing him, Al reported that he convinced himself, to an even greater degree than he had before, that the abuse was his fault:

I was nothing but the biggest liar ... those are the thoughts that went into my mind ... Because no one trusted me, and no one believed that this was happening to me ... it was like *I* was the bad person, *I* did the worst thing in the whole world (Al).

Questioning or Denying their Experience

Participants noted that prior to their disclosures, their sense of the sexual abuse experience was already fragile and uncertain. Negative professional reactions apparently contributed to the questioning of their experience and, ultimately, to its complete denial:

At the time, I felt crazy. The [professional] reaction made me feel more crazy ... I thought that they were right – the sexual abuse by my mom and sister couldn't have been that bad. It seemed like more trouble than it was worth trying to deal with this (Jacob).

David assumed that because of his credentials, the psychologist's assessment that he 'didn't have a problem' must be correct. David reported that from that moment on, despite frequent anxiety attacks, flashbacks, suicidal thoughts, and a deep mistrust of women, he tried to convince himself that he didn't have a problem:

> When I went to see [the psychologist] I really felt like he should know what he's talking about. He told me that I didn't have a problem and he laughed at me. It made me feel like what's my problem? What am I complaining about? The message that I got was there's no problem. Just shut up, don't think about it and don't worry about it. So that's what I tried doing. For the following four to five years I just tried to convince myself that I didn't have a problem (David).

Despite trying to convince himself that he did not have a problem, David continued to experience anxiety and panic attacks, had suicidal thoughts and was 'paranoid about women getting at him'. In this sense, inappropriate professional reactions left these individuals to deal with their problems alone and in isolation.

Silence and Secrecy

Another consequence that professional responses had on participants was that it imposed silence. Participants felt that if professionals would not believe them, no one would. The implicit message they received was that speaking about females who sexually abuse was taboo:

> The unspoken assumption by professionals that women heal and never hurt, silences me that much more ... It makes the validation of my feelings and my fears that much more difficult ... Abuse by women is not taboo ... because if it was it, it wouldn't be done. Speaking about it is taboo (Alexandra).

> It has silenced me. The [professional] reaction made me feel like I shouldn't talk about this. It shut me down (Jacob).

Lack of Faith in Professionals

Participants reported losing faith in helping professionals:
> I felt very betrayed by the professionals. I felt that there was nobody in the world that I could ever trust. Nobody ... I can't believe how insensitive social workers and psychiatrists and therapists can be. I didn't feel they really listened to me (Al).

> I don't believe in the [child welfare] system anymore. I have no faith in it (Dominique's step-mother).

For some, the lack of faith in professionals made it so they felt they could no longer turn to professionals for help or support:

> After that experience [with the psychologist], I decided that I didn't want to go back and see a counsellor (David).

> I felt I had no place to go. I felt like I couldn't go to the sexual assault centres and say 'I've been raped by a woman'. I didn't know if I would receive respect or if I would be told that just wasn't so (Alexandra).

It is important to note is that as much as professionals can have a damaging effect on victims of sexual abuse, with appropriate interventions, they can have a positive one. After several negative experiences, victims reported that finding a professional or a group that was supportive and acknowledged the seriousness of the abuse brought a sense of relief, broke the sense of isolation and reassured them that they were not 'crazy'. For example, after being disillusioned by the psychologist, after years of difficulty, David decided to try a self-help group. This turned out to be a very positive experience:

> The first [professional] that I went to see told me 'I just don't see what you're problem is' and this group said, 'Yes, there is a problem' ... I felt such a sense of relief. I no longer felt that sense of isolation – it was really broken down (David).

Matt discusses how helpful it was to find a therapist that took the sexual abuse by his mother seriously:

> [The second professional I saw] took it very seriously and that helped. He believed that this was a serious thing and that my mother acted completely inappropriately and shouldn't have been doing what she was doing. That was the first time I had heard [a professional] say those types of things to me. It reinforced that what I was feeling was real (Matt).

Laura also explained how a positive professional response and ongoing support can make a difference in the healing process:

> There hasn't been any hesitation in sharing anything with [my therapist]. She provides an environment that is incredibly safe and supportive. She provides me with a safe place to heal myself. I'm so fortunate to have this lady because I don't know where I would be with the people who are judgmental. I would never have got where I am today (Laura).

There is a widespread belief that professional attitudes toward child sexual abuse have progressed over the last 20 years and that there is a greater awareness and sensitivity to the issue (Elliott, 1993). These data reveal, however, that professional sensitivity and awareness may have progressed in regard to female victims of male sexual perpetrators, but perhaps less so with regard to female perpetration and its impact on victims. Professional reactions of discomfort, shock, dismissal and disbelief intensified victims' trauma, inciting secondary victimization. Given that professional sensitivity and a non-judgmental attitude are viewed as central tenets of any professional intervention (Rooney, 1992), it is disconcerting that some victims reported professional re-victimization following disclosure. Victims made great efforts to seek out professional help and took considerable risk to disclose the sexual abuse based on the assumption that they would be helped and supported. Negative responses ignored victims' needs and failed to address the fundamental issues that impacted on their level of functioning. Interestingly, the victims who consulted more than one professional were those who had experienced a negative professional response. Following a negative professional response, victims recognized that their needs were not being met and continued to search until they found a supportive professional. However, not all victims who experienced a negative professional response continued to search for a positive response. After at least one negative professional response to disclosure, three victims (20 per cent) refused, for an extended period of time, to seek further professional help. Although these victims eventually, out of desperation, sought professional help many years later, for a time, they were forced to suffer in silence. Importantly, this sample can be considered a 'clinical sample' as most respondents were in therapy during the time of interview and the majority of victims were recruited through professionals who were, for the most part, supportive of their disclosures. As such, the current sample may have excluded victims who were so negatively affected by professional responses that they never pursued further professional help. It is therefore possible that there exists a larger 'dark figure' of victims who have unmet needs as a result of negative professional responses.

It is important to note that the professional culture of denial may actually contribute to the victims' reliance on traditional sexual scripts and the process of denial. Professionals appear to hold considerable authority in the eyes of victims. As we have seen, survivors may internalize professional advice and reactions. A victim's denial and transformation of the abuse experience, as discussed earlier in the chapter, may be further intensified by professional reactions of denial. This demonstrates that the dialectical process whereby institutional ideology, in the form of professional intervention, is likely to have an important impact on the individual ideology of victims.

This chapter has explored the life histories and experiences of victims of female sex offenders. The data reveal that the majority of victims experienced severe sexual abuse at the hands of a lone female perpetrator, throwing into question the notion of the sexually passive and harmless female. It also revealed that victims, much like police officers and psychiatrists, appeared to draw upon broader cultural 'rules' to help guide their actions and constructions and ultimately transformed sexual abuse by women. The fact that broader cultural rules were simultaneously drawn upon and reproduced reveals the enactment of the duality of structure. The chapter also traced the impact and consequences of the sexual abuse on survivors and found that contrary to the professional portrayals of female sex offenders as harmless and inconsequential, survivors suffered long-term and debilitating after-effects from the sexual abuse in a variety of areas of their lives. The analysis also found that some of the professionals with whom victims came into contact denied and/or dismissed sexual abuse by women. These professional responses were found to have negative effects on survivors.

For victims, like police officers and psychiatrists, it appears to mean something different to be sexually abused by a female. The gender of the perpetrator seemed to trigger a gendered response to the sexual abuse experience. Despite severe sexual abuse and debilitating after-effects, the experience is often viewed as less representative of sexual 'abuse', is transformed or even denied. This further confirms the idea that female sex offending is viewed, assessed and understood within traditional gendered narratives and through a gendered lens. It also reveals that the transformation process and culture of denial which was found among police officers and psychiatrists, also appears to exist within the realm of survivors.

The importance of the dialectical process once again becomes apparent. Survivors, who are at the *individual level* of the dialectic, appear to draw upon, articulate and reproduce wider cultural meanings of gender, crime and sexuality in the negotiation of their experiences, reflecting Giddens' notion of the duality of structure. Survivors' perspectives and responses appear to reflect traditional sexual scripts and the broader culture of denial with regard to female sex offending.

Notes

1   All of the participant's names have been changed to ensure anonymity.
2   Although Charles did not feel damaged by the sexual abuse, he did believe that it was related to his later sexual offending against young girls. He reported sexually abusing over ten girls from age of twelve to eighteen, including the sexual abuse of his younger sister over a five year period. As an adult, he was convicted of four counts of sexual assault and spent two years in prison for sex related offences.
3   A negative professional response was one in which the victim felt re-victimized by the professional intervention.
4   Unfortunately, the participants were unsure of the specific credentials of these professionals.
5   I have included Dominique's father and step-mother's experiences with professionals in this part of the study. I was introduced to Dominique's family during my fieldwork at the Police Sexual Assault Unit. Their case was under investigation by police at the time and they expressed an interest in participating in the research. Dominique's father gave me permission to interview Dominique who was then ten years old. According to her father, Dominique was, as far as was possible, distanced from contact with professionals. Although Dominique was interviewed by police officers and social workers, it was her father and step-mother who had the majority of contact with them. As it happened, they were in the same position as the other participants – trying as best they could to gain professional attention and support for a victim of female sexual abuse.

7   Conclusion and Policy Implications

This concluding chapter provides an overview of the main research findings and considers how the research contributes to current debates about organizational cultures, criminal justice responses to female offenders, and feminist theory. It also addresses the implications of the findings for child sexual abuse policy and practice, and offers some suggestions for future research.

The Culture of Denial

The in-depth analysis of police, psychiatrists' and victim perspectives on female sex offending contained within this book has highlighted the widespread denial of women as potential sexual aggressors. Although the origins of the culture of denial, like reactions to other sexual taboos such as incest, may have their roots in a complex array of factors (as suggested in chapter two) the proposed transformation and dialectical processes, as well as the concept of the duality of structure appear to contribute to our understanding of the emergence, maintenance and reproduction of this denial.

Responses to female sex offending by the three groups under study all appear to follow closely with the transformation process: female sex offending represents a 'deviant' reality as it challenges traditional sexual scripts concerning female sexual passivity, docility and beliefs that women are 'naturally' maternal, nurturing and disinterested in sex. For police officers, psychiatrists and victims, the challenge posed by female sex offending evokes varying degrees of conflict and discomfort as it threatens the security of the traditional model of the world. To alleviate the discomfort, these three groups, either unwittingly or fully aware,[1] transformed sexual offences by women. They appeared to invoke a gendered lens, a lens whereby the offender's gender became central to the meaning of the offence. The three groups distorted the reality of female sex offending, bringing it into alignment with traditional sexual scripts of women as either harmless or not 'real' women, which ultimately worked to alleviate the initial conflict. Although there was significant overlap in the ways in which each of the three groups constructed and transformed female sex offending, for example, all three groups rendered female sex offenders as sexually passive and harmless, there were also differences. Victims relied on the notion of women as sexually harmless to transform female sex offending while the notion of not being a 'real' woman did not come into play. In contrast, both the themes of 'rendering her harmless' and not being 'a real woman' were present within psychiatrists' and police officers' constructions of female sex offenders. Both professional groups relied on notions of women as not dangerous, as aberrant and abnormal, and as not responsible for the sexual offence due to their lack of intentionality. The greatest difference to emerge between the two professional groups was that psychiatrists constructed the female sex offender around notions of psychosis and mental illness, whereas police officers portrayed the offenders as sexually out of control, and devious. These constructions of women as either 'mad' or 'bad' – as mentally ill or as sexually out of control and devious have been unwavering in societal portrayals of women for centuries. The different portrayals chosen by each professional group appeared to reflect the cultural context – the working knowledge and informal norms of their occupation. For psychiatrists, viewing female sex offenders as psychotic or mentally ill was perhaps more congruent with the nature and context of psychiatry. For police officers portraying female sex offenders as 'out of control' reflected the cultural context of police work which depicted 'normal' women as feminine, nurturing and sexually passive.

Despite some differences in the content and direction of their transformations, an overall similarity between victims, psychiatrists and police officers was that the enactment of the transformation process ultimately led to the denial of female sex offending. Moreover, the widespread nature of the denial placed female sex offending within the context of a *culture of denial* with regard to its recognition and seriousness. A dialectical process was also proposed as a possible model from which to understand how the denial of female sex offending is maintained and reproduced. I suggested that social reality, and thus cultural values, are constructed and transmitted through a dialectical process which illustrated the relationship between three carriers of culture – society, institutions and individuals. The three carriers of culture form an interdependent dialectic whereby one relies upon, and simultaneously influences and reproduces the other. The relationships and dynamics within the dialectical process are ultimately representative of Giddens' concept of the 'duality of structure' whereby humans draw upon structures in order to provide guidance for their own actions, and in doing so, reproduce them.

As society, institutions, and individuals were found to be interconnected and given that the denial of female sex offending was apparent at the societal level (as revealed in chapter one), I proposed that we should find denial at both the institutional and individual levels. Indeed, the denial of female sex offending was visible at both these levels. At the institutional level, it was found that the formal policies and practices of the police service and psychiatric institutions appeared to be drawn from broader societal meanings of gender, crime and sexuality and reflecting this context, operated within the framework of a culture of denial with regard to female sex offending. These formal policies included training initiatives which presented sexual offending as an offence committed solely by males, and the exclusion of female sex offending in both the DSM-IV, and the police Crime Analysis Report. On an individual level, it was possible to see how gendered categorizations and traditional sexual scripts of women as sexually passive and harmless were interwoven and articulated in psychiatrists' and police officers' daily talk and banter, denying a woman's potential for sexual aggression or violence. Informal professional practices such as police officers deeming case of female sex offending as unfounded sometimes without an in-depth investigation, or psychiatrists claiming that female sex offenders were not in need of treatment also contributed to the denial of the issue. These informal practices highlighted the ways in which individual psychiatrists and police officers drew upon both institutional ideology and societal ideology in order to provide guidance to their own behaviour. Reflecting Giddens' concept of the duality of structure, professionals simultaneously constructed and reproduced the culture of denial with regard to female sex offending.

In their representations of female sex offending, victims (who are at the individual level of the dialectic) also appeared to draw upon societal values and scripts of female sexual passivity and harmlessness and male sexual aggression in their negotiations of the sexual abuse experience. For example, male victims reported making conscious efforts to redefine their sexual interactions with older females not as sexual abuse, but as early initiation to sexuality, ultimately denying the severity and impact of sexual abuse by females. Other victims attempted to redefine the sexual interactions with their mothers within the context of 'caretaking'. Thus, by drawing on broader societal meanings of female sexual passivity and harmlessness, victims appeared to contribute to the construction, maintenance and reproduction of traditional sexual scripts and the culture of denial. Individuals *within* institutions (psychiatrists and police officers) as well as individuals *apart* from institutions (victims) concurrently relied upon, sustained and perpetuated the culture of denial. Exemplifying the duality of structure, individuals appeared to be both products of their contexts and, importantly, participants in the shaping of those contexts.

Organizational Cultures and the Dialectic

The study has demonstrated that the notion of a dialectic contributes to our understanding of organizational culture and its role in shaping individual practice. Two prominent ideas have tended to accompany discourses on organizations. First, organizations have often been regarded as isolated entities and impervious sub-cultures which are inaccessible and unwelcoming to outsiders or external ideologies and practices (Warren & Rasmussen, 1977; Van Maanen, 1981; Fielding, 1994). Second, organizational cultures are said to be largely constraining, and have a significant influence on the attitudes and practices of individual workers. For example, the informal police culture is often held responsible for the attitudes and practices of individual officers (Manning, 1977, 1989; Young, 1991; Fielding, 1994; Holdaway, 1996; Crank, 1998). However, the findings of this study show that organizational cultures are both constraining *and* enabling. Although formal and informal organizational 'rules' and policies may pose practical limits on individual behaviour, individuals are nonetheless capable of endorsing or resisting such rules.

This study has also demonstrated that organizational cultures are not inflexible and may not be impenetrable or all-powerful in shaping individual attitudes and practices. Rather, organizational cultures are intimately connected to broader societal values and beliefs, which, in turn, have a crucial impact on institutional policy and practice. These findings encourage us to question the utility of regarding institutions as solely constraining and self-sustaining entities set apart from other aspects of social life.

As further support for the idea that institutions are neither solely constraining nor all-powerful in their ability to transmit organizational values, we need only to look at the important role of the individual in the development and perpetuation of organizational values. Individual psychiatrists and police officers were not merely passive recipients of an all-powerful culture. Instead, they had the power to contribute to the values of their surrounding institution and could choose whether or not to embrace these values. Furthermore, the broader culture also had an important role to play in influencing individual ideology and practice. For example, police officers and psychiatrists appeared to rely upon culturally available meanings of women as sexually harmless, and as out of control in their constructions of female sex offenders. The fact that police officers and psychiatrists came from very different institutional cultures and nonetheless came to construct the female sex offender in similar ways reveals the power of societal ideology and its influence on both institutional ideology and individual ideology.

Victims of female sex offenders, who represent individuals apart from institutions, can also be seen to have a potential influence on institutions. Victims came into contact with a variety of institutions, such as the police service, mental health agencies, and child protection agencies. Their ability to influence organizational policy and practice lies in the fact that their status as victims of female sex offenders, which defies traditional sexual scripts and organizational shorthands, may compel institutions to re-examine their 'accepted' organizational values, policies and practices. Thus, individuals apart from institutions have a key role to play for the *future* development of organizational policy and practice.

There is another important implication of viewing institutions as part of a dialectical process. This relates to institutional responsibility and the capacity to facilitate long-term change. Institutions have, at times, been regarded as uniquely responsible for the dissemination of potentially harmful values such as sexism or racism. For example, as stated in chapter four, the British police service has been criticized for propagating 'institutionalized racism' following the inquiry into the death of Stephen Lawrence. A similar criticism could be made towards police and psychiatric institutions for disseminating values that implicitly deny women's potential for sexual aggression. However, keeping in mind the essence of the dialectical process whereby institutions are but one component of a larger process, it would seem inappropriate to hold the police and psychiatric institutions solely responsible for propagating the denial of women as potential sexual aggressors. Although institutions are uniquely responsible for their actions as well as their inactions, they cannot be seen in isolation from society and individuals. Thus, in order to instigate viable change and a long-term commitment to understanding female sex offending, recognition of the problem would need to be present within the other carriers of culture. Viewing institutions within the context of a dialectic may also help to promote a broader sense of responsibility with regard to addressing female sex offending.

Criminal Justice Responses to Female Offenders

Throughout history, criminological theorists and criminal justice officials have tended to rely primarily on traditional scripts and stereotypes in their depiction of female offenders (Gavigan, 1987; Morris & Wilczynski, 1993; Lloyd, 1995). In offering explanations for their offending behaviour, they have situated women into dichotomous conceptual categories: as either guarantors of idealism, passivity and virtue, or its opposite – duplicity and nihilism. In the first instance, the female offender is presented as passive and innocent – a generally pathetic or tragic individual who is not considered a danger to the community at large despite the fact that she may have committed a serious offence (Allen, 1987b; Ballinger, 1996). In the opposing portrayal, her offending behaviour is explained by reference to her duplicity, her masculinity, and her taintedness.[2]

Recent research has challenged the accuracy and utility of these traditional views of female offending. For example, in the area of sexual coercion, research has shown that women can and do engage in sexually aggressive and abusive behaviour (Struckman-Johnson, 1988; Byers & O'Sullivan, 1998; Struckman-Johnson & Struckman-Johnson, 1998) and that factors quite apart from an offender's duplicity or masculinity contribute to women's sexual aggression. Such factors include sexual arousal, a desire to hurt, or to gain power and control over a sexual partner (Anderson, 1998; Craig Shea, 1998). As an example, in her study comparing sexually coercive and non-coercive college women, Craig Shea (1998) found that:

> [sexually coercive women] were typically less accepting of traditional sex roles ... more aggressive and power-oriented [than non-coercive women]; they tend to view relationships and sex in particular as a ... means of gaining advantage and feelings of tenderness and love are not necessarily components of their sexual encounters (Craig Shea, 1998: 101).

It is interesting to note that such research findings appear to be having little practical impact on everyday conceptions of female offenders. This study has revealed that in their constructions of female sex offending, police officers, psychiatrists, and at times, victims continue to rely on traditional perceptions of women as virtuous and incapable of sexual aggression on the one hand, or as 'unreal' women (should they cross the established boundaries of 'acceptable' female behaviour) on the other. Although these conceptions may be inaccurate and do little to enrich our understanding of women's actual offending behaviour, they appear to be entrenched in contemporary thought, social policy, and practice.

There are several important implications of the continued reliance on these traditional perceptions of female offenders. In the context of this study, by constructing and portraying female sex offenders as essentially two dimensional beings – as innocuous or as unruly – the complexities that are intrinsic to cases of female sexual assault remain unexplored. These categorizations serve to distance 'real', 'feminine' women from 'out of control', unruly women, thus maintaining the security of our model of the world where women are forever nurturing and maternal. However, these constructions inhibit the development of any new discourse, insight, or convincing understandings of women who sexually offend. Instead, the actions of these women are relegated to simplistic, often inaccurate explanations or their behaviour is overlooked completely.

Moreover, viewing women suspected of sexual offences within the traditional sexual script of sexually passive and harmless may, at times, facilitate chivalrous responses to their behaviour.[3] The notion of chivalry appeared to manifest itself in different ways for the two professional groups under study. For police officers, it seemed to come in the form of failing to lay charges against a female suspected of a sexual offence – deeming the case unfounded either without having conducted an in-depth investigation, or despite evidence pointing to the contrary. Officers also appeared to deem cases unfounded based not on the suspected offence, but instead on the female suspect's femininity or her status as a mother.

For psychiatrists, 'chivalry' appeared to take on a slightly different form and thus, had different implications. As females were perceived to be sexually passive and harmless, those female sex offenders referred to psychiatrists for treatment were considered inconsequential and not in need of psychiatric attention. Moreover, psychiatrists appeared to propagate the view that unlike male sex offenders, treatment or attention which addressed the *sexual* aspect of the female offender's behaviour was unnecessary. Indeed, such beliefs could have potentially dangerous implications – namely that female sex offenders who are left untreated will not gain insight into their behaviour and may continue to pose a risk to children.[4]

Traditional representations of female offenders appear to provide little insight into the offender and her offence. These representations appear to be more of a commentary on the status of women more generally – perpetuating the eternal cliché of the exalted madonna pitted against the depraved, out of control whore. Indeed, these powerful and recurring narratives not only shape the ways in which women's sexual aggression is talked about and understood, but also how broader questions of gender are understood in this society.

Ballinger (1996) has argued that even when the female offender herself attempts to resist the stereotypical mad/bad/victim categories by presenting her own logical and rational explanations of her crimes, she is disqualified as a speaker and her accounts become 'muted' by 'expert' and commonsensical knowledge around criminal women. Having become members of a muted group, female offenders will only be 'heard' again if and when they communicate through the dominant modes of expression – as either innocuous or unruly.

Arguably, each time that a female sex offender raises her 'voice', she is reopening the space within which new knowledge and discourse can be produced about women who sexually offend. However, this study has shown that each time a female sex offender 'speaks', there are explicit attempts by criminal justice and mental health practitioners to mute her voice, her actions, and her responsibility and once again rely upon the 'known truths' about women. To do otherwise would challenge idealized beliefs about women's gentle, passive and caring 'nature'. The criminal justice responses to female offending which result in a lack of formal sanctions may, at times, be advantageous to women. However, there is a cost and it is a price which arguably all women pay.[5] Women are relegated to limiting, narrow frames of reference. They lack agency, and responsibility for their actions. Feminist discourse frequently speaks of the lack of control and agency in women's lives, that their minority voices are frequently stifled by the roots of patriarchy. If women's voices are to be heard, it would be beneficial if they could be heard in all possible forms – in compassion, in protest, as well as in violent rage.

This study has found that portrayals of female sex offenders place gender as the central feature of the offending behaviour. Ignoring gender altogether would cause us to overlook important social, economic and political factors crucial to understanding the sources and motivations for female sex offending. However, making gender and femininity the *sole* focus may be equally as dangerous, as it may encourage the reliance on traditional sexual scripts and has the capacity to fuel notions of female irresponsibility and strengthen arguments for the subordination of women. It may also diffuse the political impact of female aggression or crime and divert attention from other more promising lines of thought about female crime. The study therefore supports the need to move beyond traditional sexual scripts and organizational shorthands in relation to explanations of female offending, allowing the complexities that surround female criminality to be thoughtfully explored.

Feminist Theory

> Until feminism begins to address that women are capable of sexual abuse, until feminism begins to question the unspoken assumption that women heal and never hurt, it cannot and will not move forward (Alexandra).

As was noted in the introduction, feminist activists were largely responsible for bringing the issue of child sexual abuse to the forefront of debate. As such, the importance of feminist contributions to child sexual abuse discourse cannot be understated. However, feminist explanations which attribute all forms of sexual violence to men's power over women in a patriarchal society fall short when we are presented with the problem of women committing sexual offences against children (Young, 1993). Although feminist criminologists have been very strong in proposing paradigms of victimization in relation to women and crime, there appears to be a continuing failure to recognize agency on the part of women and accept that they too can engage in unacceptable and abusive behaviour (Allen, 1987b; Birch, 1993). In particular, there appears to be a feminist resistance to addressing the topic of female sex offending (Randall, 1992; Elliott, 1993; Wolfers, 1993; Young, 1993). Female sex offenders, as well as their victims, have rarely been subject to an in-depth feminist analysis. Birch comments on the feminist silence surrounding Myra Hindley, England's most 'notorious' female sex offender:

> I was struck by the deafening silence from feminists on the subject of Myra Hindley. On one level, of course, this is understandable. She was not a battered wife who hit back, a victim who took action to protect herself or her children. Quite the reverse. There is no easy way to appropriate her actions for the purpose of advancing the cause of women. Why, indeed, should we want to? (Birch, 1993: 34).

There may be conscious and reasonable rationales behind the feminist silence. Indeed, there may be very real dangers attached to studying female sexual offending which need to be taken into consideration. Studying sexually aggressive behaviour by women could be used to undermine the acceptance of the extent and range of men's use of violence towards women and children, drawing attention away from 'men's far more lethal aggression' (Campbell, 1993: 143).

Research findings on female sexual offending could also be distorted or exaggerated to serve anti-feminist objectives and could replicate what occurred with regard to research on battering. In 1978, Suzanne Steinmetz published an article claiming that husbands were also victims of domestic violence and that such abuse was even more under-reported than wife abuse. Following this, opponents of the women's movement used these findings to argue against funding shelters for battered women (Gelles & Straus, 1988).

Although it appears that studying female sex offending from a feminist perspective may have potentially negative implications if the research is not conducted in a careful, sensitive manner, abandoning research and attention to this area because of these potentially negative implications would be a disservice to both victims of female sex offenders and the offenders themselves. For example, victims of females have received little recognition in sexual abuse literature and the implications of this may be most evident in some of the harmful professional responses to their disclosures found in this study. In terms of female sex offenders, failure to conduct research on the topic will do little to increase our knowledge regarding their characteristics and motivations and may encourage inaccurate portrayals and misconceptions about their behaviour. Research in the area is clearly needed. However, any such research would need to pay close attention to how the research questions and the findings are framed, and would need to be contextualized. Careful and sensitive research would greatly enrich our understanding of sexual violence and aggression.

More needs to be said about feminist theory and its ability to incorporate the notion of female sex offending. Feminist analyses of sexual assault have consistently underscored that all forms of sexual violence should be viewed within the context of male power and masculinities whereby men use their power as a form of social control by denying women freedom and autonomy (Kelly, 1988; Radford & Stanko, 1996). Although sexual assault by women could be taken to reflect their powerlessness in a patriarchal society, feminist perspectives appear quite restrictive and seem to deny the possibility of female sexual aggression in isolation from explanations of male domination. In essence, the mere existence of a lone woman who sexually abuses children appears to invalidate feminist explanations of sexual assault, undermining the core aspect of feminist theory – patriarchy and its role in the subordination of women.[6]

Feminism's inability to encompass female sexual aggression within its theoretical foundations ultimately points to an inadequacy. However, this does not mean that we must reject all aspects of feminist theory with regard to sexual assault by females. If feminism in its current form cannot adequately explain female sex offending, it would follow that feminism needs to alter in order to accommodate the findings of this study which not only indicate the existence of female sex offending, but also its denial.

One way for feminism to accommodate female sex offending would be to employ the adaptive theory approach proposed by Layder (1998). Adaptive theory works to constantly fuse and accommodate aspects of prior theoretical ideas and concepts which emerge from the ongoing collection of empirical data and its analysis. The word 'adaptive' is meant to convey the idea that although an existing theory provides a scaffold which has a relatively durable form, this scaffold should not be viewed as immutable. Rather, theories are able to adapt in response to the discovery of new information or data which seriously challenges the theory's basic assumptions. In this sense, existing theories like feminism are seen to be able to expand their theoretical framework to produce new offshoots in light of incoming evidence, such as the existence of women who sexually abuse children. Layder argues that adaptive theory may thus necessitate the abandonment of certain concepts or the creation of new ones. So, while feminist concepts of patriarchy may need to be abandoned in some cases of female sex offending, new concepts, perhaps relating to existing feminist notions of power, may provide a means through which feminism can accommodate female sex offending.

Power is an important concept within feminist theory (Holland et al., 1998). In their conceptualization of power, feminists have long focused on women's lack of power and men's exercise and sometimes abuse of power within the context of broader social structures and interpersonal relationships (Shulman, 1971; Millet, 1977). As a result of feminist theory's focus on women as primarily *victims* of male power, there has been a tendency to downplay women's desire for power as well as their use and abuse of it (Young, 1993). Nonetheless, research has demonstrated that women do seek power and control in their relationships, even if obtained through coercive or abusive means (Craig Shea, 1998; Anderson, 1998). Feminist conceptualizations of power not only fail to take into account women's agency and (ab)use of power, which may be important in relation to women who sexually abuse children, but also it seems unlikely that male domination can be viewed as the *sole* source and cause of female aggression, as feminist theory in its current form would suggest. As such, if feminist concepts of power were expanded to encompass the abuse of power *by* women (apart from notions of patriarchy and male domination) this could provide the beginnings of a more balanced feminist approach to understanding women who sexually abuse children. A new feminist focus could turn to women as active agents who seek to compensate for their lack of power (which is likely to stem from a myriad of possible sources, not simply patriarchy) by attempting to gain power and control over those who are more vulnerable than themselves – children. Such explanations would not be far from the feminist explanations already in place with regard to male perpetrated sexual assault. In such cases, the assault is not perceived to be related to sex, but is instead viewed as a means for men to gain and maintain power and control over women (MacKinnon, 1996).

Clearly, feminist concepts of power and its relation to female sex offending needs to be explored to a degree that goes beyond the scope of this book. However, it seems that an adaptive approach, which could critically analyze and expand feminist concepts of power to incorporate abusive behaviours by women may provide a useful framework for future theory and research in this area.

Implications of the Culture of Denial

The presence of the culture of denial may have important consequences for female sex offenders, their victims, and for prevalence rates. First, as a result of the professional perception that female sex offending is harmless or inconsequential, professionals may fail to intervene in cases involving female perpetrators. Consequently, children in the care of, or in contact with a female sex offender may be at risk and remain outside of the realm of professional attention and statutory intervention.

Second, given that some psychiatrists' believe that female sex offending is largely inconsequential and that the offenders are generally not in need of psychiatric attention or treatment, it is possible that female sex offenders may be exonerated and left untreated. As a result, they will not gain insight into their behaviour and may continue to pose a risk to children. Moreover, in light of some psychiatrists who view cases involving female perpetrators as clinically 'uninteresting', minimal psychiatric effort and attention is likely to be placed on clinical research in the area. As a result, our knowledge of female sex offending, it aetiology and motivating factors will continue to be limited.

Third, sentencing patterns are highly influenced by the perceived seriousness of a crime. If professionals view female sex offending as harmless, sentencing outcomes in these cases may be less severe, and possibly inappropriate.

Fourth, the perceived harmlessness of female sex offending by professionals may diminish the level of harm inflicted on the victim. Therefore, the impact of the sexual abuse and the intervention needs of these victims may be ignored and disregarded. Ultimately, victims who are negatively affected by the sexual abuse may be forced to suffer in silence.

Fifth, the study has highlighted the significance of professional intervention in relation to disclosures of victims of sexual abuse by females. Professional intervention, whether positive or negative, appears to have a crucial impact on the well-being of victims. Supportive professional responses including the acknowledgement and validation of victims' experiences of sexual abuse appear to mitigate the negative effects of the sexual abuse. In contrast, unsupportive responses where professionals minimized or disbelieved victims' allegations of sexual abuse appeared to exacerbate the negative effects of the sexual abuse, ultimately inciting secondary victimization. As a result, the professional denial of female sex offending may, in some cases, increase and intensify the long-term effects of the sexual abuse on the victim. In a similar vein, negative experiences with professional denial may ultimately contribute to victim under-reporting.

Finally, if female sex offenders are bypassing criminal charges, the prevalence rates of female sexual offending may be skewed. The research revealed that compared to male sex offenders, a number of cases involving female sex offenders were deemed to be unfounded by police officers. Moreover, some of these decisions appeared to be made not based on the facts of the case, but upon traditional sexual scripts of women as sexually passive and harmless. It is therefore possible that more than one to eight per cent of sexual offences (which are cited in case report studies) are committed by women, but the official numbers reflect the (gendered) norms which shape police decision-making, which in turn are shaped by the informal working rules of the police (Ericson, 1982; McConville et al., 1991). It is unlikely that there are an inordinate number of female sexual offenders eluding criminal processing as males sexually abuse to a much greater extent than do females. However, as this study has illustrated, it is probable that *some* females may be avoiding apprehension as a result of police officers' reliance on traditional scripts and organizational shorthands concerning gender, crime and sexuality. These important implications make it essential to develop policies and practices to begin to challenge the culture of denial.

Implications for Child Sexual Abuse Policy and Practice: Countering the Culture of Denial

One implicit intention of this research has been to contribute to further discussions about child sexual abuse policy and practice. What remains clear, however, is that given the strong professional resistance to addressing the issue of female sex offending, for policies and practices to be truly effective, they would need to address the culture of denial. To begin to counter the culture of denial, several policies and practices could be implemented. These include a re-evaluation of gendered institutional policies, greater study of professional decision-making, the development of professional training and education on the issue of female sexual abuse, improving services offered to victims of female sexual abuse, and finally, re-assessing the gender specificity in the criminal law governing sexual offences. These themes, which are addressed below, are intended to encourage further discussion and debate, and any such discussions would greatly benefit from an exchange of views and experiences between police officers, psychiatrists, social workers, victims, child sexual abuse policy makers, sexual abuse support groups, legal practitioners, and other interested parties. It is important to note however, that given the pervasive nature of the culture of denial, any suggestions for policy and practice implementation are limited by the willingness of society, institutions and individuals to recognize and acknowledge the reality of female sex offending.

Re-Evaluating Gendered Institutional Policies

Formal institutional policy and training initiatives tended to present sexual offending as an offence committed by males. Introducing institutional policies and practices which generate the possibility that women are capable of sexual abuse could help in the professional recognition of female sex offending. This could include the implementation of gender neutral language within the DSM-IV and in police documents such as the Crime Analysis Report, as well as a re-examination of police investigative policies which require male-oriented forms of evidence in order to lay criminal charges against a suspected sex offender. These changes could encourage heterogeneity of thought and prevent the reliance on organizational shorthands, traditional sexual scripts and the culture of denial.

Greater Study of Professional Decision-making

The research also uncovered that police and psychiatrists hold great discretionary powers in decision-making. Moreover, once a decision has been made it is rarely re-appraised. More stringent study of decision-making practices by supervisors as well as by colleagues may have the potential to prevent organizational shorthands and scripts from entering into the decision-making process. However, any such study or monitoring would need to be done in a supportive rather than punitive way in order to ensure that counter-ideologies and practices do not go underground. Supervisors, who often act as role models, could also help by presenting alternative images of people to whom shorthands or scripts are applied, and to ensure that they are consistently reinforced when contrary ideas are articulated.[7]

Professional Education and Training: Promoting Sensitivity to Female Sexual Abuse

Examples of good police practice within the police sexual assault unit were identified in the handling of female victims of male perpetrated sexual assault. Officers appeared to uphold principles of sensitivity and a non-judgemental attitude toward these victims that were encouraged through formal police training initiatives. The adoption of a non-judgemental attitude is evidenced in the comments of the following police officer:

> You know, when I think of how I thought about things before I came here [to the unit] and how I think now, it has changed a lot. A sort of evolution has occurred. You often have to investigate sexual assault cases where it seems as though people have put themselves at risk. At the beginning, I had to investigate cases of prostitutes, and women who invited men home and things happened they didn't want to happen [sexual assault]. You realize that these people may have put themselves at risk, but also that these are what I consider vulnerable people. My having realized [this] is where I think a certain evolution happened. This work demands that you be sensitive, non-judgemental, and have an open mind (M-DS2).

A meaningful commitment to principles of sensitivity and a non-judgemental attitude require that they be directed at *all* victims, including both male and female victims of female sex offenders. By widely promoting such principles within the institutional context, this could provide guidance to professionals and help to minimize harmful professional interventions, encourage victim disclosures, and may have the potential to increase victims' confidence in the criminal justice system. Given the link between institutional ideology and individual ideology, it is not surprising that with the deliberate propagation of new ways of thinking about sexual assault within the police service (particularly as it pertained to female victims of male perpetrators) a modification in the attitudes of officers was noted. There is therefore reason to believe that the same process could occur in relation to female sexual offending.

One way to encourage greater sensitivity among professionals and institutions is through extensive training and education. Psychiatrists and police officers reported discomfort and uneasiness when dealing with female sex offending. The minimal attention and research the topic has received appeared to contribute to professional discomfort and confusion as to how to proceed. These circumstances may lead to the reliance on scripts and shorthands, as scripts may provide a sense of order and clarity in a time of uncertainty. If implemented, training initiatives could provide professionals with the needed tools to work with cases of female sex offending and could help to allay the discomfort and thus prevent the enactment of the transformation process and ultimately, the culture of denial. Any such training could occur alongside training already in place for male sex offending.

To meet the needs of victims of female sex offenders, within the context of training, professionals should be reminded that sexual abuse by females occurs and encouraged to respond in the same supportive way as the more common cases of sexual abuse by males. For professional training to be informed and effective, it would need to emphasize the importance of fostering a climate that indicates that disclosures of female sexual abuse are permissible (by both victims and offenders), the importance of validating victims' experiences, the dangers of unsupportive professional responses, as well as focusing on recovery issues which appear to be unique to victims of female sex offenders. Moreover, encouraging professionals to routinely inquire about female sexual aggression in the context of their daily practice could facilitate disclosures by unidentified offenders, as well as by victims. For example, within the context of working with victims of child sexual abuse, professionals could inquire: 'So far we've only discussed sexual abuse by males. Was there ever a time when a female had any type of unwanted sexual contact with you?' Although the immediate response may be negative, such probes establish a climate in which a client has permission to disclose such experiences later or when he or she is ready to do so (Sgroi & Sargent, 1993).

It would also be highly beneficial if knowledge concerning female sex offending was incorporated into the realm of formal education. Few helping professionals, whether police officers, psychiatrists, social workers, or psychologists, appear to be receiving formal educational training on female sexual abuse, particularly at the college or university level. Introducing students to the topic early on in their professional development could encourage an openness and awareness of the issues that could prove crucial for later professional practice.

It is important to note, however, that the recognition of and modification of professional attitudes towards female sexual abuse may be a slow and arduous process given the current political climate. Recently, I have been approached by several social workers who have told me of their desire to address the issue of women who sexually offend within their institution. However such suggestions have often been met with hostility and antagonism from their colleagues. One female social worker explained that she was preparing to present a paper on women as perpetrators of sexual offences at a conference. Prior to the presentation she was warned not to present the paper. She explained:

> Before the conference, I received threatening telephone calls from female colleagues saying: 'What are you doing? Why are you presenting this? Don't you dare present women in a bad light! Don't push back all of the gains that we have made in sexual abuse and feminism.

Another female social worker I spoke with was facilitating a therapy group for adolescent girls who were victims of sexual abuse. During the course of therapy, several girls disclosed to the group that they had recently sexually offended against a child in their care. Following these disclosures, the social worker went to her institution's Board of Directors to obtain permission to conduct a therapy group for women who sexually offend. She explained the Board's reaction to her request:

> My colleagues would not hear it. They were not open to it. I was shut down ... They said to me 'You're mother-blaming. You're woman-bashing ... You don't know what you're talking about'. I said 'Well, I'm hearing from the girls [that they are offending]. If you want it on the table, get consent from the girls and you too will hear what they are saying'. But they did not want to know any more ... They didn't believe me ... That's what was shocking to me – more than what the girls themselves were saying ... I thought Jesus Christ, I better shut up about this because I'm going to be black-balled in my [professional] community. That experience had a very significant impact on me.

This social worker's experience demonstrates that challenging the culture of denial can be both personally and professionally dangerous. In response, this social worker decided to defy the Board's decision and began, in secret, to facilitate the therapy group for female sex offenders. She explained:

> I needed to keep my therapy group secret ... The denial was so strong ... I chose to do the work with the [female sex offenders] ... but not tell the Board because

they were in such denial ... I realized that I wasn't going to get any assistance. I decided to go underground with this because [my colleagues] were not ready.

While the experiences of these social workers illustrate the difficulties and complexities of defying the culture of denial, they also demonstrate that professional training and education may not only come in the form of formal institutionally-based training, but also from the more informal realm of individual professionals educating other professionals. While challenging the culture of denial may be slow, arduous and even risky, given the reality of the dialectical process and the ability of individuals to have an impact on larger institutions and society, individual professionals who continue to take such risks and challenge institutional practices may begin to influence both the institutional and societal realms.

Over the past decade, the issue of female sex offending has begun to gain wider recognition. However, more attention to the problem is needed to understand its complexities and the diverse reactions it evokes. The negative professional responses to victim disclosures found in this study appear to be reminiscent of the professional reactions of shock and denial that were prevalent with regard to male perpetrated sexual abuse in the 1970s. The devastating impact these responses had on females reporting sexual abuse by males has been well documented (Russell, 1986). However, through professional training and awareness a modification in professional attitudes has, to varying degrees, been noted (Radford & Stanko, 1996). With greater attention and commitment to the issue on a broad scale, a similar process could occur in relation to professional responses to female sexual abuse.

Improved Services to Victims of Female Sex Offenders

Reflecting the culture of denial, several victims in this study who sought professional help were turned away by victim services and sexual assault support centres as a result of the gender of their sexual abuse perpetrator. Failing to provide adequate services to victims of female sex offenders may not only be detrimental to the victim in question, but also society at large given that some victims fear sexually abusing children and have violent sexual fantasies of harming women. In light of this, it seems clear that services offered to victims need to be improved. While the education and training of professionals (and particularly a greater awareness of the potential dangers of unsupportive or dismissive responses) could certainly assist in the quality of individual and group services offered to victims, other types of services could also be beneficial. Namely, the establishment of support groups for victims of female perpetrated abuse. Given that victims frequently spoke of their feelings of isolation and shame as a result of being sexually abused by a female, the presence of other victims dealing with similar issues could provide both comfort and validation.

As the numbers of victims of female offenders presenting themselves to agencies may be small as compared to victims of male offenders, organizations may need to engage in greater collaboration to establish solid victim referral services. I am aware of one particular Canadian agency that provides a support group for victims of female sex offenders. Given the expertise of the staff within this organization, victims of females are frequently referred there by other agencies. I have been told that there is a steady demand for service.

What remains less clear are the types of interventions needed for victims of female sex offenders. While this study has highlighted some intervention techniques that appear harmful and helpful to victims, more in-depth research is needed in the area. Particularly, it is important to consult with victims to determine, from their perspective, the techniques and forms of intervention that they deem essential to their healing and well-being.

Re-Evaluating Gender Specificity in the Criminal Law on Sexual Offences

A final comment needs to be made with regard to the implications of female sex offending in relation to the criminal law. Gender biases in the law which deny the possibility of female sex offending continue to be an issue. For example, under the current sexual offence laws in the UK men and women face different charges if they have sex with underage children with consent. Moreover, only men, and not women can be found guilty of indecent exposure (Wintour, 2000). As noted earlier in the book, such gender bias within the context of the law may act to constrain the consideration of female sex offending. The legal framework may therefore need to be altered to accommodate sexual offences by women. Such changes could help to increase the recognition of sexual offences by women. In turn, victims may feel more inclined to report sexual offences by women and professionals may become more aware of the issue. Ultimately, an official change in the law could be a step in the process of inverting the pervasive culture of denial revealed in this study.

At the time of writing, the British government has proposed a new crime of 'sexual abuse within families' as part of the first major overhaul of the law on sexual offences in England and Wales in nearly fifty years (Travis, 2000). The new offence would bring together existing crimes such as incest, rape, and indecent assault, but at the same time would make clear that the law no longer regarded such crimes as private matters. It will be interesting to see if sexual abuse by women will be addressed within the new offence. Indeed, this overhaul of the laws governing sexual offences could provide an ideal opportunity for the recognition of sexual abuse by women and the potential for some of the policies and practices suggested by this research to be implemented.

However, it may be overly optimistic to assume that the recognition of female sex offending will accompany changes to the law alone. The Canadian context informs us that simply changing the law to accommodate women who sexually offend may not be enough to instigate significant and long-term changes in relation to the culture of denial. In Canada, efforts have been made to remove the gender bias which previously existed within the law. As mentioned in chapter one, prior to 1983, a woman could not be charged or convicted of a sexual offence. For example, within the Canadian Criminal Code (CCC) the legal definition of rape (Section 143) stated that 'a *male* person commits rape when he has sexual intercourse with a *female* person ...' (emphasis added). However, definitions of sexual offences within the CCC were amended in 1983 and 1986 and replaced with gender neutral language, allowing for women to be charged and convicted of sexual offences. For example, Section 271 of the CCC which defines sexual assault now reads: '*Every one* who commits a sexual assault is guilty of an indictable offence ...' (emphasis added). Other offences within the CCC also recognize women as potential perpetrators. For example, Section 173 (2) outlining the crime of indecent exposure reads:

> Every person who, in any place, for a sexual purpose, exposes *his or her* genital organs to a person who is under the age of fourteen years is guilty of an offence punishable on summary conviction (emphasis added).

Despite changes in the definition of sexual assault and the inclusion of women within sexual offences, this study has revealed that the denial of women as potential sexual aggressors remains pervasive in Canadian culture. While one might argue that efforts to include females within the legal framework have been relatively recent and more time is needed for its full impact to be realized, it seems evident that *only* changing the law is not enough to invert the culture of denial. Although accommodating women within the legal framework can be seen as a symbolic gesture acknowledging women's potential for sexual aggression, real changes would need to come not only from structural constraints, such as the law, but also from the everyday action and interaction of individuals (particularly professionals) whose decision-making practices play a pivotal role in the recognition of female sex offending. This once again highlights the importance of avoiding dualist views of social reality which focus on either structural constraints or individual action. Instead, as suggested by Giddens, *both* action and structure need to be addressed in order to fully understand the complexity of social life.

There is a further dilemma associated with including females within the context of the sexual assault law. One needs to question whether invoking a punitive response is a viable solution to female sex offending. Although accommodating women within the sexual assault laws may to some degree increase the recognition of the issue, charging more women with sexual offences may not necessarily deter other potential female sex offenders from offending or reduce recidivism (this would also apply to male sex offenders). Moreover, the repercussions of a punitive response (that is, sending an offender to prison) may be that few such offenders will receive treatment (assuming treatment initiatives have some degree of effectiveness) and may in fact have a negative impact on the well-being of female offenders due to the difficulties associated with imprisonment. These issues underscore the need to fully explore the implications of altering the legal framework before implementing any long-term changes.

Directions for Future Research

As a result of the dearth of information on sexual abuse by females, careful and sensitive research is needed. This section offers some directions for future research, particularly as it pertains to victims, offenders, and professionals working in the area of child sexual abuse.

Victims of Female Sex Offenders

More large-scale studies of victims of female sex offenders would be helpful in ascertaining whether the experiences of victims in this study reflect those of the wider population of victims of female sexual abuse. Is disclosure problematic because of the culture of denial? Research comparing the after-effects of sexual abuse by males and abuse by females would also be beneficial. What are the similarities and differences? Moreover, what factors are present in victims who appear to have suffered less impact from the sexual abuse? What makes some survivors fare better than others subjected to comparable maltreatment? Research into such questions would add greatly to our understanding of sexual abuse and would enable practitioners and policy makers to create treatment initiatives for victims which best address their needs.

Further research is necessary into the relationship between sexual abuse by women and its impact on misogynistic views as well as later offending behaviour. Misogynistic views were noted among both male and female victims. Two victim-participants who had been convicted of sexual offences used their own victimization experience to explain their subsequent perpetration. These relationships need to be explored further to understand the context in which sexual victimization influences later offending behaviour.

Future research also needs to address whether and how factors such as race, class, age, sexual orientation and disability influence the impact of sexual abuse by females on victims and whether or not these factors affect the response of statutory and voluntary agencies.

Female Sexual Offenders

In regard to female sexual offenders, more research is needed in the areas of offender motivation. What are the motivating factors behind female sex offending? How do female offenders explain their actions? Are female offenders aroused by the children they abuse? Studies into male and female co-perpetration would also help to shed light on the dynamics of co-perpetration. A study into the similarities and differences of lone female offenders and females implicated in co-offending would be particularly helpful.

There is a need to examine the current treatment initiatives for female sex offenders. Are there many such initiatives? For those offenders who underwent treatment, what were their views on treatment and the professional approach? What are female sex offenders' experiences with professionals? Research in this area would greatly enhance our understanding of the current initiatives and assess the level of attention and seriousness these offenders are receiving from professionals.

Professionals Working in Child Sexual Abuse

In terms of professionals, several areas of inquiry appear necessary. First, a large-scale study of a variety of professional perspectives on female sex offending would confirm if the attitudes of professionals in this study are reflective of the wider professional community. How prevalent are the use of organizational shorthands in regard to sexual offending? Also, what factors influence how professionals come to understand female sex offending? Do personal characteristics such as gender, ethnicity, and race contribute to professional beliefs about female sexual offending? How and in what ways does the organizational culture shape professional ideas about female sex offenders and their victims? The isolation of these variables could help to improve our understanding of professional responses to the issue.

Finally, research into professional training and female sex offending would be useful. It appears that little training with regard to female sexual perpetration is presently being offered to professionals. Research could focus on the development of professional training initiatives and the ways in which such initiatives could be best integrated into the professional community. However, research would first need to examine the most effective types, methods, and strategic approaches to professional training. It would need to be established which organization, and who within the organization, would benefit most from training; under what circumstances training would need to take place; what approach to training would have the greatest long-term effects; what the goals of training would be; and who would lead such training. The work of Luthra and Oakley (1991) which explores the different approaches and strategies to race training within organizations provides a sound model from which such training strategies could be developed. The strengths of the model lie in the diversity of approach and the fact that the authors have drawn on their own subjective training experience. Moreover, they address both the strengths and limitations of race training within the organizational context and provide long-term suggestions for promoting race awareness. The model is also broad enough that it can also be applied to different organizational contexts and professional groups. The strategies outlined in Luthra and Oakley's model, which include involving activists in training, ensuring that training be cross-professional, that it be monitored and evaluated, that it should only be done within organizations that are committed to change, and that trainers need to be empowered as change agents, could easily be applied to training in relation to female sex offending.

What is essential to all of the suggestions for future research, policy, and practice is that they be done in a way that does not arouse a moral panic concerning the issue of female sex offending. This is one of the dangers associated with giving attention to a 'new' and under-recognized issue. The events in Cleveland, England in 1987, now referred to as the 'Cleveland scandal', illustrate the potential dangers of moral panics and their relationship to sexual abuse.[8] In Cleveland, during a six-week period of time, 121 children were removed from their homes by the social service department under suspicion of being victims of sexual abuse. The children, many of whom had been brought to the hospital by their parents for other ailments, were judged to have been sexually abused on the basis of a controversial medical test called the 'anal dilatation test' which was thought to indicate anal penetration (Hobbs & Wynne, 1986). Most of these diagnoses were made by a newly appointed consultant, Dr. Higgs. The Government report into the events in Cleveland contains detailed accounts of the serious, negative effects on both the innocent families and families where sexual abuse occurred (Home Office, 1988) which included children undergoing eight medical examinations in two weeks, some children being awakened at night to have their anuses examined, and sick children who were *not* suspected of being abused having their anuses examined so the doctors could determine what a 'normal' anus looked like. Moreover, a child's failure to admit sexual abuse was interpreted as a desire to protect the family perpetrator, and some children did not see their parents for many weeks (Cooper, 1990). Bell's (1988) book *When Salem Came to the Boro* describes the events in Cleveland and likens the actions of the Cleveland professionals to the witch hunts in Salem, Massachusetts. The incidents in Cleveland not only demonstrate professionals' potential for iatrogenic trauma, but also how moral panics may often accompany responses to sexual abuse.

In conclusion, although the pervasive denial of female sex offending is likely to have an impact on the recognition of the problem (and the low rates of female sex offending in official sources need to be understood within this context) there is no substantive evidence to refute the common assumption that males represent the vast majority of child sexual abuse perpetrators. Although women do sexually abuse, and it is clear that the issue demands more attention, cause for panic in searching out the 'new' and 'previously undetected' female sex offender is unwarranted. What is essential, however, is that the possibility of female sexual abuse be considered, especially by professionals who play a critical role in the identification and management of cases of sexual abuse. Although female sexual abuse may be representative of a small group of offenders and victims, the small numbers do warrant attention. It is through an examination of *all* types of child sexual abuse that we may increase our awareness and understanding of a complex issue.

Notes

1   This is not necessarily *conscious* discrimination in favour of women. Rather, there are times when professionals and victims, without intending to

discriminate in favour of women, are aware that they are realigning the female sex offender and her offence within the framework of more culturally 'acceptable' notions of female behaviour.

2   See for example Lombroso (1895), Pollak (1961), and Klein (1973).

3   Chivalry theory suggests that criminal justice professionals are influenced by a patriarchal culture that defines women as dependent and as needing to be protected rather than punished (Pollak, 1961; Anderson, 1976; Chesney-Lind, 1977; Moulds, 1980). As such, women who come into contact with the criminal justice system are said to be afforded less harsh treatment than their male counterparts. It should be noted however, that the issue of chivalry is highly controversial and there is evidence which both supports and rejects chivalric responses to female offenders (Nagel and Hagan, 1983). Figures have shown chivalry operating in women's favour (Walker, 1968) and have also shown the reverse (Smart, 1976). Thus, the extent to which women are dealt with leniently by the police remains unclear. While a myriad of factors may mediate the notion of chivalry (Hedderman & Gelsthorpe, 1997), lenient treatment does appear to be dependent upon conformity to traditional role stereotypes. That is, lenient dispositions may be reserved for passive, unaggressive, remorseful, white middle-class women (Morris, 1987). Incidentally, these were often the characteristics which professionals in this study used to describe female sex offenders, which may explain their seemingly chivalric responses.

4   It is important to recognize that the notion of treatment for sex offenders is highly complex due to the controversy concerning the overall effectiveness of such treatment (Marques, 1999). One cannot assume that treatment initiatives will be successful in the prevention of further offending or are a viable solution to the problem of sex offending. While a range of target areas for treatment of male sex offending have been put forward in areas such as impaired relationships with adults (McFall, 1990), lack of empathy (Freeman-Longo & Pithers, 1992), the degree and nature of anger (Prentky, 1995), cognitive distortions (Murphy, 1990, Marshall, 1993), deviant sexual arousal (Abel and Blanchard, 1974) and anti-social personality factors (Hall, 1988; Prentky et al., 1995), there continues to be little consensus as to what treatments actively reduce recidivism in male sex offenders (Quinsey et al., 1993; Polizzi, MacKenzie & Hickman 1999). The issue of treatment is even more complex for female sex offenders as little empirical research has focused on developing suitable treatment initiatives for this population (Mathews et al., 1989). Although it seems wholly inappropriate for female sex offenders to be denied access to treatment, treatment initiatives offered to this population would need to be demonstrably effective and address their particular clinical needs.

5   Chivalrous treatment always presents a 'double-edged' sword for women (Wilczynski, 1997: 426). Women who conform to gender stereotypes can benefit from 'assumptions of good intention, moral purity and blameless victimization' (Gordon, 1988: 92). However, those who do not are apt to be

treated much more severely (i.e. – receive a punishment of imprisonment as opposed to probation) (Worrall, 1981).

6   Although some female sex offenders may be victims of male power and domination (for example, women who are coerced or threatened into committing sexual offences by a male partner), feminist explanations which view a*ll* forms of sexual violence within the context of patriarchy and male power fail to account for women who sexually abuse children alone and of their own volition.

7   It is important to note that supervisors themselves may rely on organizational shorthands and traditional sexual scripts in the context of their everyday work. As such, it may be beneficial for those in supervisory roles to undergo training in the area of female sexual perpetration which could increase their awareness and recognition of the issue and its implications for professional practice. The issue of training is addressed in the next section.

8   For further discussions of moral panics in relation to sexual abuse see La Fontaine (1997) and de Young (1999).

References

Allen, C.M. (1990) 'Women as perpetrators of child sexual abuse: Recognition barriers', in Horton, A., Johnson, B., Roundy, L. and Williams, D. (eds.) *The incest perpetrator: A family member no one wants to treat*, Newbury Park, CA: Sage Publications.

Allen, C.M. (1991) *Women and men who sexually abuse children: A comparative analysis*, Orwell: The Safer Society Press.

Allen, H. (1987a) *Justice Unbalanced: Gender, psychiatry and judicial decisions*, Milton Keynes: Open University Press.

Allen, H. (1987b) 'Rendering them harmless: The professional portrayal of women charged with serious violent crimes', in Carlen, P. and Worrall, A. (eds.) *Gender, crime and justice*, Milton Keynes: Open University Press.

Allison, D. and Roberts, M. (1998) *Disordered mother or disordered diagnosis: Munchausen by proxy syndrome*, London: The Analytic Press.

American Psychiatric Association (1968) *Diagnostic and statistical manual of mental disorders, 2nd ed.*, Washington, DC: American Psychiatric Association.

American Psychiatric Association (1994) *Diagnostic and statistical manual of mental disorders, 4th ed.*, Washington, DC: American Psychiatric Association.

Anderson, P. (1998) 'Women's motives for sexual initiation and aggression', in Anderson, P. and Struckman-Johnson, C. (eds.) *Sexually aggressive women*, London: Guilford Press.

Anderson, P. and Struckman-Johnson, C. (eds.) (1998) *Sexually aggressive women*, London: Guilford Press.

Armstrong, L. (1993) *And they call it help: The psychiatric policing of America's children*, Reading, MA: Addison-Wesley.

Atkinson, P. (1983) 'Reproduction of the professional community', in Dingwall, R. and Lewis, P. (eds.) *The sociology of the professions: Lawyers, doctors and others*, London: Social Science Research Council.

Atkinson, R. (1998) *The life story interview*, London: Sage Publications.

Attias, R. and Goodwin, J. (1985) 'Knowledge and management strategies in incest cases: A survey of physicians, psychologists and family counselors', *Child Abuse and Neglect*, 9: 165-74.

Babbie, E. (1986) *The practice of social research*, Belmont: Wadsworth Publishing.

Babiker, G. and Arnold, L. (1997) *The language of injury: Comprehending self-mutilation*, Leicester: BPS Books.

Bachmann, K., Moggi, F. and Stirnemann-Lewis, F. (1994) 'Mother-son incest and its long-term consequences: A neglected phenomenon in psychiatric practice', *Journal of Nervous and Mental Disease*, 182(12): 723-5.

Badgley, R. (Chairman) (1984) *Sexual offences against children. Report of the committee of sexual offences against children and youths*, Ottawa: National Health and Welfare.

Ballinger, A. (1996) 'The guilt of the innocent and the innocence of the guilty', in Myers, A. and Wight, S. (eds.) *No angels: Women who commit violence*, London: Harper Collins.

Banning, A. (1989) 'Mother-son incest: Confronting a prejudice', *Child Abuse and Neglect*, 13(4): 549-63.

Bash, H. (1995) *Social problems and social movements: An exploration into the sociological construction of alternative realities*, New Jersey: Human Press International.

Bayer, R. and Spitzer, R. (1985) 'Neurosis, psychodynamics and DSM-III: A history of the controversy', *Archives of General Psychiatry*, 42: 187-95.

Beck, R. (1999) 'Rape from afar: Men exposing to women and children'. in Brookman, F., Noaks, L. and Wincup, E. (eds.) *Qualitative research in criminology*, Aldershot: Ashgate.

Becker, D. (1997) *Through the looking glass: Women and borderline personality disorder*, Colorado: Westview Press.

Bell, S. (1988) *When salem came to the Boro*, London: Pan.

Berg, B. and Budnick, K. (1986) 'Defeminisation of women in law enforcement: A new twist in the traditional police personality', *Journal of Police Science and Administration*, 14(4): 314-9.

Berger, P. and Luckmann, T. (1966) *The social construction of reality*, New York: Anchor Books.

Bickel, J. (1996) 'Leveling the playing field', in Wear, D. (ed.) *Women in medical education*, Albany: State University of New York Press.

Binder, A. and Geis, G. (1983) *Methods of research in criminology and criminal justice*, London: McGraw-Hill.

Birch, H. (1993) 'If looks could kill: Myra Hindley and the iconography of evil', in Birch, H. (ed.) *Moving targets: Women, murder and representation*, London: Virago Press.

Bittner, E. (1967) 'The police on skid row: A study of peace keeping', *American Sociological Review*, 32: 699-715.

Bolton, F.G., Morris, L.A. and MacEachron, A.E. (1989) *Males at risk: The other side of child sexual abuse*, Beverly Hills: Sage Publications.

Borden, T. and Laterz, J. (1993) 'Mother/daughter incest and ritual abuse: The ultimate taboos', *Treating Abuse Today*, 3(4): 5-8.

Brandon, S., Boakes, J., Glaser, D. and Green, R. (1998) 'Recovered memories of childhood sexual abuse', *British Journal of Psychiatry*, 172: 296-307.

Brannen, J. (1988) 'The study of sensitive subjects', *Sociological Review*, 36: 552-63.

Brenner, M., Brown, J. and Canter, D. (eds.) (1985) *The research interview: Uses and approaches*, London: Academic Press.

Brewer, J. (1991) 'Hercules, hippolyte and the amazons – or policewomen in the R.U.C', *British Journal of Sociology*, 42(2): 231-47.

Brewer, J. (1993) 'Sensitivity as a problem in field research: A study of routine policing in Northern Ireland', in Renzetti, C. and Lee, R. (eds.) *Researching sensitive topics*, London: Sage Publications.

Briere, J. (1992) *Child abuse trauma*, Newbury Park: Sage Publications.

Briere, J., Evans, D., Runtz, M. and Wall, T. (1988) 'Symptomatology in men who were abused as children: A comparison study', *American Journal of Orthopsychiatry*, 58: 457-61.

Briere, J. and Zaidi, L. (1989) 'Sexual abuse histories and sequelae in female psychiatry emergency room patients', *American Journal of Psychiatry*, 148: 55-61.

Brookman, F. (1999) 'Accessing and analysing police murder files', in Brookman, F., Noaks, L. and Wincup, E. (eds.) *Qualitative research in criminology*, Aldershot: Ashgate.

Broussard, S., Wagner, N.G., and Kazelskis, R. (1991) 'Undergraduates students' perceptions of child sexual abuse: the impact of victim sex, perpetrator sex, respondent sex, and victim response', *Journal of Family Violence*, 6: 267-78.

Brown, G.R. and Anderson, B. (1991) 'Psychiatric morbidity in adult inpatients with childhood histories of sexual and physical abuse', *American Journal of Psychiatry*, 148: 55-61.

Brown, P. (1990) 'The name of the game: Toward a sociology of diagnosis', *Journal of Mind and Behavior*, 11: 385-406.

Browne, A. and Finkelhor, D. (1986) 'Impact of child sexual abuse: A review of the research', *Psychological Bulletin*, 99(1): 66-77.

Browne, D. (1993) 'Race issues in research on psychiatry and criminology', in Cook, D. and Hudson, B. (eds.) *Racism and criminology*, London: Sage Publications.

Brownmiller, S. (1975) *Against our will: Men, women and rape*, New York: Simon & Schuster.

Buchanan, D., Boddy, D. and MacCalman, J. (1988) 'Getting in, getting on, getting out and getting back', in Bryman, A. (ed.) *Doing research in organisations*, London: Routledge.

Bucher, R. and Stelling, J. (1977) *Becoming professional*, London: Sage.

Bunker Rohrbaugh, J. (1981) *Women: Psychology's puzzle*, London: Abacus.

Burnam M.A., Stein J.A., Golding J.M., Siegel J.M., Sorenson S.B., Forsythe A.B. and Telles, C.A. (1988) 'Sexual assault and mental disorders in a community population', *Journal of Consulting and Clinical Psychology*, 56: 843-50.

Busfield, J. (1996) *Men, women and madness: Understanding gender and mental disorder*, London: MacMillan Press.

Byers, E. (1996) 'How well does the traditional sexual script explain sexual coercion? Review of a program of research', *Journal of Psychology and Human Sexuality*, 8: 6-26.

Byers, E., and O'Sullivan, L. (1996) 'Introduction', *Journal of Psychology and Human Sexuality*, 8: 1-5.

Byers, E., and O'Sullivan, L. (1998) 'Similar but different: Men's and women's experiences of sexual coercion', in Anderson, P. and Struckman-Johnson, C. (eds.) *Sexually aggressive women*, London: The Guildford Press.

Cain, M. (1973) *Society and the policeman's role*, London: Routledge and Kegan Paul.

Campbell, A. (1993) *Men, women and aggression*, New York: Basic Books.

Canadian Centre for Justice Statistics (2001) Crime Statistics in Canada, *Juristat*, 21, 8.

Caplan, P. (1995) *They say you're crazy: How the world's most powerful psychiatrists decide who's normal*, Reading, MA: Addison-Wesley.

Carlson, S. (1990) 'The victim/perpetrator: Turning points in therapy', in M. Hunter (ed.) *The Sexually Abused Male: Vol. 2, Application of treatment strategies*, Lexington, MA: Lexington.

Cashmore, E. (1996) *Dictionary of race and ethnic relations*, London: Routledge.

Cavaiola, A. and Schiff, M. (1989) 'Self-esteem in abused chemically dependent adolescents', *Child Abuse and Neglect*, 13: 327-34.

Cavanaugh-Johnson, T. (1989) 'Female child perpetrators: Children who molest other children', *Child Abuse and Neglect*, 13: 571-85.

Chan, J. (1996) Changing police culture, *British Journal of Criminology*, 36(1): 109-34.

Chan, J. (1997) *Changing police culture: Policing in a multi-cultural society*, Cambridge: Cambridge University Press.

Charmaz, K. (1983) 'The grounded theory method: An explication and interpretation', in Emerson, R. (ed.) *Contemporary field research*, Toronto: Little Brown and Company.

Chasnoff, I., Burns, W., Schnoll, S., Burns, K., Chissum, G. and Kyle-Spore, L. (1986) 'Maternal-neonatal incest', *American Journal of Orthopsychiatry*, 56(4): 577-80.

Chesler, P. (1972) *Women and madness*, New York: Doubleday.

Chesney-Lind, M. (1977) 'Judicial paternalism and the female status offender: Training women to know their place', *Crime and Delinquency*, 23: 121-30.

Child Abuse Studies Unit, (1993) *Abuse of women and children: A feminist response*, London: University of North London Press.

Cicourel, A.V. (1968) *The social organisation of juvenile justice*, New York: John Wiley and Sons.

Clark, R., and Hatfield, E. (1989) 'Gender differences in receptivity to sexual offers', *Journal of Psychology and Human Sexuality*, 2: 39-55.

Coffey, P., Leitenberg, H., Henning, K., Turner, T. and Bennett, R. (1996) 'Mediators of the long-term impact of child sexual abuse: Perceived stigma, betrayal, powerlessness, and self-blame', *Child Abuse and Neglect*, 20(5): 447-55.

Coleman, D. and Baker, F.M. (1994) 'Misdiagnosis of schizophrenia in older, black veterans', *Hospital and Community Psychiatry*, 47(45): 527-8.

Comack, E. and Brickley, S. (eds.) (1991) *The Social Basis of Law: Critical Readings in the Sociology of Law*, Halifax: Garamond Press.

Condy, S.R., Templer, D.I., Brown, R. and Veaco, L. (1987) 'Parameters of sexual contact of boys with women', *Archives of Sexual Behaviour*, 16: 379-94.

Connell, R. (1987) *Gender and power: Society, the person and sexual politics*, Stanford: Stanford University Press.

Cooper, A., Swaminath, S., Baxter, D. and Poulin, C. (1990) 'A female sexual offender with multiple paraphilias: A psychologic, physiologic (laboratory sexual arousal) and endocrine study', *Canadian Journal of Psychiatry*, 35(4), 334-7.

Cooper, I, (1990) 'Child sexual abuse: Abusive professional responses', in Stephanis, C. (ed.) *Psychiatry: A world perspective*: Elsevier Science Publishers.

Cooper, I. and Cormier, B. (1990) 'Incest', in Blugrass and Bowden (eds.) *Principles and practices of forensic psychiatry*, London: Churchill Livingstone.

Cope, R. (1989) 'The compulsory detention of Afro-Caribbeans under the Mental Health Act', *New Community*, 15(3): 343-56.

Coward, R. (1993) 'Culture obsessed with abuse', *The Observer*, 6 June.

Craig Shea, M. (1998) 'When the tables are turned: Verbal sexual coercion among college women', in Anderson, P. and Struckman-Johnson, C. (eds.) *Sexually aggressive women*, London: Guilford Press.

Crank, J.P. (1998) *Understanding police culture*, Cincinnati: Anderson Publishing.

Crawford, C. (1997) *Forbidden femininity: Child sexual abuse and female sexuality*, Aldershot: Ashgate.

Crewdson, J. (1988) *By silence betrayed: Sexual abuse of children in America*, Boston: Little Brown.

Crews, F. (1997) *The memory wars*, London: Granta.

Crimlisk, H. and Welch, S. (1996) 'Women and psychiatry', *British Journal of Psychiatry*, 169: 6-9.

Curra, J. (2000) *The relativity of deviance*, London: Sage Publications.

Daniels, A. (1972) 'Military psychiatry: The emergence of a subspecialty', in Freidson, E. and Lorber, J. (eds.) *Medical men and their work*, Chicago: Aldine.

Davenport, W. (1977) 'Sex in cross-cultural perspective', in Beach, F. (ed.) *Human sexuality in four perspectives*, Boston: John Hopkins University.

Davin, P., Hislop, J., and Dunbar, T. (1999) *Female sexual abusers*, Vermont: Safer Society Press.

Deer, B. (1988) 'Why we must look: The Cleveland inquiry', *The Sunday Times*, 10 July: C2-C3.

De Mause, L. (1974) 'The evolution of childhood', in De Mause, L. (ed.) *The history of childhood: The evolution of parent-child relationships as a factor in history*, London: Souvenir Press.

De Young, M. (1982) *The sexual victimization of children*, London: McFarland and Co.

De Young, M. (1999) *The devil goes abroad: The export of ritual abuse moral panic*, paper presented at the British Society of Criminology Conference, Liverpool, UK.

Dhaliwal, G., Gauzas, L., Antonowicz, D. and Ross, R. (1996) 'Adult male survivors of childhood sexual abuse: Prevalence, sexual abuse characteristics, and long-term effects', *Clinical Psychological Review*, 16(7): 619-39.

Dickstein, L. (1996) 'Overview of women physicians in the United States', in Wears, D. (ed.) *Women in medical education*, Albany: State University of New York Press.

Diethelm, O. (1971) *Medical dissertations of psychiatric interest before 1750*, Basel: Karger.

Dietz, C. and Craft, J. (1980) 'Family dynamics of incest: A new perspective', *Social Casework*, 61: 602-9.

Dimock, P. (1988) 'Adult males sexually abused as children', *Journal of interpersonal Violence*, 3: 191-203.

Donat, P. and D'Emilio, J. (1997) 'A feminist redefinition of rape and sexual assault: Historical foundations and change', in O'Toole, L. and Schiffman, J. (eds.) *Gender violence*, New York: New York University Press.

Douglas, J. (1985) *Creative interviewing*, London: Sage Publications.

Douglas, M. (1966) *Purity and danger: An analysis of the concepts of pollution and taboo*, London: Routledge and Kegan Paul.

Driver, E. and Droisen, A. (eds.) (1989) *Child sexual abuse: feminist perspectives*, Basingstoke: Macmillan Education.

Duffin, J. (1996) 'Lighting candles, making sparks', in Wear, D. (ed.) *Women in medical education*, Albany: State university of New York.

Eaton, J.S.J. (1980) 'The psychiatrist and psychiatric education', in Kaplan, H. and Freedman, A. (eds.) *Comprehensive textbook of psychiatry*, Baltimore: Williams & Wilkins.

Edwards, S. (1984) *Women on trial*, Manchester: Manchester Publishing.

Elliott, M. (ed.) (1993) *The female sexual abuse of children*, London: Guilford Press.

Elshtain, J. (1993) *Democracy on trial*, Concord, Ontario: House of Anansi Press.

Emerson, R. (1983) *Contemporary field research*, Boston: Little, Brown.

Ericson, R.V. (1982) *Reproducing order: A study of police patrol work*, Toronto: University of Toronto Press.

Essed, P. (1991) *Understanding everyday racism*, London: Sage Publications.

Etherington, K. (1995) *Adult male survivors of childhood sexual abuse*, London: Pitman.

Evert, K. (1987) *When you're ready: A woman's healing from physical and sexual abuse by her mother*, Maryland: Launch Press.

Faller, K. (1987) 'Women who sexually abuse children', *Violence and Victims*, 2(4): 263-76.

Faller, K. (1989) 'Characteristics of a sample of sexually abused children: How boys and girl victims differ', *Child Abuse and Neglect*, 13: 281-91.

Favazza, A.R. and Rosenthal, R.J. (1993) 'Diagnostic issues in self-mutilation', *Hospital and Community Psychiatry*, 44(2): 134-40.

Fehrenbach, P.A. and Monastersky, C. (1988) 'Characteristics of female adolescent sexual offenders', *American Journal of Orthopsychiatry*, 58(1): 148-51.

Fernando, S. (1988) *Race and culture in psychiatry*, Tavistock: Routledge.

Fielding, N. (1988) *Joining forces: Police training, socialization and occupational competence*, London: Routledge.

Fielding, N. (1994) 'Cop canteen culture', in Newburn, T. and Stanko, E. (eds.) *Just boys doing business: Men, masculinity and crime*, London: Routledge.

Fielding, N. and Fielding, J. (1991) 'Police attitudes to crime and punishment', *British Journal of Criminology*, 31(1): 39-53.

Finkelhor, D. (1983) 'Removing the child: Prosecuting the offender in cases of sexual abuse: Evidence from the National Reporting System for Child Abuse and Neglect', *Child Abuse and Neglect*, 7(2): 195-205.

Finkelhor, D. (ed.) (1984) *Child sexual abuse: New theory and research*, New York: Free Press.

Finkelhor, D. (1986) *A sourcebook on sexual abuse*, Newbury Park, CA: Sage Publications.

Finkelhor, D. and Russell, D. (1984) 'Women as perpetrators', in Finkelhor, D. (ed.) *Child sexual abuse: New theory and research*, New York: Free Press.

Finkelhor, D., Williams, L. and Burns, N. (1988) *Nursery crimes: Sexual abuse in daycare*, Beverly Hills: Sage Publications.

Fontana, A., and Frey, J. (1994) 'Interviewing: The art of science', in Denzin, N. and Lincoln, Y. (eds.) *Handbook of qualitative research*, London: Sage Publications.

Fook, J., Ryan, M. and Hawkins, L. (1994) 'Becoming a social worker: Educational implications from preliminary findings of a longitudinal study', *Social Work Education*, 13(2): 5-26.

Foster, P. (1996) 'Observational research', in Sapsford, R. and Jupp, V. (eds.) *Data collection and analysis*, London: Sage Publications.

Freedman, A., Kaplan, H. and Sadock, B. (1975) *Comprehensive textbook of psychiatry*, Baltimore: Williams & Wilkins.

Freel, M. (1995) *Women who sexually abuse children*, Norwich: Social Work Monographs.

Freeman-Longo, R. and Pithers, W. (1992) *A structured approach to preventing relapse: A guide for offenders*, Orwell, Vermont: The Safer Society Press.

Freud, S. (1962) 'The aetiology of hysteria', in Strachey, J. (ed.) *The standard edition of the complete psychological works of Sigmund Freud*, London: Hogarth Press (Original work published in 1896).

Freund, K., Heasman, G., Racansky, I,G. and Glancy, G. (1984) 'Pedophilia and heterosexuality vs, Homosexuality', *Journal of Sex and Marital Therapy*, 10(3): 193-200.

Freyd, J. (1996) *Betrayal trauma: The logic of forgetting childhood abuse*, Cambridge, Mass: Harvard University Press.

Friedman, S. (1988) 'A family systems approach to treatment', in L.E.A. Walker (ed.) *Handbook on the sexual abuse of children*, New York: Springer.

Fritz, G.S., Stoll, K. and Wagner, N.N. (1981) 'A comparison of males and females who were sexually molested as children', *Journal of Sex and Marital Therapy*, 7: 54-9.

Fromuth, M. and Burkhart, B. (1987) 'Childhood sexual victimization among college men: Definitional and methodological issues', *Violence and Victims*, 2(4): 241-53.

Fromuth, M. and Burkhart, B. (1989) 'Long-term psychological correlates of childhood sexual abuse in two samples of college men', *Child Abuse and Neglect*, 13: 533-42.

Fromuth, M., Burkhart, B. and Webb Jones, C. (1991) 'Hidden child molestation: An investigation of adolescent perpetrators in a nonclinical sample', *Journal of interpersonal Violence*, 6(3): 376-84.

Fromuth, M. and Conn, V. (1997) 'Hidden perpetrators: Sexual molestation in a nonclinical sample of college women', *Journal of interpersonal Violence*, 12(3): 456-65.

Gagnon, J. and Simon, W. (1974) *Sexual conduct*, London: Hutchinson.

Galligan, P.T. (1996) *Report to the attorney general of Ontario on certain matters related to Karla Homolka*, Toronto: ADR Chambers.

Garb, H. (1996) 'The representativeness and past-behavior heuristics in clincial judgment', *Professional Psychology: Research and Practice*, 27: 272-7.

Gavigan, S. (1987) 'Women's crime: New perspectives and old theories', in Adelberg, E. and Currie, C. (eds.) Vancouver: Press Gang Publishers.

Gelles, R.J. and Straus, M.A. (1988) *Intimate violence*, New York: Simon & Schuster.

Gelsthorpe, L. (1989) *Sexism and the female offender*, London: Gower.

Gentry, C.E. (1978) 'Incestuous abuse of children: The need for an objective view', *Child Welfare*, 57(6): 355-64.

Giddens, A. (1976) *New rules of sociological method*, London: Hutchison.

Giddens, A. (1979) *Central problems in social theory*, London: Macmillan.

Giddens, A. (1984) *The constitution of society*, Cambridge: Polity Press.

Gilgun, J. (1992)'Definitions, methodologies and methods', in Daly, K. (ed.) *Qualitative methods in family research*, London: Sage Publications.

Glaser, B. and Strauss, A. (1967) *The discovery of grounded theory*, Chicago: Aldine Publishing.

Goodwin, J. and DiVasto, P. (1979) 'Mother-daughte incest', *Child Abuse and Neglect*, 3: 953-7.

Goodwin, J. and DiVasto, P. (1982) 'Female homosexuality: A sequel to mother-daughter incest', in Goodwin, J. (ed.) *Sexual abuse: incest victims and their families*, London: John Wright.

Grier, P., Clark, M. and Stoner, S. (1993) 'Comparative study of personality traits of female sex offenders', *Psychological Reports*, 73: 1378.

Griffiths, C.T. and Verdun-Jones, S. (1989) *Canadian criminal justice*, Toronto: Butterworths.

Groneman, C. (1994) 'Nymphomania: The historical construction of female sexuality', *Signs: Journal of Women in Culture and Society*, 19(21): 337-67.

Groth, N. (1979) 'Sexual trauma in the life histories of rapists and child molesters', *Victimology*, 4: 10-16.

Hall, G. (1988) 'Criminal behaviour as a function of clinical and actuarial variables in a sexual offender population', *Journal of Consulting and Clinical Psychology*, 56: 773-5.

Hall, R. (1982) *Organizations: Structure and process*, New Jersey: Prentice-Hall.

Hammersley, M. (1989) *The dilemma of qualitative method: Herbert Blumer and the Chicago tradition*, London: Routledge.

Hammersley, M. and Atkinson, P. (1995) *Ethnography: Principles in practice*, London: Routledge.

Hedderman, C. and Gelsthorpe, L. (1997) *Understanding the sentencing of women*, London: Home Office.

Heisel, D. (1996) 'Training and education in forensic psychiatry', in Benedek, E. (ed.) *Emerging issues in forensic psychiatry*, San Fransisco: Jossey-Bass.

Heney, J. (1990) *Report on self-injurious behaviour in the Kingston Prison for Women*, Ottawa: Correctional Service of Canada.

Herman, J. (1981) *Father-daughter incest*, Cambridge, Mass: Harvard University Press.

Herman-Giddens, M. and Berson, N. (1994) 'Enema abuse in childhood: Report from a survey', *Treating Abuse Today*, 4: 45-9.

Herrington, N. (1997) 'Female cops – 1992', in Dunham, R. and Alpert, G. (eds.) *Critical issues in policing*, Prospect Heights, IL: Waveland Press.

Hetherton, J. and Beardsall, L. (1998) 'Decisions and attitudes concerning child sexual abuse: Does the gender of the perpetrator make a difference to child protection professionals?', *Child Abuse and Neglect*, 22(12): 1265-83.

Higgs, D., Canavan, M. and Meyer, W. (1992) 'Moving from defense to offense: The development of an adolescent female sex offender', *The Journal of Sex Research*, 29(1): 131-9.

Hobbs, C.J. and Wynne, J.M. (1986) 'Buggery in childhood: A common syndrome of child sexual abuse', *Lancet*, 2(8510, 4 Oct): 792-6.

Holdaway, S. (1983) *Inside the British police: A force at work*, Oxford: Oxford University Press.

Holdaway, S. (1996) *The racialisation of British police*, London: Macmillan Press.

Holdaway, S. (1997) 'Constructing and sustaining 'race' within the police workforce', *British Journal of Sociology*, 48(1): 19-34.

Holdaway, S. (1999) 'Understanding the police investigation of the murder of Stephen Lawrence: A mundane sociological analysis', *Sociological Research Online*, 4(1).

Holland, J., Ramazanoglu, C., Scott, S., Sharpe S., and Thomson, R. (1998) 'Don't die of ignorance I nearly died of embarrassment: Condoms in context', in Jackson, S. and Scott, S. *Feminism and Sexuality*, New York: Columbia University Press.

Holmes, G. and Offen, L. (1996) 'Clinicians' hypotheses regarding clients' problems: Are they less likely to hypothesize sexual abuse in male compared to female clients?', *Child Abuse and Neglect*, 20(6): 493-501.

Holmes, G., Offen, L. and Waller, G. (1997) 'See no evil, hear no evil, speak no evil: Why do relatively few male victims of childhood sexual abuse receive help for abuse-related issues in adulthood?', *Clinical Psychological Review*, 17(1): 69-88.

Home Office (1988) *Report of the inquiry into child abuse in Cleveland, 1987* (HMSO).

Home Office (1997) *Sex Offenders Act 1997, chapter 51* (HMSO).

Home Office (2001) *Statistics on women and the criminal justice system* (HMSO).

Hopkins, K. (1980) 'Brother-sister marriage in Roman Egypt', *Comparative Studies in Society and History*, 22: 304.

Hosking, D. and Morley, I, (1991) *A social psychology of organizing: People, processes and contexts*, London: Wheatsheaf.

Howitt, D. (1992) *Child abuse errors: When good intentions go wrong*, London: Harvester Wheatsheaf.

Hunt, J. (1990) 'The logic of sexism among the police', *Women and Criminal Justice*, 1: 3-30.

Hunter, J.A. (1991) 'A comparison of the psychosocial maladjustment of adult males and females sexually molested as children', *Journal of interpersonal Violence*, 6: 205-17.

Hunter, M. (1990) *Abused boys: The neglected victims of sexual abuse*, Lexington, MA: Lexington.

Institute of Race Relations (1999) *Evidence, Submitted for Part 2 of the inquiry into matters arising from the death of Stephen Lawrence*.

Jackson, S. (1978) 'The social context of rape: Sexual scripts and motivation', *Women's Studies international Quarterly*, 1: 27-38.

Jenkins, P. (1998) *Moral panic: Changing concepts of the child molester in modern America*, London: Yale University Press.

Jenkins, R. (1996) *Social identity*, London: Routledge.

Jennings, K. (1993) 'Female child molestation: A review of the literature', in Elliott, M. (ed.) *The female sexual abuse of children*, London: Guilford Press.

Johnson, J. (1975) *Doing field research*, New York: Free Press.

Johnson, R. and Shrier, D. (1985) 'Sexual victimization of boys: Experience at an adolescent medicine clinic', *Journal of Adolescent Health Care*, 6: 372-6.

Johnson, R. and Shrier, D. (1987) 'Past sexual victimization by females of male patients in an adolescent medicine population', *American Journal of Psychiatry*, 144(5): 650-2.

Jones, D. (1996) 'Father knows best?' in Wear, D. (ed.) *Women in medical education*, Albany: State University of New York Press.

Jones, M. (1980) *Organisational aspects of police behaviour*, Farnborough: Gower.

Jones, S. (1985) 'The analysis of depth interviews', in Walker, R. (ed.) *Applied qualitative research*, London: Gower.

Jorgensen, D. (1989) *Participant observation: A methodology for human studies*, London: Sage Publications.

Jupp, V. and Norris, C. (1993) 'Traditions of documentary analysis', in Hammersley, M. (ed.) *Social research: Philosophy, politics and practice*, London: Sage Publications.

Justice, B. and Justice, R. (1979) *The last taboo: Sex in the family*, New York: Human Sciences Press.

Kappeler, V., Sluder, D. and Alpert, G. (1994) *Forces of deviance: The dark side of policing*, Prospect Heights, IL: Waveland Press.

Karpman, B. (1954) *The sexual offender and his offenses: Etiology, pathology, psychodynamics and treatment*, New York: Julian Press.

Kasl, C.D. (1990) 'Female perpetrators of sexual abuse: A feminist view', in Hunter, M. (ed.) *The sexually abused male: Vol. 1, Prevalence, impact and treatment*, Lexington, MA: Lexington Books.

Kastrup, M. and Petersson, B. (1986) 'Working conditions of male and female psychiatrists', *Acta Psychiatrica Scandinavica*, 74(1): 84-90.

Keenan, C. and Maitland, L. (1999) *Literature review of research into the law on sexual offences against children and vulnerable people*, Development and Statistics Directorate of the Home Office for the Review of Sexual Offences (HMSO).

Keith, M. (1993) *Race, riots and policing: Lore and disorder in a multi-racist society*, London: UCL Press.

Kelley, S. (1990) 'Responsibility and management strategies in child sexual abuse: A comparison of child protective workers, nurses and police officers', *Child Welfare*, LXIX(1): 43-51.

Kelly, L. (1988) *Surviving sexual violence*, Cambridge: Polity Press.

Kelly, L., Burton, S. and Regan, L. (1994) 'Researching women's lives or studying women's oppression? Reflections on what constitutes feminist research', in Maynard, M. and Purvis, J. (eds.) *Researching women's lives from a feminist perspective*, London: Taylor and Francis.

Kendall-Tackett, K., Simon A. (1987) 'Perpetrators and their acts: data from 365 adults molested as children', *Child Abuse and Neglect*, 11: 237-45.

Kidder, L. (1981) *Research methods in social relations*, New York: Holt-Saunders.

King, H. (1994) 'Sowing the field: Greek and Roman sexology', in Porter, R. and Teich, M. (eds.) *Sexual knowledge, sexual science: The history of attitudes to sexuality*, Cambridge: Cambridge University Press.

King, R., Koopman, C. and Millis, D. (1999) 'Training on ethnic and gender issues in psychiatric residency programs', *Academic Psychiatry*, 23(1): 20-29.

Kirk, S. and Kutchins, H. (1992) *The selling of DSM: The rhetoric of science in psychiatry*, New York: Aldine De Gruyter.

Klein, D. (1973) 'The etiology of female crime: A review of the literature', *Issues in Criminology*, 8: 3-30.

Klerman, G. (1984) 'The advantages of DSM-III', *American Journal of Psychiatry*, 141: 539-42.

Knopp, F.H. and Lackey, L.B. (1987) *Female sexual abusers: A summary of data from 44 treatment providers*, Orwell, VT: Safer Society Press.

Koonin, R. (1995) 'Breaking the last taboo: Child sexual abuse by female perpetrators', *Australian Journal of Social Issues*, 30(2): 195-210.

Koss, M. and Harvey, M. (1991) *The rape victim*, London: Sage Publications.

Krug, R.S. (1989) 'Adult males report of childhood sexual abuse by mothers: Case descriptions, motivation and long-term consequences', *Child Abuse and Neglect*, 13: 111-9.

Kushnick, L. (1999) 'Over policed and under protected: Stephen Lawrence, institutional and police practices', *Sociological Research Online*, 4(1).

Kutchins, H., and Kirk, S. (1997) *Making us crazy: DSM the psychiatric bible and the creation of mental disorders*, London: The Free Press.

Kvale, S. (1996) *InterViews*, London: Sage Publications.

La Barbara, J., Martin, J. and Dozier, J. (1980) 'Child psychiatrists' view of father-daughter incest', *Child Abuse and Neglect*, 4(3): 147-52.

La Fontaine, J.S. (1997) *Speak of the devil: Tales of satanic abuse in contemporary England*, Cambridge: Cambridge University Press.

Langsley, D. (1987) 'The education of tomorrow's psychiatrists', in Nadelson, C. and Robinowitz, C. (eds.) *Training psychiatrists for the 90s*, Washington: American Psychiatric Press.

Larson, N. and Maison, S. (1987) *Psychosexual treatment program for female sex offenders*, St-Paul, MN: Minnesota Correction Facility – Shakopee.

Lawson, C. (1991) 'Clinical assessment of mother-son sexual abuse', *Clinical Social Work Journal*, 19(4): 391-403.

Lawson, C. (1993) 'Mother-son sexual abuse: rare or underreported? A critique of the research', *Child Abuse and Neglect*, 17: 261-9.

Layder, D. (1994) *Understanding social theory*, London: Sage Publications.

Layder, D. (1998) *Sociological practice*, London: Sage Publications.

Lee, R. and Renzetti, C. (eds.) (1993) *Researching sensitive topics*, London: Sage Publications.

Leibenluft, E., Dial, T., Haviland, M. and Pincus, H. (1993) 'Sex differences in rank attainment and research activities among academic psychiatrists', *Archives of General Psychiatry*, 150(5): 849-51.

Lemert, E. (1976) 'Records in the juvenile court', in Wheeler, S. (ed.) *On record: Files and dossiers in American life*, New Jersey: Transaction Books.

Levine, S. and Kamin, L. (1974) 'Sexism and psychiatry', *American Journal of Orthopsychiatry*, 44(3): 327-36.

Lévi-Strauss, C. (1969) *The elementary structures of kinship*, Boston: Beacon Press.

Lew, M. (1990) *Victims no longer: Men recovering from incest and other sexual child abuse*, New York: Harper & Row.

Light, D. (1980) *Becoming psychiatrists: The professional transformation of self*, London: W.W. Norton & Company.

Lloyd, A. (1995) *Doubly deviant, doubly damned: Society's treatment of violent women*, London: Penguin.

Locke, H.G. (1996) 'The color of law and the issue of color: Race and the abuse of police power', in Geller, W.A. and Toch, H. (eds.) *Police violence: Understanding and controlling police abuse of force*, New Haven: Yale University Press.

Lombroso, C. (1895) *The female offender*, New York: Appleton.

Longdon, C. (1993) 'A survivor's and therapist's viewpoint', in Elliott, M. (ed.) *The Female Sexual Abuse of Children*, London: Guilford Press.

Loring, A. and Powell, B. (1988) 'Gender, race, and DSMIII: A study of the objectivity of psychiatric diagnostic behaviour', *Journal of Health and Social Behaviour*, 29: 1-22.

Luchetti, C. (1998) *Medicine women: The story of early American women doctors*, New York: Crown Publishers.

Lunbeck, E. (1987) 'A new generation of women: Progressive psychiatrists and the hypersexual female', *Feminist Studies*, 13(3): 513-43.

Luthra, M., and Oakley, R. (1991) *Combating racism through training: A review of approaches to race training in organisations*, Coventry: Centre for Research in Ethnic Relations.

MacKinnon, C. (1996) 'Feminism, marxism, method and the state: An agenda for theory', in Jackson, S. and Scott, S. *Feminism and Sexuality*, New York: Columbia University Press.

Macpherson, S.W. (1999) *The Stephen Lawrence inquiry: Report of an inquiry by Sir William Macpherson of Cluny*, London, The Stationery Office.

Maltz, W. and Holman, B. (1987) *Incest and sexuality: A guide to understanding and healing*, Lexington: Lexington Books.

Manning, P. (1977) *Police work*, Cambridge, MA: MIT Press.

Manning, P. (1989) 'Occupational culture', in Bailey, W.G. (ed.) *The encyclopedia of police science*, New York: Garland.

Margolin, L. (1987) 'The effects of mother-son incest', *Lifestyles*, 8: 104-14.

Margolis, M.I, (1984) 'A case of mother-adolescent incest: A follow-up study', *Psychoanalytic Quarterly*, 53: 355-85.

Marques, J. (1999) 'How to answer the question: "Does sex offender treatment work"?', *Journal of interpersonal Violence*, 14(4): 437-51.

Marshall, W. (1993) 'A revised approach to the treatment of men who sexually assault adult females', in Nagayama Hall, G., Hirschman, R., Graham, J. and Zaragoza, M. (eds.) *Sexual aggression: Issues in etiology, assessment and treatment*, Washington: Taylor and Francis.

Martin, S. (1979) 'POLICEwomen and policeWOMEN: Occupational role dilemmas and choices of female offenders', *Journal of Police Science and Administration*, 7: 314-23.

Martin, S. (1980) *Breaking and entering: Policewomen on patrol*, Berkeley, CA: University of California Press.

Martin, S. (1997) 'Women officers on the move: An update of women in policing', in Dunham, R. and Alpert, G. (eds.) *Critical issues in policing*, Illinois: Waveland Press.

Martin, S. and Jurik, N. (1996) *Doing justice, doing gender*, London: Sage Publications.

Marvasti, J. (1986) 'Incestuous mothers', *American Journal of Forensic Psychiatry*, 7(7): 63-9.

Mason, J. (1996) *Qualitative researching*, London: Sage Publications.

Masson, J.M. (1984) *The assault on truth: Freud's suppression of the seduction theory*, London: Faber & Faber.

Mathews, F. (1996) *The invisible boy: Revisioning the victimization of male children and teens*, Ottawa: Minister of Supply and Services.

Mathews, R., Matthews, J. and Speltz, K. (1989) *Female sexual offenders: An exploratory study*, Orwell, VT: Safer Society Press.

Mathis, J.L. (1972) *Clear thinking about sexual deviation*, Chicago: Nelson Hall.

Maxmen, J. (1985) *The new psychiatry: How modern psychiatrists think about their patients, theories, diagnoses, drugs, psychotherapies, power, training, family and private lives*, New York: William Morrow and Company.

May, T. (1993) *Social research: Issues, method and process*, Buckingham: Open University Press.

Mayer, A. (1983) *Incest: A treatment manual for therapy with victims, spouses and offenders*, Holmes Beach, FL.: Learning Publications.

Mayer, A. (1992) *Women sex offenders: Treatment and dynamics*, Florida: Learning Publications.

McCarty, L. (1986) 'Mother-child incest: Characteristics of the offender', *Child Welfare*, 65: 447-58.

McConville, M., Sanders, A. and Leng, R. (1991) *The case for the prosecution: Police suspects and the construction of criminality*, London: Routledge.

McFall, R. (1990) 'The enhancement of social skills: An information processing analysis', in Marshall, W., Laws, D. and Barbaree, H. (eds.) *Handbook of sexual assault: Issues, theories and treatment of the offender*, New York: Plenum Press.

Mead, M. (1968) 'Incest', *International encyclopedia of social sciences*, New York: Macmillan and Free Press.

Meehan, A. (1986) 'Record-keeping practices in the policing of juveniles', *Urban Life*, 15(1): 70-102.

Meiselman, K. (1978) *Incest: A psychological study of causes and effects with treatment recommendations*, San Francisco: Jossey-Bass.

Mendel, M.P. (1995) *The male survivor: The impact of sexual abuse*, London: Sage Publications.

Messner, K. and Kimmel, M. (eds.) *Men's lives*, New York: Macmillan.

Mies, M. (1983) 'Toward a methodology for feminist research', in Bowles, G. and Duelli Klein, R. (eds.) *Theories of women's studies*, London: Routledge and Keagan Paul.

Miles, M. and Huberman, A.M. (1994) *Qualitative data analysis: An expanded sourcebook*, London: Sage Publications.

Miller, A. (1985) *Thou shalt not be aware: Society's betrayal of the child*, London: Pluto.

Millet, K. (1977) *Sexual politics*, London: Virago.

Mitchell, J. and Morse, J. (1998) *From victims to survivors: Reclaimed voices of women sexually abused in childhood by females*, New York: Accelerated Development.

Mitterauer, M. (1994) 'The customs of the Magians: The problem of incest in historical societies', in Porter, R. and Teich, M. (eds.) *Sexual knowledge, sexual science: The history of attitudes to sexuality*, Cambridge: Cambridge University Press.

Mohr, J. (1977) 'The paedophilias: Their clinical, legal and social implications', in B. Schlesinger (ed) *Sexual behaviour in Canada: patterns and problems*, Toronto: University of Toronto Press.

Morris, A. (1987) *Women, crime and criminal justice*, Oxford: Basil Blackwell.

Morris, A. and Wilczynski, A. (1993) 'Rocking the cradle: Mothers who kill their children', in Birch, H. (ed.) *Moving targets: Women, murder and representation*, London: Virago Press.

Moulds, E. (1980) 'Chivalry and paternalism: disparities of treatment in the criminal justice system', in Datesman, S. and Scarpitti, F. (eds.) *Women, crime and society*, Oxford: Oxford University Press.

Mrazek, P. (1981) 'Definition and Recognition of Sexual Child Abuse: Historical and Cultural Perspectives', in Mrazek, P. and Kempe, C. (eds.) *Sexually abused children and their families*, Oxford: Pergamon.

Mullen, P., Martin, J., Anderson, J., Romans, S. and Herbison, G. (1996) 'The long-term impact of the physical, emotional, and sexual abuse of children: A community study', *Child Abuse and Neglect*, 20(1): 7-20.

Murphy, W. (1990) 'Assessment and modification of cognitive distortions in sex offenders', in Marshall, W. Laws, D., and Barbaree, H. (eds.) *Handbook of sexual assault: Issues, theories and treatment of the offender*, New York: Plenum Press.

Myers, M. (1989) 'Men sexually assault as adults and sexually abused by boys', *Archives of Sexual Behaviour*, 18(3): 203-15.

Nagel, I. and Hagan, J. (1983) 'Gender and crime: Offence patterns and criminal court sanctions', in Tonry, M. and Morris, N. (eds.) *Crime and justice, Vol. 4*, Chicago: University of Chicago Press.

Nasjleti, M. (1980) 'Suffering in silence: The male incest victim', *Child Welfare*, 59(5): 269-76.

Nava, M. (1992) *Changing cultures: feminism, youth and consumerism*, London: Sage Publications.

Naylor, B. (1995) 'Women's crime and media coverage: Making explanations', in Dobash, R.E., Dobash, R.P. and Noaks, L. (eds.) *Gender and Crime*, Cardiff: University of Wales Press.

Nelson, E. (1994) 'Females who sexually abuse children: A discussion of gender stereotypes and symbolic assailants', *Qualitative Sociology*, 17(1): 63-87.

Nolen-Hoeksema, S. (1990) *Sex differences in depression*, Stanford: Stanford University Press.

O'Connor, A.A. (1987) 'Female sex offenders', *British Journal of Psychiatry*, 150: 615-20.

O'Hagan, K. (1989) *Working with child sexual abuse*, Milton Keynes: Open University Press.

Olson, P.E. (1990) 'The sexual abuse of boys: A study of the long-term psychological effects', in Hunter, M. (ed.) *The sexually abused male: Prevalence, impact and treatment*, Lexington, MA: Lexington Books.

Pearson, P. (1997) *When she was bad: Violent women and the myth of innocence*, Toronto: Random House of Canada.

Penfold, P.S. and Walker, G.A. (1984) *Women and the psychiatric paradox*, Milton Keynes: Open University Press.

Petrovich, M. and Templar, D. (1984) 'Heterosexual molestation of children who later became rapists', *Psychological reports*, 54: 810.

Pidgeon, N. (1996) 'Grounded theory: Theoretical background', in Richardson, J.T.E. (ed.) *Handbook of research methods for psychology and the social sciences*, Leicester: BPS Books.

Pierce, R. and Pierce, L.H. (1985) 'The sexually abused child: A comparison of male and female victims', *Child Abuse and Neglect*, 9: 191-9.

Pilgrim, D. and Rogers, A. (1993) *A sociology of mental health and illness*, Buckingham: Open University Press.

Piliavin, I. and Briar, S. (1964) 'Police encounters with juveniles', *American Sociological Review*, 70: 206-14.

Pipe, R., Bhat, A., Matthews, B. and Hampstead, J. (1991) 'Section 136 and African/Afro-Caribbean minorities', *International Journal of Social Psychiatry*, 37(1): 14-23.

Plummer, K. (1981) 'Paedophilia: Constructing a sociological baseline', in Cook, M. and Howells, K. (eds.) *Adult Sexual interest in Children*, London: Academic Press.

Polizzi, D., MacKenzie, D. and Hickman, L. (1999) 'What works in adult sex offender treatment? A review of prison-non-prison-based treatment programs', *International Journal of Offender Therapy and Comparative Criminology*, 43(3): 357-74.

Pollak, O. (1961) *The criminality of women*, New York: A.S. Barnes.

Prentky, R. (1995) 'A rationale for the treatment of sex offenders: Pro Bono Publico', in McGuire, J. (ed.) *What works: Reducing reoffending*, New York: John Wiley and Sons.

Prentky, R., Knight, R., Lee, A. and Cerce, D. (1995) 'Predictive validity of lifestyle impulsivity for rapists', *Criminal Justice and Behaviour*, 22: 106-28.

Quinsey, V., Harris, G., Rice, M. and Lalumiere, M. (1993) 'Assessing treatment efficacy in outcome studies of sex offenders', *Journal of interpersonal Violence*, 8(4): 512-23.

Rack, P. (1982) *Race, culture, and mental disorder*, London: Tavistock.

Radford, J. and Stanko, B. (1996) 'Violence against women and children: The contradictions of crime control under patriarchy', in Hester, M., Kelly, L. and Radford, J. (eds.) *Women, violence and male power*, Buckingham: Open University Press.

Ramsay-Klawsnik, H. (1990) *Sexual abuse by female perpetrators: Impact on children*, paper presented at the National Symposium on Child Victimization, Atlanta, GA.

Randall, J. (1992) *Childhood and sexuality: a radical Christian approach*, Pittsburgh: Dorrance.

Redlich, F. (1982) 'Two new approaches to psychiatric teaching', in Yager, J. (ed.) *Teaching psychiatry and behavioral science*, New York: Grune & Stratton.

Reiner, R. (1991) *Chief constables*, Oxford: Oxford University Press.

Reiner, R. (2000) 'Police research', in King, R. and Wincup, E. (eds.) *Doing research on crime and justice*, Oxford: Oxford University Press.

Reinhart, M. (1987) 'Sexually abused boys', *Child Abuse and Neglect*, 11: 229-35.

Reinharz, S. (1979) *On becoming a social scientist: From survey research and participant observation to experiential analysis*, San Francisco: Jossey-Bass.

Reinharz, S. (1992) *Feminist methods in social research*, Oxford: Oxford University Press.

Renvoize, J. (1982) *Incest: A family pattern*, London: Routledge & Kegan Paul.

Risin, L.I. and Koss, M.P. (1987) *The sexual abuse of boys: Frequency and descriptive characteristics of childhood victimizations reported by a national sample of male post-secondary students*, Kent, OH: Kent State University.

Ritchie, J. and Spencer, L. (1994) 'Qualitative data analysis for applied policy research', in Bryman, A. and Burgess, R.G. (eds.) *Analyzing qualitative data*, London: Routledge.

Roane, T. (1992) 'Male victims of sexual abuse: A case review within a child protection team', *Child Welfare*, 3: 231-39.

Roesler, T.A. (1994) 'Reactions to disclosure of childhood sexual abuse: The effect on adult symptoms', *Journal of Nervous and Mental Disease*, 182: 618-24.

Rohsenow, D., Corbett, R. and Devine, D. (1988) 'Molested as children: A hidden contribution to substance abuse?', *Journal of Substance Abuse Treatment*, 5: 13-18.

Rooney, R. (1992) 'The ethical foundation for work with involuntary clients', in Rooney, R. (ed.) *Strategies for work with involuntary clients*, New York: Columbia University Press.

Rosencrans, B. (1997) *The last secret: Daughters sexually abused by mothers*, Vermont: Safer Society Press.

Rothstein, A. (1979) 'Oedipal conflicts in narcissistic personality disorders', *International Journal of Psychoanalysis*, 30: 189-99.

Rowan, E.L., Rowan, J.B. and Langelier, P. (1990) 'Women who molest children', *Bulletin of the American Academy of Psychiatry and the Law*, 18(1): 79-83.

Rubin, H. and Rubin, I, (1995) *Qualitative interviewing: The art of hearing data*, London: Sage Publications.

Rudin, M., Zalewski, C. and Bodmer-Turner, J. (1995) 'Characteristics of child sexual abuse victims according to perpetrator gender', *Child Abuse and Neglect*, 19(8): 963-73.

Rush, F. (1980) *The best kept secret: Sexual abuse of children*, New York: Prentice-Hall.

Russell, Denise (1995) *Women, madness and medicine*, London: Polity Press.

Russell, Diana (1975) *The politics of rape: the victim's perspective*, New York.

Russell, Diana (1983) 'The incidence and prevalence of intrafamilial and extrafamilial sexual abuse of female children', *Child Abuse and Neglect*, 7: 133-46.

Russell, Diana (1984) *Sexual Exploitation*, Beverly Hills: Sage Publications.

Russell, Diana (1986)*The secret trauma: incest in the lives of girls and women*, New York: Basic Books.

Saradjian, J. (1996) *Women who sexually abuse children: From research to clinical practice*, London: Wiley.

Sarrel, P., and Masters, W. (1982) 'Sexual molestation of men by women', *Archives of Sexual Behaviour*, 11(2) 117-31.

Scavo, R. (1989) 'Female adolescent sex offenders: A neglected treatment group', *Social Casework*, 70(2): 114-7.

Schecter, M. and Roberge, L. (1976) 'Sexual exploitation', in Helfer, R. and Kempe, C. (eds.) *Child abuse and neglect: The family and the community*, Cambridge, MA: Ballinger.

Schoettle, U., Cantwell, D. and Yager, J. (1982) 'Child psychiatry in the general psychiatric residency program', in Yager, J. (ed.) *Teaching psychiatry and behavioral science*, New York: Grune & Stratton.

Schultz, L. (1982) 'Child sexual abuse in a historical perspective', in Conte, J. and Shore, D. (eds.) *Social Work and Child Sexual Abuse*, New York: Haworth Press.

Scott, A. (1996) *Real events revisited: Fantasy, memory and psychoanalysis*, London: Virago.

Scott, J. (1990) *A matter of record*, Cambridge: Polity.

Scott, S. (1984) 'The personable and the powerful: Gender and status in sociological research', in Bell, C. and Roberts, H. (eds.) *Social researching: Politics, problems, practice*, London: Routledge and Kegan Paul.

Seeman, M. (1995) *Gender and psychopathology*, Washington: American Psychiatric Press.

Sgroi, S. (1975) 'Child sexual molestation: The last frontier in child abuse', *Children Today*, 44: 18-21.

Sgroi, S. and Sargent, N. (1993) 'Impact and treatment issues for victims of childhood sexual abuse by female perpetrators', in Elliott, M. (ed.) *The female sexual abuse of children*, London: Guilford Press.

Shaw, M. (1995) 'Conceptualizing violence by women', in Dobash, R.E., Dobash, R. and Noaks, L. (eds.) *Gender and crime*, Cardiff: University of Wales Press.

Shearing, C. and Ericson, R.V. (1991) 'Culture as figurative action', *British Journal of Criminology*, 42(4): 481-506.

Shepher, J. (1971) 'Mate selections among second generation kibbutz adolescents and adults: incest avoidance and negative imprinting', *Archives of Sexual Behaviour*, 1: 293.

Showalter, E. (1987) *The female malady: Women madness and English culture 1830-1980*, London: Virago.

Shrier, D. and Johnson, R. (1988) 'Sexual victimization of boys: An ongoing study of an adolescent medicine clinical population', *Journal of the National Medical Association*, 80(11): 1189-93.

Shulman, A. (1971) 'Organs and orgasms', in Gornick, V. and Moran, B. *Women in a sexist society: Studies in power and powerlessness*, New York: Mentor Books.

Sieber, J. (1993) 'The ethics and politics of sensitive research', in Lee, R. and Renzetti, C. (eds.) *Researching sensitive topics*, London: Sage Publications.

Sillen, T. (1979) *Racism and psychiatry*, New Jersey: Citadel.

Sleek, S. (1996) 'Ensuring accuracy in clinical decisions', *The APA Monitor*, 26: 30.

Smart, C. (1976) *Women, crime and criminology*, London: Routledge.

Smith, D. (1975) 'The social construction of documentary reality', *Sociological inquiry*, 44(4): 257-68.

Smith, D.J. and Gray, J. (1986) *Police and people in London: the PSI report*, Avebury: Aldershot.

Smith, R., Pine, C. and Hawley, M. (1988) 'Social cognition about adult male victims of female sexual assault', *Journal of Sex Research*, 24: 101-12.

Snyder, H. (2000) *Sexual assault of young children as reported to law enforcement: Victim, incident and offender characteristics*, Bureau of Justice Statistics: US Department of Justice.

Solomos, J. (1993) 'Constructions of black criminality: Racialisation and criminalisation in perspective', in Cook, D. and Hudson, B. (eds.) *Racism and Criminology*, London: Sage Publications.

Stacey, J. (1988) 'Can there be a feminist ethnography?', *Women's Studies international Quarterly*, 11: 21-7.

Steffensmeier, D. and Terry, R. (1973) Deviance and respectability: An observational study of reactions to shoplifting, *Social Forces*, 51: 417-26.

Stein, J., Golding, J., Siegel, J., Burnam, M.A. and Sorenson, S. (1988) 'Long-term psychological sequelae of child sexual abuse: The Los Angeles Epidemiologic Catchment Area Study', in Wyatt, G., and Powell, G. (eds.) *Lasting effects of child sexual abuse*, Newbury Park, CA: Sage Publications.

Storer, H. (1856) 'Cases of nymphomania', *American Journal of Medical Science*, 32(10): 378-87.

Strauss, A., and Corbin, J. (1990) *Basics of qualitative research*, London: Sage Publications.

Struckman-Johnson, C. (1988) 'Forced sex on dates: It happens to men too', *The Journal of Sex Research*, 24: 234-41.

Struckman-Johnson, C. and Struckman-Johnson, D. (1998) 'The dynamics and impact of sexual coercion of men by women', in Anderson, P. and Struckman-Johnson, C. (eds.) *Sexually aggressive women*, London: Guilford Press.

Sudnow, D. (1964) 'Normal crimes: Sociological features of the penal code in a public defender office', *Social Problems*, 12: 255-76.

Swiggert, V. and Farrel, R. (1977) 'Normal homicides and the law', *American Sociological Review*, 42: 16-32.

Tantam, D. and Whittaker, J. (1992) 'Personality disorder and self-wounding', *British Journal of Psychiatry*, 161: 451-64.

Testa, M., Miller, B.A., Downs, W.R. and Panek, D. (1992) 'The moderating impact of social support following childhood sexual abuse', *Violence and Victims*, 7: 172-86.

The Fifth Estate (1998) *Karla Homolka*, Toronto: Canadian Broadcasting Corporation.

Tiefer, L. (1989) 'In pursuit of the perfect penis', in Messner, M. and M. Kimmel (eds.) *Men's Lives*, New York: MacMillan Publishing Company.

Travin, S., Cullen, K. and Protter, B. (1990) 'Female sex offenders: Severe victims and victimizers', *Journal of Forensic Sciences*, 35(1): 140-150.

Travis, A. (2000) 'New crime of sexual abuse within families likely in overhaul of act', *The Guardian*, 4 May.

Travis, A. (2002) 'Overhaul of ancient legislation widely welcomed', *The Guardian*, 20 November.

Trivelpiece, J.W. (1990) 'Adjusting the frame: Cinematic treatment of sexual abuse and rape of men and boys', in Hunter, M. (ed.) *The sexually abused male: Vol. 1, Prevalence, impact and treatment*, Lexington, MA: Lexington.

U.S. Department of Justice (2002) *Crime in the United States 2001*, Washington: Federal Bureau of Investigation.

Ussher, J. (1991) *Women's madness: Misogyny or mental illness?* London: Harvester Wheatsheaf.

Van Maanen, J. (1981) 'The informant game: Selected aspects of ethnographic research in police organizations', *Urban Life*, 9: 469-94.

Van der Mey, B. (1988) 'The sexual victimization of male children: a review of previous research', *Child Abuse and Neglect*, 12: 67-72.

Waddington, P.A.J. (1984) *The training of prison governors: Role ambiguity and socialization*, London: Croom Helm.

Waegel, W. (1981) 'Case routinization in investigative police work', *Social Problems*, 28(3): 263-75.

Walker, N. (1968) *Crime and punishment in Britain*, Edinburgh: University of Edinburgh Press.

Walklater, S. (1995) *Gender and crime: An introduction*, London: Prentice Hall.

Walsh, B.W. and Rosen, P.M. (1988) *Self-mutilation: Theory, research and treatment*, London: Guilford Press.

Walsh, M.R. (1977) *Doctors wanted: no women need apply*, New Haven: Yale University Press.

Walton, J. (1857) 'Case of nymphomania successfully treated', *American Journal of Medical Science*, 33(1): 47-50.

Warren, C. and Rasmussen, P. (1977) 'Sex and gender in field research', *Urban Life*, 6(3): 349-68.

Watkins, B. and Bentovim, A. (1992) 'The sexual abuse of male children and adolescents: A review of current research', *Journal of Child Psychology and Psychiatry*, 33(1): 197-248.

Weinberg, S.K. (1955) *Incest behavior*, New York: Citadel.

Welldon, E. (1988) *Mother, madonna, whore: The idealization and denigration of motherhood*, London: Free Association Books.

Wilczynski, A. (1997) 'Mad or bad? Child killers, gender and the courts', *British Journal of Criminology*, 37(3): 419-36.

Williams, L. and Farrell, R. (1990) 'Legal response to child sexual abuse in day care', *Criminal Justice and Behavior*, 17(3): 284-302.

Wincup, E. (1999) 'Researching women awaiting trial: Dilemmas of feminist ethnography', in Brookman, F., Noaks, L. and Wincup, E. (eds.) *Qualitative research in criminology*, Aldershot: Ashgate.

Wintour, P. (2000) 'Go-ahead for reform of sex laws', *The Guardian*, 19 May.

Wolfe, F. (1985) *Twelve female sexual offenders*, paper presented at Next Steps in Research on the Assessment and Treatment of Sexually Aggressive Persons, St, Louis, MO.

Wolfers, O. (1993) 'The paradox of women who sexually abuse children', in Elliott, M. (ed.) *The female sexual abuse of children*, London: Guilford Press.

Wolff, K. (1950) *The sociology of Georg Simmel*, New York: Free Press.

Wolfram, S. (1987) *Inlaws and outlaws: Kinship and marriage in England*, London: Croom Helm.

Worden, R.E. (1989) 'Situational and attitudinal explanations of police behaviour: A theoretical reappraisal and empirical reassessment', *Law and Society*, 23(4): 667-711.

Worden, R.E. (1996) 'The causes of police brutality: Theory and evidence on police use of force', in Geller, W.A. and Toch, H. (eds.) *Police violence: Understanding and controlling police abuse of force*, New Haven: Yale University Press.

Worrall, A. (1981) 'Out of place: female offenders in court', *Probation Journal*, 28(3): 90-93.

Yager, J. (1982a) 'Supervising psychiatric residents for eclectic practice', in Yager, J. (ed.) *Teaching psychiatry and behavioral science*, New York: Grune & Stratton.

Yager, J. (1982b) 'Teaching and learning psychiatry and behavioral science', in Yager, J. (ed.) *Teaching psychiatry and behavioral science*, New York: Grune & Stratton.

Young, M. (1991) *An inside job: Policing and police culture in Britain*, Oxford: Clarendon.

Young, V. (1993) 'Women abusers – a feminist view', in Elliott, M. (ed.) *The female sexual abuse of children*, London: Guilford Press.

Index